Genesis

John C. Jeske

Publishing House
St. Louis

The interior illustrations were originally executed by James Tissot
(1836-1902).

Commentary and pictures are reprinted from GENESIS (The People's
Bible Series), copyright © 1991 by Northwestern Publishing House.
Used by permission.

Scripture is taken from The Holy Bible: NEW INTERNATIONAL
VERSION, © 1973, 1978, 1984 by the International Bible Society.
Used by permission of Zondervan Bible Publishers.

Copyright © 1992 Concordia Publishing House
3558 S. Jefferson Avenue, St. Louis, MO   63118-3968
Manufactured in the United States of America

1 2 3 4 5 6 7 8 9 10   01 00 99 98 97 96 95 94 93 92

CONTENTS

THE EARLY HISTORY OF GOD'S GRACIOUS DEALINGS WITH MANKIND

ILLUSTRATIONS

PREFACE

The People's Bible Commentary is just what the name implies—a Bible and commentary for the people. It includes the complete text of the Holy Scriptures in the popular New International Version. The commentary following the Scripture sections contains personal applications as well as historical background and explanations of the text.

The authors of *The People's Bible Commentary* are men of scholarship and practical insight gained from years of experience in the teaching and preaching ministries. They have tried to avoid the technical jargon which limits so many commentary series to professional Bible scholars.

The most important feature of these books is that they are Christ-centered. Speaking of the Old Testament Scriptures, Jesus himself declared, "These are the Scriptures that testify about me" (John 5:39). Each volume of *The People's Bible Commentary* directs our attention to Jesus Christ. He is the center of the entire Bible. He is our only Savior.

We dedicate these volumes to the glory of God and to the good of his people.

The Publishers

INTRODUCTION

Name and Purpose

Genesis is the name given to the first book of the Bible, the first of the five books of Moses. In the Hebrew Bible this book is named after the first word of the book, "in the beginning." "Genesis" is a Greek word meaning "origin," and that's an appropriate name. This first book of the Bible gives us information about the origin of the universe and of the human race. It records the tragic details of the origin of sin and its ugly consequences. Genesis also records the origin of God's gracious work of undoing the damage sin had caused, beginning with his first promise of the Savior. By far the largest section of Genesis (chapters 12-50) records the origin of God's special people of Israel.

This important book of beginnings is not intended to be a general history of the ancient world. The specific purpose of Genesis is to trace God's saving activity. Genesis is the first chapter in the history of God's magnificent rescue operation which we call his plan of salvation. It is interesting and instructive to note how Genesis describes God's redemptive work — not by formulating statements of doctrine, but by relating the biographies of people. In the lives of these people we can see God at work with the message of his law, and with message of his love.

Author

There is no direct reference in Genesis to its author. This does not mean, however, that we must regard the book as anonymous.

The Scripture does not treat Genesis as a separate book. From earliest times the Hebrew people considered Genesis and the four books that follow it to be a unit. They called these five books "the Torah of Moses." "Torah" (usually translated as "Law") means "instruction," "teaching." This "Law of Moses" is also commonly referred to as the Pentateuch ("five books"). The ancient Jewish community often called the Pentateuch "the five fifths of the Law."

The premise from which this commentary is written is that Moses is the author of the first five books of the Bible. The rest of the Old Testament and all of the New Testament simply take for granted that a written book known as the "Law of Moses" was in existence, whose contents were given to Moses by God himself. The Bible knows of only one human author of the Pentateuch, and that author is Moses. Jesus settled the question of the authorship of Genesis and of the entire Pentateuch once for all when he told his critics: "If you believed Moses, you would believe me, for he wrote about me" (John 5:46).

This immediately raises the question: "How did Moses receive the information he wrote in the Pentateuch?" Most of what is written in the books of Exodus, Leviticus, Numbers and Deuteronomy happened during the lifetime of Moses. He could have drawn on his own personal experience to write these things. What is recorded in Genesis, however, from the account of the creation to the death of Joseph, took place long before Moses was born. How could he have received this material?

Since there were no human eyewitnesses to the creation of the world, information about this could have come to Moses only by the miracle of divine revelation. God miraculously gave Moses information about how the world came into existence, information which Moses could have received in no other way. The Pentateuch was a part of the Old Testament Scripture of which St. Paul said: "All Scripture is God-breathed" (2 Timothy 3:16).

A related question we must address is this: when God revealed the material of Genesis to Moses, did he do so directly? Or could Moses have made use of existing written documents which had come down to him? In reporting the travels of the patriarch Abraham, for example, is it possible that Moses may have had access to records which Abraham himself kept? Luther once made the comment: "I think that Abraham composed a little book or a brief account from Adam up to his own time," a record which Moses might very well have used (LW 4:308). Although nothing definite can be said about whether or not Moses used existing documents, there is no reason why a Bible-believing Christian should deny this possibility. If God saw fit to use a little boy's lunch to feed the 5000, and a virgin's womb to give the world a Savior, why should he not have been able to use previously written documents when revealing his truth for Moses to write down?

Our position on the divine inspiration and the divine authority of the Scripture in general, and of Genesis in particular, *flows from the presuppositions of the Christian faith*. The Bible's message of God's law and its message God's love have convinced us that God has miraculo spoken to us in Genesis and that what he says is true cannot lie. The Son of God was referring specifically Scripture of the Old Testament when he sai Scripture cannot be broken" (John 10:35).

It will come as no surprise to the reader to learn that not all Bible students approach the study of Genesis from these same presuppositions. In the view of many the Pentateuch was not written by one author, but is the result of joining at least four earlier, independent documents, code-named the Jahwist, the Elohist, the Deuteronomist, and the Priestly source. The Jahwist (J) is thought to have been a theologian who lived in the southern kingdom about 850 B.C. and who usually referred to God as Jahweh. The Elohist (E) is said to have lived in the northern kingdom about 750 B.C. His contribution to the Pentateuch can be identified by its preponderant use of the name Elohim for God. The Deuteronomist (D) is said to have been a person or a school or a group in northern Israel who wrote after the capital of Samaria had fallen to the Assyrians, perhaps some time around 625 B.C. The Priestly source (P), we are told, was composed by a writer or writers who addressed Israel in the Babylonian Exile or later (500 B.C., give or take a century). It retells the story of Israel's ancestors and outlines the way Israel was to worship God. Genealogical tables, tribal lists and worship regulations are usually assigned to this Priestly source, since those are the sorts of things a priestly writer 'd have been especially interested in.

ding to this Documentary Theory the Pentateuch is ⁓ a literary mosaic, scissored-and-pasted togeth- ` documents written earlier. This view main- ⁓uch reached its present form perhaps ⁓ the time of Christ, more than a Let it be restated that this com- ⁓e conviction that Moses is the ⸃oks of the Bible.

Structure

To appreciate the unique structure of the book of Genesis it will be helpful to remember that Moses arranged his literary material in ten sections, each introduced by the formula: *"This is the account of. . . ."* These ten "accounts" are mini-histories and illustrate how from the very beginning of time God has been interested and active in establishing a family of believers. Nine of these ten "accounts" or histories are named after people; the very first is the "account of heaven and earth" (2:4). In each case, the "account" does not tell us of the *origin* of the person or thing named, but of its *subsequent history*, and always with reference to God's great plan of salvation. Here is a summary of the ten "accounts":

1. *The account of heaven and earth* (Genesis 2:4-4:26) explains what happened when evil invaded God's perfect creation. Through Satan's temptation Adam and Eve were led to doubt God's love and to rebel against his good will, thereby bringing the curse of death and damnation upon the human family. The history of the Cainites (chapter 4) shows how rapidly evil advanced once it entered the world. In pure grace, however, God set about to restore his good creation. He promised that the Savior (the woman's "offspring") would destroy Satan's power and free his captives.

2. *The account of Adam* (5:1-6:8) traces the ancestry of the promised Messiah from Adam to Noah. Luke 3:36-38 confirms that this is history, not folk legend. A prominent theme in this "account" is *death*. Everyone named here died, with the single exception of a man who walked with God. The tragic conclusion of this "account" records how the descendants of Seth gradually joined the Cainites in lives of self-glorification and moral abandonment, and God had to announce universal judgment. Only Noah found grace to remain faithful to God.

3. *The account of Noah* (6:9-9:29) gives us an awesome double message. While destroying all life outside the ark through a worldwide flood, the Lord graciously preserved the messianic line through Noah and his family. The same floodwaters which brought God's judgment down on sin and hardened unbelief lifted the ark and its precious cargo above the death and destruction. After the flood the Lord used Noah to announce that the Messianic line would be continued through Shem.

4. *The account of the sons of Noah* (10:1-11:9) emphasizes the unity of the human race by tracing the distribution of Noah's three sons into various nations and languages. This "Table of Nations" surveys the world of nations that were familiar to ancient Israel. Those with whom God's chosen people had more contact are listed in greater detail. The "account" concludes with the dispersion at Babel. Those who sought their own glory instead of glorifying the name of the LORD again fell under God's judgment.

5. *The account of Shem* (11:10-26) gives us the forefathers of the Messiah, narrowing the Savior's ancestry from the line of Shem to Terah, father of Abraham.

These first five "accounts" trace the early history of God's saving activity *in the ancient world*. The second set of five "accounts" traces God's saving activity *among the patriarchs*.

6. *The account of Terah* (11:27-25:11) is one of the longest "accounts," covering almost a quarter of the book of Genesis. It records how, after the human race had forsaken the gospel (Genesis 6:5-7; 11:1-9) God determined a new program of faithful love for his sinful creatures. He chose Abram, of the family of Terah, to be the father of his special nation of Israel. God called Abram out of a culture where idolatry was practiced, and trained him to trust com-

pletely in God's promise. Through this faith Abram became "the father of believers."

7. *The account of Ishmael* (25:12-18) is the shortest of Moses' ten "accounts," since the descendants of Ishmael, Abraham's son by the slave girl, constituted not the chosen line but a side line in the Old Testament history of God's saving grace. This six-verse "account" documents how God kept his promise that twelve tribal rulers would descend from Ishmael. God keeps all his promises.

8. *The account of Isaac* (25:19-35:29) carries the fulfillment of the Messianic promise through the two generations that followed Abraham. Unlike his illustrious father, Isaac had a quiet, retiring nature. He and his wife had twin sons. Even before their birth the Lord announced that the older (Esau) would serve the younger (Jacob). Contrary to what might have been expected, Jacob was the son chosen by God to carry on the line from which the Savior would be born. Unfortunately, in his early life Jacob showed a tendency to rely for success on his own cleverness. This "account" documents how Jacob had to learn the hard way to cast himself completely on God's saving grace. When Jacob had learned this, God changed his name to Israel, the one who in faith had power with God and man.

9. *The account of Esau* (36:1-37:1) again constitutes a side line. It tells us, first of all, of the development of Esau's line and, secondly, of the development of the Edomites, Israel's neighbors to the south.

10. *The account of Jacob* (37:2-50:26) is the last and longest of Moses' ten "accounts." It records how Jacob's twelve sons and one daughter grew into a family of seventy souls who, together with their households, moved to Egypt. God's grace worked in a mysterious way to bring this about, using the cruelty of Joseph's brothers to advance his wonderful plans for his chosen nation. This "account" explains

how the twelve tribes happened to be in Egypt and sets the stage for the narrative of Exodus.

We see, then, that in recording the early history of God's gracious dealings with mankind Moses divides his material into two unequal parts. The first eleven chapters of Genesis describe God's saving activity *in the original world* — among the first two people, among the descendants of Adam and Eve, and then among the descendants of Noah.

The last thirty-nine chapters of Genesis describe God's saving activity *among the patriarchs*: Abraham, Isaac and Jacob. After the account of Noah's descendants ended in idolatry and rebellion against God (11:1-9) God introduced a new program of his saving love. He lovingly chose and trained the patriarchs Abraham, Isaac and Jacob to raise up his special people of Israel. It was through this chosen nation that God resolved to carry out his marvelous plan to rescue the whole human race from sin. This saving love of God, then, is the grand theme of the entire Bible, from the first word of Genesis to the last word of Revelation.

Christ's Genelogy
Matt 1 - Joseph/Abraham
Luke 3 - Mary/Jesus

PART I

THE HISTORY OF GOD'S GRACIOUS DEALINGS WITH MANKIND IN THE ORIGINAL WORLD

GENESIS 1:1 — 11:26
THE CREATION OF THE WORLD
GENESIS 1:1 — 2:3

Nobody can be considered truly wise who has not learned the answers to the basic questions of life. Who am I? A chemical accident? A creature up from the jungle wearing a dress or a three-piece suit — you know, from cave-man to space-man in half a billion years? An insignificant combination of bone and blood and muscle and nerve, surrounded by the infinite immensity of outer space? By whose order do I live on this planet? Was it by accident, or by design? What is the purpose of my life? To survive as comfortably as I can? Mark Twain called life "a rather discreditable incident on one of the minor planets." Was he right?

We could never answer these questions correctly if God had not answered them for us. In the very first chapter of the Bible God comes to us, since we were unable to come to him. He tells us things we never in a million years would have been able to find out by ourselves — important truths about himself, and about us, and about how we happen to be where we are, about why we're here and where we're headed.

Don't misunderstand. God has not told us everything we might like to know. After all, the purpose of the Bible is not to satisfy our curiosity, but to enable us to live this life with real meaning and to find our place at the side of the Father. As we begin reading the Genesis narrative of creation we'll want to remember this is the only absolutely reliable information we have about the beginning of the universe and of the human race.

1 **In the beginning God created the heavens and the earth.**

"In the beginning God...." God is the first-named subject in the book of Genesis, and that's appropriate. The universe in which we live had a beginning. Prior to that starting point, there was no universe. There was no up and no down, no here and no there. Just nothing — except God. He always was. Before creation God alone existed. The Hebrew word translated "God" has been identified as coming from a verb meaning "to fear." The God who existed from all eternity and who at one point created time and space is awesome, and deserves to be held in reverence by his creatures. Everything exists for his sake, including the human race. You and I do not exist of ourselves or for ourselves. We have a right to exist only as we remain in harmony with the majestic Creator and his plan for us.

We humans have birthdays and deathdays, beginnings and endings; God has neither. He alone is eternal; nobody and nothing else is eternal. There was no bubble of gas, no cosmic dust which could have kindled the germ of life. The earliest forms of life did not originate in a blob of slime on some prehistoric pond. The elements, the materials from which our universe is made up, are not eternal. They came into existence only when God so ordered. The word order of this first sentence of the Bible seems perfectly normal in English, but Hebrew sentences normally begin with the verb. Here the word order is inverted, for the sake of emphasis. Moses wants to emphasize that there was a point of absolute beginning, when only God was in existence.

"God *created* the heavens and the earth." The Hebrew verb translated "created" is a very special one. In the Bible that verb 1) is used only of God's activity, and 2) always expresses the origin of something extraordinary, absolutely unique. Sometimes God creates by using existing material; when he created Adam, for example, he used the dust of the ground. But if the activity described in this opening verse took place at *the beginning*, when only God existed, it must have been a creation *out of nothing*.

The expression "the heavens and the earth" denotes the universe in its initial state. For his own reasons God did not see fit to make his creation in its completed form. By an act of his will God created all of the components which would later constitute the universe as we know it, including matter, energy, space and time. On the first day God created all of his raw materials, just as a home builder assembles all his building materials at the site before assembling them into a house.

²Now the earth was formless and empty, darkness was over the surface of the deep, and the Spirit of God was hovering over the waters.

Once again the order of the Hebrew sentence, which normally begins with the verb, is inverted. Moses wants to focus our attention on just one part of the universe — the earth, the home God has designed for the human race.

The piles of concrete block and sand and lumber a builder assembles at the construction site aren't very pretty. Neither was the earth after God's initial creative act. Moses lists four conditions which God was going to modify during that creation week. If in subsequent discussion, these four conditions are referred to as deficiencies, this is not to be understood as suggesting that God's original creation was not good. The following are the four conditions which were temporary and which God would modify during the creation week:

formlessness (The universe was a shapeless blob of material);

emptiness (The universe lacked the vegetation and the creatures God would later supply);

darkness (This would be removed only when God announced: "Let there be light!");

the deep (A fluid mass covered everything).

Christians confess that *God the Father* Almighty is the maker of heaven and earth. This is not to be understood as though the other persons of the Trinity had nothing to do with creating the universe. The Apostle John says concerning *God the Son*: "Through him all things were made; without him nothing was made that has been made" (John 1:3). *God the Holy Spirit* was also active at creation. He is described as "hovering" over the waters. Moses uses this verb elsewhere to describe the action of a mother eagle hovering over her nest, providing for her young and protecting them. The life-giving Spirit of God was active at the creation, preserving what God had created, preparing the universe for what God had in mind. The work of creation, then, is a work in which all the members of the Trinity share.

³And God said, "Let there be light," and there was light. ⁴God saw that the light was good, and he separated the light from the darkness. ⁵God called the light "day," and the darkness he called "night." And there was evening, and there was morning — the first day.

If the earth was to be the home of the human race, the darkness which enveloped the earth had to be modified. God did that with the majestic word: "Let there be light!" "He spoke and it came to be" (Psalm 33:9). For the first time light blazed out on a world which up to then had been in pitch darkness. Without light, life as we know it would be impossible.

The question has been asked: "How could there have been light on the first day if the sun and the stars weren't created until the fourth day?" The Hebrew language distinguishes between the *substance of light* (energy in the form of particles, or waves, or a combination of the two) and the heavenly *lightbearers*, just as we distinguish between the light produced by a reading lamp and the lighting fixture itself. Light itself was created on the first day; the bodies which regulate light were not created until three days later.

"God saw that the light was good." It served the purpose perfectly for which God designed it. Surely this is a valuable reminder when we hear learned people today argue that our world progressed from lower and imperfect forms to higher and better forms. This first chapter of Genesis will remind us seven times that what came from the Creator's hand was perfect .

God separated the light from the darkness. He did not destroy darkness, since he realized that like light, it would serve a salutary purpose. God therefore regulated it, providing for regular and predictable periods of light and of darkness. The light period God called "day"; the period of darkness he called "night." The first light period was followed by a period of darkness. The NIV translates: "There was evening." The word here translated "was" is better translated "became," "came on." After the period of light, evening came. Evening set in, bringing the light period to an end.

Moses continues: "There was morning," or perhaps better: "Morning set in," "morning followed," bringing the period of darkness to a close. Like every day of our lives, that very first day of the world's history consisted of a period of daylight followed by a period of darkness.

The reader may have noticed that Moses used the word "day" in two different senses in verse 5. The first time it refers to the *light period* that followed God's command. The second time Moses used the word "day" he used it in a wider sense. He called *the period of light plus the period of darkness* a day. In the very next chapter (2:4) he will use the word "day" in a still wider sense, to express *"time when."* Moses defined his terms precisely and used them carefully. It's a basic rule of Bible interpretation that the Bible must be permitted to interpret itself. The meaning of a word is determined by the way it's used and by the context in which it's used. Although the Bible uses the word "day" in various meanings, it nowhere uses the word to denote a period which is millions or even thousands of years in length. Those who want to read eons of time into the creation week do violence to the language of Genesis.

⁶And God said, "Let there be an expanse between the waters to separate water from water." ⁷God made the expanse and separated the water under the expanse from the water above it. And it was so. ⁸God called the expanse "sky." And there was evening, and there was morning — the second day.

The universe God created was formless, shapeless. Now God remedied that by creating an expanse, with water above and water beneath. God stated the purpose of this huge expanse: "...to separate water from water." God called the expanse "sky." That isn't a very scientific term; Moses doesn't define precisely what the expanse included. We get the impression that it did include not only what we call earth's atmosphere, but everything we see when we look into the heavens, including the region of the stars and planets.

With this creative act God took another step to prepare the earth as a home for his animal and human creatures. The expanse serves us in many different ways. It provides air for all breathing life. It diffuses the light from sun, moon, and stars. This huge layer of gases insulates earth's inhabitants from the extremes of heat by day and cold at night. We know that after a heavy rainfall the expanse above us serves a valuable function in evaporating moisture and returning it to the clouds.

This raises the question about exactly what is meant by the expression "*the water above the expanse*," which God separated from the "water below the expanse." There are those who think that "the water above the expanse" consisted of the clouds, the huge quantities of atmospheric water vapor which are held in suspension and are periodically precipitated in the form of rain or snow, only in turn to evaporate and return to the clouds This is the hydrologic system under which we live today, and there are those who believe this same system was in operation on the second day of creation.

There are many, however, who have difficulty with that view. In Genesis 2:5 we learn that "the LORD God had not sent rain on the earth." How long did that rainlessness last? Is it possible that the hydrologic system initiated on the second day of creation was completely different from the one under which we live?

Many have found support for this in 2 Peter 3:3-7. Here Peter refers to *three* great events of world history bringing about earth-shaking changes. Two of these events lie in the past; one is still in the future. The first is *creation*; the second is the *flood*; the third is *the end of the world*. It's easy to see the tremendous changes God's creation brought about — calling into existence things that were not. And the Scripture tells us to look for similar changes at the end of the world, when the present form of the earth will be destroyed. But what comparable changes did the flood, the third-named phenomenon, produce? The great flood at the time of Noah produced changes in the earth's crust, to be sure, but isn't the universe after the flood basically the same as the one that existed before the flood?

Perhaps not. Many have seen in St. Peter's words an indication that the flood brought about a basic change in earth's hydrologic system. In that case the "water above the expanse" may well have been a vast transparent canopy of water vapor (cf. Whitcomb and Morris, *The Genesis Flood*, pp. 253-258). This huge canopy would have provided a uniformly warm temperate climate and a healthful environment for earth dwellers. At the time of the flood the floodgates of the heavens which were opened (Genesis 7:11) would then have been the vapor canopy which released enormous quantities of water upon the earth. If the "water above the expanse" were in fact some sort of vapor canopy, the rainbow God gave Noah would then have been the first rainbow ever seen on earth.

"Evening came, and morning came — the second day." Once again Moses describes a day as consisting of a light period, daytime, plus a dark period, nighttime — in that order, exactly as we think of a day. Moses describes this as "the second day." The ordinal numeral "second" is significant. Since only similar entities may be enumerated as "second" or "third," calling this the second day indicates that it was the same kind of time period as was Day One or, for that matter, any of the creation days.

⁹**And God said, "Let the water under the sky be gathered to one place, and let dry ground appear. " And it was so. ¹⁰God called the dry ground "land," and the gathered waters he called "seas." And God saw that it was good.**

¹¹**Then God said, "Let the land produce vegetation: seedbearing plants and trees on the land that bear fruit with seed in it, according to their various kinds." And it was so. ¹²The land produced vegetation: plants bearing seed according to their kinds and trees bearing fruit with seed in it according to their kinds. And God saw that it was good . ¹³And there was evening, and there was morning — the third day.**

On the second day God had made a partial separation of the waters which had blanketed the earth, a *vertical* separation. God had put some of the water above the expanse, and some below. Now God made a second separation of the water, this time a *horizontal* one: water from soil. Since the land surface consisted of a fluid mass, a sort of mud, it was uninhabitable by the creatures God was about to design.

God therefore said: "Let the water under the sky be gathered to one place, and let dry ground appear." The geological implications of this command are considerable. Rocks were uplifted as land masses and continents were assembled. As God carved out basins for the oceans and lakes, there was erosion and redepositing of earth and rock. The psalmist paints a vivid picture of God's activity on the third day of creation:

At your rebuke the waters fled,
        at the sound of your thunder they took to flight;

> they flowed over the mountains,
>> they went down into the valleys,
>> to the place you assigned for them.
> You set a boundary they cannot cross;
>> never again will they cover the earth.
>
> (Psalm 104:7-9)

The bodies of water which had now been gathered God called "seas." The term is general and includes oceans, lakes and rivers. From the account of the flood (Genesis 7-8) we learn also that some of the water was stored in huge underground deposits.

Now that dry land had appeared, God proceeded to clothe it with growing things. This vegetation is divided by Moses into two broad classifications: seed-bearing plants and fruit trees whose fruit is seed-bearing. "Let the land produce vegetation," God commanded. It's interesting to note that the word translated "land" is the same word translated "earth" in verses 1 and 2. There the term referred to the entire earth; here it is clearly restricted to dry land. We're reminded once again how carefully Moses defines his terms.

At God's command a splendid profusion of plant life appeared on earth — everything from violets to sequoia trees. Earth was to be the home of God's highest creature, and God wanted it to be a beautiful home. He endowed each species with the unique power to produce another generation of its own kind. After creating the first generation of trees and plants God determined not to repeat that creative act. That reproductive function would now be carried on by the seed produced by the parent plant, but within definite limits. Reproduction would be "according to their various kinds." It's that orderly provision of the Creator which assures us we can expect to pick flowers, not tomatoes, from our rosebush, and which enables farmers to produce a nation's food supply. Reproduction "after its kind" speaks against the claim of evolutionists that all vegetation on earth today developed from a single initial organic cell.

It's interesting and instructive to note that God's creative command produced mature trees, trees bearing fruit. Normally it takes several years for an apple tree to reach fruit-bearing stage. God created trees that had that capability instantly. If on the third day of creation one of those trees had been cut down and its tree rings counted, it would have been hard to believe that tree was only a few hours old. God created his first creatures, animate and inanimate, *with the appearance of age.*

Like a skilled craftsman, God surveyed what he had just completed and was pleased with it. He pronounced it good. Everything about God's creation was perfect. Night fell, and when the darkness was dispelled by dawn the following morning, the third day of the world's history had ended.

[14]And God said, "Let there be lights in the expanse of the sky to separate the day from the night, and let them serve as signs to mark seasons and days and years, [15] and let them be lights in the expanse of the sky to give light on the earth." And it was so. [16]God made two great lights — the greater light to govern the day and the lesser light to govern the night. He also made the stars. [17]God set them in the expanse of the sky to give light on the earth, [18] to govern the day and the night, and to separate light from darkness. And God saw that it was good. [19]And there was evening, and there was morning — the fourth day

The creation of trees and plants brought about the need for modifying the light which had been created on the first day. God therefore provided lightbearers. He made a "greater light to govern the day and the lesser light to govern the night." God hung two great lamps in the expanse to determine the rhythm of day and night. Although we know that the sun is smaller than many of the other stars, Moses' description represents the viewpoint of someone living on earth. This is sometimes called "phenomenal language," language reflecting things as they appear to our senses.

It may seem strange that the creation account does not name the sun and the moon. The reason may very well be that many of Israel's neighbors in the ancient Near East considered the sun, moon, stars and planets to be gods who governed the course of human affairs. Ancient people also practiced astrology, believing that the course of the planets and stars determines life on this earth down to the smallest detail. God wanted to prevent his children from worshiping the heavenly bodies. He also wanted to free his people from believing that their fate depended upon the orbit of the stars. He therefore indicated in considerable detail the precise functions these lightbearers were designed to serve.

Their first purpose was to *separate day from night*. In addition, they were to *serve as signs* marking seasons, days and years. And finally they were to *give light* on earth.

And so the fourth day came to an end, the first day regulated by the heavenly bodies. Yet it is described in the same way as the first three were, consisting of day and night, in that order. It was, like all of the creation days, what we understand as a normal day.

20And God said, "Let the water teem with living creatures, and let birds fly above the earth across the expanse of the sky."

21So God created the great creatures of the sea and every living and moving thing with which the water teems, according to their kinds, and every winged bird according to its kind. And God saw that it was good.

22God blessed them and said, "Be fruitful and increase in number and fill the water in the seas, and let the birds increase on the earth."

²³**And there was evening, and there was morning — the fifth day.**

Three of the deficiencies which had characterized God's initial creation had now been corrected. The *darkness* had been replaced by a whole skyful of stars and planets. Instead of being a *formless mass*, the universe was now ordered and well formed. And the *mass of water* which had made the earth unfit for habitation had been confined behind barriers — some above the sky, some behind established shorelines, some beneath the earth's surface. Now God addressed the fourth deficiency.

At creation the universe was *void of life*. It would no longer be. A word from the lips of God filled the waters with the vast variety of marine life — from guppies to blue whales — and the sky with birds. The Creator endowed each of these new forms of life with the capability of passing on life to the next generation — again after its own kind. This divine restriction does not allow for new kinds, as the theory of evolution proposes. Evolution builds its case on mutations. But the study of genetics has demonstrated that mutations, traceable to damaged reproductive cells, are slight and regressive and do not develop new kinds.

This reproductive capability of birds and sea creatures was possible because "God blessed them." This divine blessing was more than a pious wish; it was an effective act, enabling the creature to be and to do what the Creator had designed. When God said, "Be fruitful and increase in number and fill the water in the seas, and let the birds increase," he was expressing more than just hope. He was giving his creatures the capability, as well as the mating impulse to carry out his command to reproduce.

²⁴And God said, "Let the land produce living creatures according to their kinds: livestock, creatures that move along the ground, and wild animals, each according to its kind." And it was so.

²⁵God made the wild animals according to their kinds, the livestock according to their kinds, and all the creatures that move along the ground according to their kinds. And God saw that it was good.

The sixth day of the creation week was a busy day and a blessed one, for it brought the climax of God's creative activity. God first of all created the land animals, which Moses lists under three categories: livestock (which can be tamed and domesticated); animals which live and move close to the ground (reptiles, insects, worms); and wild animals (those with freedom of movement). The classification is not necessarily intended to be exhaustive; it simply emphasizes certain characteristics. Genesis 2:19 informs us that God used earth as his material for creating the animals. Once again the Creator expressed his approval of this new phase of his creation.

²⁶Then God said, "Let us make man in our image, in our likeness, and let them rule over the fish of the sea and the birds of the air, over the livestock, over all the earth, and over all the creatures that move along the ground." ²⁷ So God created man in his own image, in the image of God he created him; male and female he created them. ²⁸ God blessed them and said to them, "Be fruitful and increase in number; fill the earth and subdue it. Rule over the fish of the sea and the birds of the air and over every living creature that moves on the ground."

The stage was now set for the climax of God's creative activity. God said: "Let us make man." Long before we humans ever thought about God he was thinking about us and making plans for us to share life with him, to live with him as members of his family.

God approached the creation of this highest creature in a manner different from any other of his creative activity. Here he gave no simple creative order: "Let there be!" Before creating the first human, God engaged in solemn deliberation. The reader will note the plurals (Let *us* make...in *our* image...in *our* likeness"). The New Testament makes it clear that the three persons of the Holy Trinity were all active in the work of creation. In writing the creation account Moses consistently used language which would be in complete harmony with the information God would subsequently reveal to us about the plurality of persons in the Godhead.

God stated clearly what his purpose was in designing this highest creature. He was to exercise rule over the rest of the creation, "over all the earth." This divine program for the human race makes it clear that God's human creatures were not just another species of animal. Mankind — male and female — is clearly distinguished from the animals, set apart for a function different from the one the Creator assigned to these lower creatures. Mankind was to manage the earth for God. All of earth's resources were placed under his jurisdiction. When God blessed the human race (Genesis 1:28) he ordered it to subdue the earth, to rule over it.

The fall into sin has greatly modified this dominion over God's creation. The created world is no longer completely subordinate to fallen mankind. Animals attack and kill him; water drowns him; and finally earth covers him. But God's authorization "Subdue the earth and rule over it!" has never been revoked.

"So God created man in his image." It is noteworthy that here, for the third time in this chapter, Moses uses the verb "created." This Hebrew verb is used only when God is the author of an action, and only of an action which is unique and unprecedented. Previously Moses had used this verb only when describing God's creating the universe (1:1) and the first living creatures to move about by their own volition (1:21). Here this special verb is used to describe the creating of the crown and climax of God's creative activity. Let it be stated again that the verb "create" does not in itself imply a making out of nothing. God did use a lump of earth to create Adam.

To equip his first human creatures for the awesome assignment of managing the earth for him God created them in his image, in his likeness. Here is the ultimate evidence that mankind, whom God created male and female, is pre-eminent in God's creation. Some Bible students have seen in "the image of God" only a reference to man's humanness, his self-consciousness, his intellect. But that is clearly not the biblical meaning of the term. (Even after Adam and Eve fell into sin and lost the divine image, they retained their human personality and their powers of intellect.) The image of God cannot describe a physical resemblance to God, since God is a spirit. The New Testament describes the divine image as a special *knowledge*, knowing God to be the source of every blessing (Colossians 3:10). It describes the divine image as *holiness*, an absence of sinfulness (Ephesians 4:24).

In trying to understand the concept of the image of God, it may be helpful to describe the effect the divine image had on the personality of Adam and Eve — on their intellect, emotions and will. Unlike the mental dullness and ignorance we bring with us into the world, Adam and Eve understood perfectly with their *intellect* what God wanted them to know. While they possessed the image of God their *emotions* were also in tune with God's; they found their greatest happiness in God. And unlike the rebellious will each of us brought into the world, their *will* was in complete harmony with God; what he wanted was what they wanted. Every impulse and desire of theirs was in tune with God's good will. Created in the image of God, they were human replicas of what God is like.

We know that this beautiful relationship with God was destroyed when Adam and Eve doubted God's love, disobeyed his command, and dragged the whole human race down with them. All of the descendants of Adam and Eve, with a single exception, brought a sinful image with them into the world — a *mind* ignorant of God's good plan for them, *emotions* that find joy in things that displease God, and a *will* which rebels against God's good and gracious will. The New Testament brings us the wonderful news, however, that through faith in Christ the image of God is again created in the sinner, who is thereby restored to that precious relationship Adam and Eve once enjoyed with God.

As long as we live in a sinful world, the image of God is only partially restored in us by faith. That new nature created in us by the Holy Spirit must coexist with the sinful image we received from our parents. St. John assures us, however: "When (Christ) appears, we shall be like him, for we shall see him as he is" (1 John 3:2). When the believer enters eternal life, the image of God in him will be completely restored.

"Male and female he created them." It is significant that immediately following this statement (which, incidentally, is not made about any of the animals) God gave his first two human creatures the blessing: "Be fruitful and increase in number...fill the earth."

Jesus referred to this statement in a conversation with the Pharisees recorded in Matthew 19:4-6. There Jesus made it clear that human procreation is not just a biological matter, simply the result of a union of male and female. As God sees it (and as God wants us to see it) human conception and birth are to be considered only in conjunction with the marital union of a man and a woman pledged to each other for life. Jesus' words to the Pharisees combine quotations from Genesis 1 and 2: "At the beginning the Creator made them male and female, and said: 'For this reason a man will leave his father and mother and be united to his wife, and the two will become one flesh.' So they are no longer two, but one. Therefore what God has joined together, let man not separate." In contrast to the animals, which propagate by means of random mating, a wise Creator designed human reproduction to be the result of a lifetime commitment of two people in marriage. The fact that in our society almost half of all marriages end in divorce does not change the fact that God has made his intentions clear. And one more thing is clear. God will have the last word in history, as he had the first at creation.

It's important to remember that the first two human beings came from the hand of their Creator not as half-animals but as royalty, with unrestricted dominion over all of God's creation. Since through sin we have lost this dominion, it's difficult for us to appreciate what this meant for Adam and Eve. In the sinful world in which we live dominion usually signals conquest and often exploitation. God's two perfect children were to rule everything God had created not in order to dominate it or take advantage of it, but to protect and preserve it for God. Similarly Christians, who look upon themselves as stewards of our natural environment, will be sensitive to waste and abuse of the world's natural resources.

²⁹Then God said, "I give you every seed-bearing plant on the face of the whole earth and every tree that has fruit with seed in it. They will be yours for food. ³⁰And to all the beasts of the earth and all the birds of the air and all the creatures that move on the ground — everything that has the breath of life in it — I give every green plant for food." And it was so.

³¹God saw all that he had made, and it was very good. And there was evening, and there was morning — the sixth day.

At creation God assigned a vegetarian diet to man and beast. He specified "every seed-bearing plant...every green plant." Many years later, after the great flood, God told Noah and his family that the beasts of the earth, the birds of the air and the fish of the sea were to be food for them. "Just as I gave you the green plants, I now give you everything," God told Noah (Genesis 9:3).

Does this mean that during all the years from creation to the flood humans were vegetarians? The Scripture does not answer that question directly. Bible students have called attention to the fact that the garments of skin God later made for Adam and Eve required the taking of animal life, as did the sacrifices Abel offered to God. Remember, too, that at the time of the flood (Genesis 7:12) Noah was aware of the distinction between "clean" and "unclean" animals (those acceptable for food and for sacrifice, and those not acceptable). Is it possible that the meat of animals was used for food prior to the flood? Since we have no clear word of God in this matter we must leave the question unanswered.

Night fell on that eventful sixth day of the creation week. And when, hours later, the dawn of a new day appeared, the sixth day was history. God looked back on all he had made and was pleased with what he saw. All individual units of his creation were perfect, and together all formed a harmonious whole. Everything was perfectly suited for the role the Creator had assigned to it.

In God's verdict "Good!" the perceptive Christian will again sense the conflict between the creation account and the theory of the evolutionary origin of the world. The first traces the world's history from initial perfection to subsequent imperfection. Evolution, however, reverses that direction, and instead argues for a development from initial imperfection to gradual perfection. Let there be no misunderstanding: the two viewpoints are irreconcilable. In the introduction to a series of sermons Martin Luther wrote on the creation of the world, he made the observation: "When Moses writes that God created heaven and earth in six days, let his words stand. ... If, however, you cannot understand how this could have been done in six days, then give the Holy Spirit the honor of being more learned than you are" (LW III:20f).

2 Thus the heavens and the earth were completed in all their vast array. ²By the seventh day God had finished the work he had been doing; so on the seventh day he rested from all his work. ³And God blessed the seventh day and made it holy, because on it he rested from all the work of creating that he had done.

Here we have the striking conclusion to Moses' account of the creation. Unfortunately, our Bibles separate these three verses from the creation account and instead list them as the opening verses of Genesis 2. Actually they form an effective conclusion to the creation and rightly belong in Genesis 1. It will be helpful to remember that the chapter and verse divisions we have in our English Bibles are not a part of the Scriptures given by inspiration of God to the original writers. Chapter divisions were added to the text in the thirteenth century by Stephen Langton, archbishop of Canterbury.

It has been noted earlier that Moses divided the subject matter of Genesis into ten sections, each of which he introduces with the formula: "This is the account of...." The first of these ten "accounts," or mini-histories, begins at Genesis 2:4: "This is the account of the heavens and the earth when they were created." This verse, therefore, properly belongs at the head of Genesis 2. It follows, then, that whatever precedes Genesis 2:4 is introductory and rightly belongs to the first chapter.

"Thus the heavens and the earth were completed in all their vast array." The universe had now been created. A whole skyful of stars and planets had been put into orbit. The earth was blanketed with trees and plants. The earth's surface, as well as the waters surrounding it and the skies above it, were inhabited by creatures great and small. And managing all this for God were a perfect man and a perfect woman. God had also completed that segment of creation which is invisible to the naked eye — the world of the atom and the molecule, for example. God "thought up" energy — solar, electrical, atomic. I am told there is enough energy in this sheet of paper that if it could be released it could power an ocean liner across the Atlantic. The forces of nature — gravity, for example — which God initiated during creation week are still operative. Highest of God's invisible creation are the angels, God's secret agents. Moses' summary term, "a vast array," has to be an understatement.

Since God's creative work was completed on the first six days, what remained for the seventh day of the creation week? Moses describes this with three verbs.

"God *rested* from all the work of creating that he had done. Since God's creation was absolutely perfect and totally effective, God stopped creating. It's important to emphasize, however, that God did not stop working. The universe would have collapsed, the sun would have stopped shining, two human hearts would have stopped beating if God had not been ceaselessly active, preserving what he had created. But the creating was finished, and as God surveyed his handiwork he found satisfaction in it. The seventh day of that creation week was, therefore, not a day of creative activity. It has been called "the great dedication day of the universe."

"God *blessed* the seventh day...." Since there was nothing further to be created, God made his completed creation a source of ongoing blessing, especially for his human creatures.

Furthermore, God not only blessed that great dedication day, he "*made it holy*." God hallowed that seventh day for the human race. As he had found satisfaction in what he had made, so his sons and daughters are to find joy in their gracious God and in what his hands have made. This would seem to be the reason why the seventh day is not formally closed with the same formula with which Moses concluded his description of each of the first six days. The happy satisfaction God's children find in the Creator, whom they have learned to call "Father," is an ongoing thing.

It's important to note that Genesis 2:2, 3 says nothing about the seventh day of *every* week. Moses is speaking only of the seventh day that followed the six days of creation. To see these verses as setting apart *every* seventh day as a day of rest for all people is to read something into the Scripture. The Sabbath law was first given to the nation of Israel when they reached Mt. Sinai, on their way to their Promised Land (Exodus 20:8-11).

The Bible-believing Christian will appreciate the first chapter of the Bible not only because of what it tells him about the *history of the universe*, but also because of what it tells him about *God*. Just as your fingerprints and footprints tell something about you, so the creation record gives us some important information about God.

There were no eyewitnesses to the creation, no reporters, no TV cameras. But God was there, because he is *eternal*. If a word from his lips can call planets and people into existence, he is *almighty*. When we study the orderly functioning of the solar system or, for that matter, of the human body, we're struck by the *wisdom* of the Creator. When you consider, for example, what an astonishing concept the idea of human sexuality is, you're struck by the wisdom of the One who thought that up. When you touch the softness of a baby's cheeks or marvel at the brilliant oranges and reds of a summer sunset, you realize what boundless *imagination* the Creator demonstrated. And when we focus our attention on God's two highest creatures, designed in God's perfect image, equipped for a useful and meaningful life as children and coworkers of God, we see how God showed himself to be a God of *love*. Long before we ever thought about God, he was thinking about us and making plans for us.

We'll want to remember that the creation account is not an isolated piece of information, inserted into the Scripture just for its own sake. It emphasizes how from the very beginning God's love has been at work on behalf of the human race, the very crown of his creation. This love is apparent *before* God's children rebelled against a loving heavenly Father. This love becomes even more apparent *after* they rebelled and fell into sin.

THE FIRST ACCOUNT:
OF THE UNIVERSE
GENESIS 2:4-4:26

The opening chapter of the book of Genesis has drawn us a picture of the beautiful world the Creator designed and put together at the beginning of time. You can't read the description of that world without comparing it with the world in which we live. Every day's newspaper, it seems, brings us an additional dose of bad news — about things like crooked business and terrorist attacks and bone cancer. A question that must rise in the mind of every thinking person is: "What happened? What happened to change God's perfect world into our bandaged and bleeding world?"

This is the question Moses answers in the first of the ten "accounts" or "histories" which make up the book of Genesis. The story which this first "account" has to tell is not a completely happy one. It begins by describing the loving relationship which existed between the Creator and his highest creatures. The Creator's love is demonstrated by all he did to make Adam and Eve happy. But this foremost of God's creatures rebelled against God's good will. By so doing he cut himself loose from God and dragged down the entire human race — and even the creature world — with him into an existence of frustration and decay — and death.

The creature could break off a beautiful relationship with God, but he was not able to repair and restore that relationship. This first "account," *the account of heaven and earth,* therefore, proceeds to show how God, in an amazing display of his free and faithful love, promised to restore his human creatures to the position of honor the Creator had originally intended for them.

Some Bible students view Genesis 2 as a second creation account, written by an author different from the one who wrote Genesis 1 and in conflict with certain details mentioned in chapter 1. This view, however, is unacceptable, for several reasons. It destroys the unity of the book of Genesis, pitting one portion against another. And it ignores the author's ten-part outline for the book. Genesis 1 is a chronological narrative; Genesis 2 is not. Instead Genesis 2 selects a number of items from the creation week (a man, a garden, two trees, and a woman) for special emphasis, thereby providing necessary background for chapter 3. Together with chapters 3-4 it shows what happened to the perfect world described in Genesis 1.

⁴This is the account of the heavens and the earth when they were created. When the LORD God made the earth and the heavens — ⁵ and no shrub of the field had yet appeared on the earth and no plant of the field had yet sprung up, for the LORD God had not sent rain on the earth and there was no man to work the ground, ⁶ but streams came up from the earth and watered the whole surface of the ground.

The first of Moses' ten "accounts" begins by drawing a lovely picture of the relationship that existed between the Creator and his first children. It shows us a God intent on making them happy.

In verses 4 and 5, Moses introduces us to a new name for God. The Hebrew name consists of the four consonants YHWH, originally pronounced "*Yahweh.*" Throughout the Old Testament this was the name that distinguished the God of Israel from the idols of surrounding nations. The Greek translation of the Old Testament translates Yahweh as *kyrios*, meaning "Lord." To enable the reader of the English Bible to distinguish between this special Yahweh name and another divine name which means "Lord and Master," our English Bibles consistently spell the translation of Yahweh with capital letters, "LORD."

In a conversation with Moses at Mt. Sinai centuries later, God explained the meaning of the name Yahweh. Here was his explanation: "The LORD, the LORD, the compassionate and gracious God, slow to anger, abounding in love and faithfulness, maintaining love to thousands, and forgiving wickedness, rebellion and sin." (Exodus 34:6-7).

Yahweh, then, the LORD, is the special name of Israel's covenant God. It's God's Old Testament Savior name. It stresses especially two qualities about God: his absolute self-sufficiency or *independence*, and his absolute *constancy*. The LORD is the God of free and faithful love. Here Moses combines the name *Yahweh*, the LORD, with *Elohim*, his Creator-name. In his treatment of Adam and Eve, God displayed his faithful mercy as well as his awe-inspiring power.

One of the consequences of the fall into sin was that God told Adam: "Cursed is the ground because of you. ...It will produce thorns and thistles for you, and you will eat the plants of the field" (Genesis 3:17f). The expression "plants of the field," the same expression used here in 2:5, must therefore refer to the cereal grains, which man after the fall was to cultivate and from which he was to make his bread. This leads to the conclusion that these grains were not on the earth prior to the fall in the same form in which we know them. Moses notes that as yet it had not rained on earth. In the absence of rainfall a system of springs kept rising from the earth to provide the moisture trees and plants needed. (Incidentally, we don't know how long that rainlessness on earth continued. The possibility that it may have

34

lasted until the time of the flood will be treated in connection with Genesis 7.)

⁷The LORD God formed the man from the dust of the ground and breathed into his nostrils the breath of life, and the man became a living being. ⁸Now the LORD God had planted a garden in the east, in Eden; and there he put the man he had formed. ⁹And the LORD God made all kinds of trees grow out of the ground — trees that were pleasing to the eye and good for food. In the middle of the garden were the tree of life and the tree of the knowledge of good and evil.

God formed man from the ground by a separate creative act. These words are clear, and they are significant. They provide a problem for those who try to reconcile the biblical account with evolution and who claim that you and I developed from the animals. Moses supplements what he had told us in Genesis 1 about the creation of the human race. The Hebrew verb ("The LORD God *formed*...") describes the activity of a potter. Its use here emphasizes the personal interest and care which the Creator demonstrated in fashioning this highest of his creatures.

The words "...he breathed into his nostrils the breath of life" hint that there is a second component to a human being, besides his body. Genesis 1:26, 27 has already supplied the details. With loving care and intelligent purpose the Creator shaped a lump of earth into his highest creature and breathed the life principle into him. The writer is again emphasizing the distinctiveness and the superior dignity of God's human creatures, who received the Creator's own breath. These words of Moses help us to understand what happens at death and why it's natural to fear death. Death, the separation of body and soul, is a violent intrusion into God's good work of creation. Moses' words, incidentally, are also a sobering reminder that we have precious little to boast of. What are we, after all, but dirt plus the breath of God?

The garden home God provided served a number of purposes for Adam. It satisfied his physical needs, his needs for food and shelter. It satisfied his emotional needs; Adam received mental stimulation as he studied the secrets of God's creation and marveled at its beauty. And in this lovely home God also provided kinship and love for Adam by creating a helper for him in the person of Eve.

Moses now directs our attention to two trees which God planted in the middle of the garden, where Adam and Eve could not fail to notice them. The *tree of the knowledge of good and evil* will be discussed in connection with verses 16 and 17. The other tree was the *tree of life*. Not much is said about it, since it never got to serve the purpose God intended for it. It would have served its purpose if Adam and Eve has resisted Satan's temptation. Judging from what God said in 3:22, the purpose of the tree of life was to confirm Adam and Eve in the possession of physical life. According to Revelation 2:7, when we one day live in God's presence in heaven, then we will eat of the tree of life, and nothing will ever be able to interrupt that perfect life.

[10]A river watering the garden flowed from Eden; from there it was separated into four headwaters. [11]The name of the first is the Pishon; it winds through the entire land of Havilah, where there is gold. [12](The gold of that land is good; aromatic resin and onyx are also there.) [13]The name of the second river is the Gihon; it winds through the entire land of Cush. [14]The name of the third river is the Tigris; it runs along the east side of Asshur. And the fourth river is the Euphrates.

To appreciate this description of the garden home God prepared for his children, remember that Moses wrote this book for the Hebrews, who lived in a part of the world that has minimal water resources. A stream, apparently originating from some underground source in the garden, branched out at the edge of the garden and became four headwaters, providing an abundant water supply for the entire area.

Moses establishes a connection between the four rivers and several well-known rivers of his day. Havilah was most likely the coast of Arabia; Cush is south of Egypt, perhaps present-day Sudan. Since the great flood changed the face of the earth, however, the geographical details in these verses cannot be used to pinpoint the precise location of the garden home.

[15]The LORD God took the man and put him in the Garden of Eden to work it and take care of it. [16]And the LORD God commanded the man, "You are free to eat from any tree in the garden; [17] but you must not eat from the tree of the knowledge of good and evil, for when you eat of it you will surely die."

Sir James Barrie once said: "Doubtless the Almighty could have provided us with better fun than hard work, but I don't know what it is." Satisfying activity was one of the joys God's highest creatures enjoyed in paradise. They could put all their abilities of mind and body to work for God. Living, as we do, in a culture which tends to view work as a necessary evil, we need this reminder that work is not something that entered the world because of the fall into sin. Work was part of God's original intent for his human creatures.

Reference has been made earlier to two special trees which the LORD God planted in the garden: the *tree of life* and the *tree of the knowledge of good and evil*. Moses now supplies us with additional information about the purpose of that second tree.

People who know how this story comes out have asked: "Why did God have to put that tree with the forbidden fruit in the garden in the first place? Since Adam and Eve weren't permitted to eat of its fruit, why put it there at all?" Let the text speak for itself.

"You are free to eat from any tree of the garden." God was not selfish in dealing with his highest creature. Adam had a wide range of foods to pick from, and the command to abstain from one tree was neither irritating nor burdensome.

But God did make it very clear: "You must not eat of the tree of the knowledge of good and evil, for when you eat of it you will surely die." When Adam received this command from God he was, in the fullest sense of the term, alive. He was bound to God by the most intimate bond of love and trust. In the language of the Scripture, that's being *alive*.

That bond would be broken if Adam refused to obey God. By that act he would separate himself from God. In the strong language of the Scripture, that's being *dead*. And as evidence that this highest creature had cut himself off from his loving Creator, he would then also be subject to physical death, the separation of body and soul.

Since that tree had such fateful consequences for Adam and the the entire human race, why did God plant it in the garden? Was it just to test Adam, to see what he would do when confronted with temptation? That cannot be a satisfactory explanation. All of Genesis 2 speaks of what God did to make his children happy, and this special tree was no exception.

God never designed humans to be puppets or robots whom he regulates by pulling strings or pressing buttons. By placing the tree of the knowledge of good and evil in the garden God was giving Adam the opportunity of his own free will to obey God. In so doing God realized the risk involved, that Adam might choose to disobey him. When Adam came from the hand of his Creator, he was in a state of *created innocence.* By giving Adam the command not to eat, God was offering him the opportunity to progress from created innocence to *conscious holiness.* God wanted his highest creature to be holy by choice, not just by accident.

Martin Luther used an illustration here which makes God's intent clear. "This tree of the knowledge of good and evil was Adam's church, his altar, his pulpit. Here he was to yield to God the obedience he owed, to give recognition to the word and will of God, to give thanks to God, and to call upon God for aid against temptation" (LW 1:95). That tree in the middle of the garden was Adam's place to worship God. Here he was reminded of God's goodness to him; here he could thank God for his mercy; here he could respond by giving God glad obedience.

The Creator had endowed Adam with a free will, the inborn freedom to do what pleased God. God wanted him now to exercise that free will. If he had, the experience would have produced a knowledge of good and evil similar to that which God himself has. Adam's *intellect* would have become more keenly aware of what God wanted and what he didn't want. His *emotions* would have found joy in the Creator's will and would have convinced him what a dreadful thing it would be to rebel against God. And Adam's *will* would have consciously chosen to follow God's command to have nothing to do with the forbidden fruit.

The Institution of Marriage

¹⁸The LORD God said, "It is not good for the man to be alone. I will make a helper suitable for him." ¹⁹Now the LORD God had

formed out of the ground all the beasts of the field and all the birds of the air. He brought them to the man to see what he would name them; and whatever the man called each living creature, that was its name. ²⁰So the man gave names to all the livestock, the birds of the air and all the beasts of the field. But for Adam no suitable helper was found. ²¹So the LORD God caused the man to fall into a deep sleep; and while he was sleeping, he took one of the man's ribs and closed up the place with flesh. ²²Then the LORD God made a woman from the rib he had taken out of the man, and he brought her to the man. ²³The man said,

> "This is now bone of my bones
> and flesh of my flesh;
> she shall be called 'woman,'
> for she was taken out of man."

²⁴For this reason a man will leave his father and mother and be united to his wife, and they will become one flesh. ²⁵The man and his wife were both naked, and they felt no shame.

It was mentioned earlier that Genesis 2 is not a second creation account, but that it supplies additional details about the creation which we need to understand Genesis 3. We've already learned about the *garden* of delight and about the two special *trees*. Now Moses supplies background information about the *woman* who played such a key role in the account of the fall.

It had never been the Creator's intent to have Adam live alone. In the Creator's view, this was "not good." And so God designed a special creature whose role is described as "a helper suitable for him." This is God's order of creation: man was designed to be the head, woman to be his helper.

God did not force his companion on the man. God had created animals of all kinds and now brought them to Adam to have him name them. One reason for God's doing this was to provide Adam an opportunity to share God's thoughts about his loneliness and to develop a longing for the special gift God was about to give him.

As Adam selected appropriate names for each of the animals and birds, he noted that each of them had a mate. Adam also recognized that no animal was suited for intimate companionship with him. He had no one with whom he could share the joy of living in paradise. It was then that God caused him to fall into a deep sleep. While Adam was asleep God took a bone of his body and by a special creative act formed it (Hebrew: "built it") into a woman.

In his first recorded words Adam expressed his joy over God's gift who, like him, had been created in God's image (Genesis 1:27). Adam's reaction to Eve shows that he possessed the image of God. Even though he'd been asleep, he *understood* where she had come from and what her relationship was to him. He *rejoiced* at this magnificent gift; he *agreed* with God that here was a helper suitable for him in every way.

This, then, was the first marriage. God designed a special creature from a part of Adam's body and brought her to Adam. Adam received her as his wife, and she was willing to be his wife. That this blessed transaction was not a one-time thing, but a basic divine establishment for the whole human race of all time becomes clear from God's statement in verse 24, a statement which he apparently made through Adam: "For this reason a man will leave his father and mother and be united to his wife, and they will become one flesh."

The marital relationship begins when two people freely pledge themselves unconditionally to each other and give evidence of this by breaking off a close family bond in order to establish a new one. To express their unconditional commitment these two people enjoy a physical union which then becomes God's way of passing on the gift of life to the next generation. In God's view, sexual union is anything but casual. Marriage, then, is not a human arrangement, or the product of human progress or social development. It was God's idea, his gift to his highest creatures. It follows, then, that people do not have the right to set their own standards for marriage, to determine their own rules for terminating it, or to devise alternate lifestyles to replace it.

Adam and Eve enjoyed their new relationship. Even though they were naked they felt no shame, because they were in full control of their sexual impulses, and expressed them in perfect love to God and in unselfish love to each other.

The First Sin

A question that has to bother every thinking person is "Why is there evil in the world?" Why do people die of cancer? Why do terrorists bomb airports, killing and maiming innocent bystanders? Why do our nation's divorce courts keep cranking out their ungodly statistics? Who would deliberately set man against man, husband against wife, management against labor and labor against management, nation against nation? Surely this is not the way God designed life on earth to be.

Every day's newspaper provides new evidence that we are not part of a nice neat creation set in motion by a loving God. Instead, we're part of a mutinous world where rebellion against God is the order of the day. The mutiny started when one of God's angels rebelled against God. Since he realized he was powerless to harm God, he showed the mentality of a terrorist by taking innocent hostages. Genesis 3 tells the tragic story of how this evil angel managed to get God's children away from him.

The day God's first children turned away from him, in an attitude of unbelief and of defiance, has to be the saddest day in history. This chapter gives us the only answer — though an incomplete one — to the question: "Why is there evil in the world?"

3 Now the serpent was more crafty than any of the wild animals the LORD God had made. He said to the woman, "Did God really say, 'You must not eat from any tree in the garden'?"

The normal word order of the Hebrew sentence is inverted here. The writer wants to emphasize that a new figure, a snake, is the subject of the action. Since this was one of God's creatures, its craftiness dare not be viewed as an evil quality. This intelligent animal was the one Satan chose to use as his instrument to drive a wedge between God and his children.

"He said to the woman, 'Did God really say...'?" Who is speaking here? Snakes don't have vocal cords. The Lord Jesus identified the evil force behind the snake when he told his Jewish opponents: "You belong to your father, *the devil.* ... He was a murderer from the beginning, not holding to the truth, for there is no truth in him. ... He is a liar and the *father of lies*" (John 8:44). Revelation 12:9 and 20:2 also call Satan "that ancient serpent."

"Did God really say...?" The question sounds innocent enough, doesn't it? "Eve, are you sure you got that straight?" Is it possible that a loving God would deny his highest creatures the pleasure of eating any kind of fruit in the garden? Satan's question was, however, not an innocent one. His purpose was to raise doubt in Eve's mind — doubt as to exactly what God had said, as well as doubt about the fairness of God's prohibition.

The first thing we note about Satan is that he operates in disguise. He pretended to be interested in Eve's well-being. He didn't say to her (and he doesn't say to us): "Come, I'll teach you how to sin." What he does say is: "Let me help you to a happier, more exciting life. Surely God wants you to be happy. Why would he put this beautiful fruit on the tree if you weren't supposed to eat it? God wants you to live life to the fullest. He's different from what you think!"

²The woman said to the serpent, "We may eat fruit from the trees in the garden, ³ but God did say, 'You must not eat fruit from the tree that is in the middle of the garden, and you must not touch it, or you will die.' "

In Eve's response we can detect the very beginnings of mankind's fall into sin. She knew that snakes can't talk. She knew also that animals have no sense of right and wrong. She should have recognized immediately that an evil spirit was involved here. And yet Eve entered in on a discussion of God's word and God's goodness with the snake. His insinuation that God was not being faithful to her is one she should immediately have rejected. This was going to be a costly conversation for Eve; she would end up paying an awful price.

Before looking at Eve's answer to Satan we might ask: "What good reason could God possibly have had for permitting his highest creature to be tempted? If he hadn't permitted the devil to tempt Eve in the first place, couldn't the tragedy of the fall into sin have been avoided?" By permitting his highest creatures to be tempted to sin, God was once again providing *another opportunity for them to glorify him* — in this case, *by consciously choosing good* where the possibility of choosing evil existed.

When she answered the devil Eve restated the broad *per-mission* God had granted ("Of all the trees of the garden you may eat freely..."), although it may be significant that she omitted the word "all." And when she restated God's *prohibition* she added "... neither shall you touch it...." Some have seen in these words an unwarranted addition to God's original command. But it's just as possible that Eve was paraphrasing God's prohibition. Touching the fruit would be the prelude to eating it.

⁴"You will not surely die," the serpent said to the woman. ⁵"For God knows that when you eat of it your eyes will be opened, and you will be like God, knowing good and evil.'

If up to this point Eve had imagined this was a harmless conversation, the next words of Satan must surely have shown her otherwise. For one thing, he denied the reality of the punishment God had threatened, calling *God's truthfulness* into question.

And then he called *God's love* into question. He put God's prohibition in an ugly light. He pictured God, the giver of all good gifts, as selfish and envious, rather than unbelievably gracious and generous. "God has forbidden you to eat the fruit only because he knows eating it would endow you with a secret knowledge, the knowledge that you can live without God. Eve, God doesn't want you to discover the tremendous potential that lies in your human reason. Instead he wants to keep you ignorant."

Satan offered Eve two alternatives, both of which should have been unacceptable to her:
1. either God had not forbidden her to eat the fruit, or
2. he was not the loving God he pretended to be.

45

Here is the basic lie of Satan: "God and his will are not really good." "God has known all along that eating the fruit would make you his equals, and he doesn't want that."

God had been unbelievably generous to Adam and Eve, but there was one thing he had not given them — equality with himself. They were not God. God had designed them to live *under* him, not *alongside* him. Here is the bait Satan dangled before Eve's eyes, knowing that there were no earthly gifts he could offer her which God had not already given his beloved children. Satan had sowed two poisonous seeds in Eve's heart. First, he persuaded her *not to take God too seriously.* Second, he made her *doubt God's goodness.* At that point Satan broke off the temptation. He waited to give his poison time to take effect.

It is an oversimplification, then, to say that Eve's sin was *disobedience.* Her sin was *unbelief.* She refused to believe what God had said about himself. She doubted his love, choosing rather to believe Satan's lie.

⁶When the woman saw that the fruit of the tree was good for food and pleasing to the eye, and also desirable for gaining wisdom, she took some and ate it. She also gave some to her husband, who was with her, and he ate it. ⁷Then the eyes of both of them were opened, and they realized they were naked; so they sewed fig leaves together and made coverings for themselves.

We can detect the change that had taken place in the entire personality of Eve. As long as she possessed the image of God, she knew everything God wanted her to know. Now her *intellect* told her that the tree was good for food and desirable for making her wise. Her *emotions* had also been misled; Eve no longer found joy in unblinking obedience to her Father's word. Her *will*, which had been in perfect harmony with God's will, now led her to do what

The Fall

God had forbidden and to tell her husband to do the same. Eve had permitted Satan's lie to take possession of her mind, heart and will.

We notice also that in the fall both Adam and Eve *abandoned their God-given roles*. Eve, designed by God to be a helper for the man, presumed to act as leader of the family — and spiritual leader, no less. And Adam, designed to be the spiritual head of the family, abandoned his leadership role and listened to his wife instead of to God.

Satan's promise to Eve had turned out to be a lie. She and Adam had not become like God. In another sense, however, Satan's word had come true. Their eyes had been opened, all right, except not in the beneficial way Satan had promised. They now knew *good* as something they had lost. And they now knew *evil* as something that controlled them. For the first time in their lives they felt a sense of shame at their nakedness. Adam and Eve realized they were no longer in full control of their sexual impulses. They were no longer able to direct them only according to God's will and to his glory. They therefore made immediate, though ineffective, efforts to clothe themselves.

It's instructive to note Satan's method of operation when he tempted Eve, because his methods haven't changed all that much down through the millennia of history. His basic lie is still: "God is not good. He's withholding from you privileges that you, as an individual, are entitled to — the privilege, for example, of deciding for yourself what's good for you." He still tempts us to turn God's plans for us topsy-turvy by playing God. He leads us to imagine that we, after all, are in charge of our lives, that we are the masters of our fate, the captains of our soul.

Satan is still whispering: "You will not surely die!" He has persuaded many to believe that hell does not exist, that after a person dies he simply ceases to exist. If a person is strong enough to withstand that lie, Satan will offer the lie that God will give everybody a second chance after death. Still another variation on the "You will not die" theme is universalism, which argues that ultimately all people will be saved, and nobody will be damned.

⁸Then the man and his wife heard the sound of the LORD God as he was walking in the garden in the cool of the day, and they hid from the LORD God among the trees of the garden. ⁹But the LORD God called to the man, "Where are you?" ¹⁰He answered, "I heard you in the garden, and I was afraid because I was naked; so I hid."

A feeling of *shame* was the first result Adam and Eve experienced because of their sin. There would be other results, and these became obvious when the LORD God came into the garden. "The LORD God" — what an appropriate name! The divine visitor was, first of all, the *LORD*, the Savior-God, who lovingly sought out his fallen creatures and revealed his faithful love. But Adam's and Eve's visitor was also God, the Creator whose majesty had been attacked by his two highest creatures, and who had come to show them their guilt.

In their sin and shame Adam and Eve were not looking for God, but he was looking for them. And how did they respond when they heard the sound of his footsteps? "They hid themselves." The second result of their sin was *fear*, an emotion they'd never felt before. But they surely had good reason to feel it now. The garden had been a place of joyful fellowship with God, but now they ran from him and hid. Here, surely, are symptoms of a frightfully serious condition: foolishly imagining they could by their own efforts protect themselves from God's punishment.

"Where are you?" Here is the call, first of all, *of anxious love*. The Savior-God was moving to restore his fallen children to himself. But these words are also a call *of stern justice*. The Creator was demanding an answer from his rebellious creatures. "What have you done that you should be hiding?"

Adam's answer, "I was afraid because I was naked, and so I hid," was a half-truth. It was evasive and deceptive, and it shows the ugly effects of the damage sin had caused.

[11]And he said, "Who told you that you were naked? Have you eaten from the tree that I commanded you not to eat from?" [12]The man said, "The woman you put here with me — she gave me some fruit from the tree, and I ate it." [13]Then the LORD God said to the woman, "What is this you have done?" The woman said, "The serpent deceived me, and I ate."

The Bible says: "He who conceals his sin does not prosper" (Proverbs 28:13). God therefore continued to question Adam, and his questions became more pointed as he sought to bring the sin of these two trembling sinners out into the open. "Have you eaten of the forbidden fruit?" Instead of accepting the blame for his action, Adam now sought to shift the blame to Eve, yes even to God himself. Here, surely, is another result of sin. A lack of love for God will inevitably result in a lack of love for one's fellow human being. And when the searchlight of God's justice focused on Eve she attempted to shift the blame to the serpent: "The serpent deceived me, and I ate."

In Eve's answer we note something else that must have been distressing to God. Both she and Adam were concentrating on the sinful *deed* of eating. God was much more concerned about the sinful *attitude* that produced the sinful deed. After all, sin does not begin with the hand but with

50

the heart. Sin is just as deceptive in our lives today; we sense its results much more readily than the attitude which produced the results.

As you read this tragic account, remember that this is *your* family history. You and I are sons and daughters of Adam and Eve. From our first parents we, too, have learned to love ourselves and to fight for ourselves, even if that means disagreeing with the faithful God who has come to save us — for himself, and for his family, and for an eternal home.

The First Announcement of God's Plan of Rescue

¹⁴So the LORD God said to the serpent, "Because you have done this,

> "Cursed are you above all the livestock
> and all the wild animals!
> You will crawl on your belly
> and you will eat dust
> all the days of your life.
> ¹⁵And I will put enmity
> between you and the woman
> and between your offspring and hers;
> he will crush your head,
> and you will strike his heel.''

Adam's and Eve's pitiful attempts to excuse themselves didn't deserve an answer from God and didn't get one. Instead God now turned to the serpent and announced a curse. The serpent's method of movement was henceforth to be changed; from now on he would crawl on his belly.

If this seems unfair, remember that God was doing this to teach the two people who were still blushing from the first sin. The snake's unusual method of moving along the ground was to serve as a constant reminder to them and to

51

us that this is the animal Satan used to drag the crown of creation down to his level. Crawling in the dust would also symbolize Satan's defeat and humiliation. Adam and Eve heard the words God spoke to Satan; they were to know that although Satan had won his little victory here he would not triumph permanently.

The LORD God then addressed some even more significant words to Satan, words in which he announced a new program of his faithful love. Martin Luther said of Genesis 3:15: "This passage contains in itself everything noble and glorious that is to be found anywhere in the Scriptures." These words furnished light for the early believers, and they will do the same for us. But the precious truths these words convey were spoken in a form which partly veiled the full measure of truth, thus challenging believers then and now to think about the words.

God spoke about enmity, enmity on three different levels. He told Satan: "I will put enmity *between you and the woman.*" There had been friendship between Eve and Satan. She regarded him as her friend; she believed her "friend" when he spoke. And if God had not intervened, Eve and all her descendants would have gone to live forever with her "friend." God's promise to send a Savior to redeem lost sinners created faith in Eve's heart, and that friendship which she had felt toward Satan was now replaced with enmity. What a blessing that you and I have learned to look upon Satan as our enemy!

The enmity God announced was going to extend further. God promised it would expand to involve coming generations of both Satan's "offspring" and Eve's "offspring." God foretold the ongoing hostility between Satan's followers and those of Eve's descendants who would share her opposition to the evil one and her trust in God's grace. This is the hostility which exists *between God's believing children and the unbelieving world* down to this day.

This enmity would reach its climax in one of Eve's descendants, here identified only as "he." God warned Satan:

"He will crush your head,
and you will strike his heel."

The prophecy culminates in the enmity *between Satan and Christ*. It was at this one descendant of Eve that Satan directed his most vicious enmity, realizing how much was at stake. "You will strike his heel." We see the fulfillment of this promise early in the Savior's life when Herod tried to kill him. We see another fulfillment when immediately after Christ's public inauguration into his work Satan tempted him to forget his Father's plan. And on that evil Friday that Christians call "Good" Satan struck his Enemy's heel with a ferocity that cost the Savior his life.

But Satan's enmity against the woman's offspring was futile, because "he will crush your head." The serpent's crushed head spells defeat. As it was through the woman that Satan brought sin and death into the world, so it was through the woman's offspring that God would conquer sin, death and Satan. "The reason the Son of God appeared was to destroy the devil's work" (1 John 5:8).

¹⁶To the woman he said,
"I will greatly increase your pains in childbearing;
with pain you will give birth to children.
Your desire will be for your husband,
and he will rule over you."

¹⁷To Adam he said, "Because you listened to your wife and ate from the tree about which I commanded you, 'You must not eat of it,'

"Cursed is the ground because of you;

> through painful toil you will eat of it
> all the days of your life.
> ¹⁸It will produce thorns and thistles for you,
> and you will eat the plants of the field.
> ¹⁹By the sweat of your brow
> you will eat your food
> until you return to the ground,
> since from it you were taken;
> for dust you are
> and to dust you will return."

The LORD God had announced his long-range plan for punishing the old evil foe. But the heavenly Father now had to deal with some children who had doubted his love, disobeyed him, tried to hide from him and even to deceive him. God now had some words for them, in which he announced appropriate discipline for both Eve and Adam.

Christian teaching has consistently distinguished between suffering which God in *anger* allots to someone who has violated his majesty, and suffering which God allots out of *love* and for a corrective purpose. The former we call God's *punishment*; the latter we call God's *chastisement*, his *discipline*.

God first addressed Eve. It was she who had first believed Satan's lie that following him would bring blessing. Every time Eve or one of her daughters would bring a child into the world the pain of childbirth would be a reminder that sin brings sorrow and suffering instead of satisfaction.

In the fall Eve had sought to act independently of her husband. She had assumed a position of leadership in that family. And so God reminded her that his creation order still stood, and would continue to stand: "Your desire will be for your husband, and he will rule over you." Although sin and selfishness would now enter the wife's relationship to her husband, and his to her, yet sin has not changed God's original design for headship in the family. The New Testament reaffirms this and asks Christian women to find joy and contentment fulfilling God's role for them (1 Timothy 2:11-15).

The LORD God now addressed Adam and announced a discipline suited to his particular misdeed. Adam, you remember, had surrendered to Eve his leadership role in marriage. Because he had submitted to his wife instead of leading in love and had gone contrary to God's command not to eat of the forbidden fruit, he would experience insubordination on the part of the soil (which up to now had been under his complete control). To remind Adam of his sin and to help him in his daily battle with his sinful nature, the Creator cursed the ground. Adam (and his children in generations to come) would experience misery and difficulty wringing a livelihood out of the soil.

God had given Adam dominion over his creation, in order to protect and preserve it. That had been Adam's attitude while he still possessed the image of God. But a terrible change came over Adam when he lost God's image and instead took on a sinful image. You remember how Adam had tried to hide from God, how he lied to God, how he tried to take advantage of his wife by shifting his blame to her. We see these same trends in the human race today. God's human creatures, originally designed to exercise God-like dominion over creation, now take advantage of it and exploit it. Ugly words have entered our vocabulary — words like smog and pollution and acid rain and endangered species and abortion. It's clear why God would not want such creatures to have unlimited dominion over his creation.

The final penalty God announced for Adam's sin was that his body, into which the Creator had breathed the breath of life, would one day return to the material from which it had originally been made. What a shattering message for Adam to hear! "Dust was your origin; dust will be your destiny!" In God's solemn announcement we see the reason people are afraid to die. Death is something that should never have been, something totally unnatural, a violent intrusion into God's good plan.

The faithful God had appeared to Adam and Eve in an amazing display of his mercy. Not only had he exposed their sin, he had announced his great good plan of deliverance from their sin, and he had designed appropriate discipline for each of them. What was their response?

[20]Adam named his wife Eve, because she would become the mother of all the living. [21]The LORD God made garments of skin for Adam and his wife and clothed them. [22]And the LORD God said, "The man has now become like one of us, knowing good and evil. He must not be allowed to reach out his hand and take also from the tree of life and eat, and live forever." [23]So the LORD God banished him from the Garden of Eden to work the ground from which he had been taken. [24]After he drove the man out, he placed on the east side of the Garden of Eden cherubim and a flaming sword flashing back and forth to guard the way to the tree of life.

Adam gave his wife a name meaning "living" or "life." Surely with this name Adam was saying more than that Eve would have offspring; that would hardly seem significant enough to mention. The term "life" is often used in the Scripture to describe union with God (what we sometimes refer to as "salvation"). The term "death," on the other hand, connotes separation from God ("damnation"). Since Eve would in a very real sense be the mother of all human beings, the One who would restore life in its fullest sense would also be her descendant. In naming his wife, therefore,

Adam showed his faith in the promise God had spoken.

God now proceeded to show his love for his children in another way. When Adam and Eve felt the first blush of shame at their nakedness (Genesis 3:7) they took immediate but unsatisfactory steps to cover themselves with fig leaves. By providing more adequate clothing for them God strengthened their sense of shame, to aid them in their struggle against temptation.

A statement God made here may puzzle the reader: "The man has now become like one of us." Luther remarked: "God says this in holy irony." After Adam and Eve had eaten the forbidden fruit they knew from experience what good and evil were, but that knowledge was a caricature of the knowledge God had intended them to have. They now knew *good* as something they had forfeited and lost. They now knew *evil* as something which permeated their whole being, a built-in enemy against which they would have to struggle even after they had been brought to faith.

It follows, then, that there was one more thing God had to do, and it required of God what we sometimes call "tough love." He had to drive two people out of their garden home. The two verbs Moses used to describe God's action are intensive verbs, and one gets the impression Adam and Eve were unwilling and had to be compelled to leave. God's stated reason for driving them out of Eden was that now he did not want them in their sin-stained condition to eat of the tree of life, for that would have perpetuated their present form of life. God didn't want them to live permanently in bodies enslaved to sin, like the damned in hell; that would have made Christ's great work of restoration impossible.

To block any attempt Adam and Eve might make to reenter their garden home, God stationed cherubim with a flashing sword at the entrance. By so doing God was announcing that life is no longer a continual *paradise* but rather a *time of grace*, a period God gives us in which we can find our way back to God through Jesus Christ. The last book of the Bible promises us that when we one day enjoy the perfect fellowship of God in heaven we will "eat from the tree of life, which is in the paradise of God" (Revelation 2:7).

The Two Divisions of the Human Family

To many people the sin of Adam and Eve in the garden of Eden does not seem terribly serious. Perhaps the best answer to that objection is: "Look at the results their action had!" Chapter 4 of Genesis illustrates the truth of St. Paul's statement: "Sin entered the world through one man, and death through sin, and in this way death came to all men, because all sinned" (Romans 5:12).

4 Adam lay with his wife Eve, and she became pregnant and gave birth to Cain. She said, "With the help of the LORD I have brought forth a man." ²Later she gave birth to his brother Abel. Now Abel kept flocks, and Cain worked the soil.

Old Testament and New Testament writers both use a special form of the verb "to know" as a delicate euphemism for the sexual relationship between husband and wife. "Adam *knew* his wife." The verb connotes knowing from experience. Adam recognized Eve's special nature and function; he knew her as his very own. God blessed their union with a child, a baby boy.

As Eve held her little son in her arms she spoke some significant words. Unfortunately, several of her words each have two different meanings. Luther understood Eve to say: "*I have gotten a man, the LORD.*" According to this translation, Eve thought that her little son was the Savior, the promised Descendant who would crush the serpent's head.

An alternate and probably better translation of Eve's words is: *"Together with the LORD I have produced a man."* If that's the way Eve's words are to be understood, then she was, first of all, expressing her amazement and gratitude over the miracle of the first human birth. God had actually permitted her to share in his creative work! It's also worth noting that in choosing a name for God Eve did not choose his Creator-name but his Savior-name. By giving Eve a son, the God of the covenant was serving notice that he wasn't about to let the human race die out. Eve rejoiced at this evidence that her family line would continue, so that at the proper time its most famous Descendant would be born. The translation of the King James Version ("I have gotten a man from the LORD") is impossible without emending the Hebrew text.

To prepare us for the tragic narrative which lies immediately ahead, Moses records the birth of a second son. We also learn that after a time Cain became a farmer and Abel a shepherd. Adam and Eve had other sons and daughters (Genesis 5:4), but with a single exception we don't know their names.

³**In the course of time Cain brought some of the fruits of the soil as an offering to the LORD. ⁴But Abel brought fat portions from some of the firstborn of his flock. The LORD looked with favor on Abel and his offering, ⁵ but on Cain and his offering he did not look with favor. So Cain was very angry, and his face was downcast.**

⁶**Then the LORD said to Cain, "Why are you angry? Why is your face downcast? ⁷If you do what is right, will you not be accepted? But if you do not do what is right, sin is crouching at your door; it desires to have you, but you must master it."**

⁸**Now Cain said to his brother Abel, "Let's go out to the field." And while they were in the field, Cain attacked his brother Abel and killed him.**

It doesn't surprise us to learn that the two sons of Adam and Eve brought sacrifices to the LORD, perhaps at the time of harvest. Those two God-fearing parents would have taught their children to worship God. Cain brought his offering from the produce of his field, Abel from the first and best of his flock.

We have no way of knowing whether God had commanded this particular form of worship. It seems unlikely that it was self-chosen, since the Bible records a number of different forms of worship which originated in the mind of sinful man, and they're downright appalling. We hear, for example, of *worshiping sun and moon.* In ancient times parents actually *offered their children as living sacrifices* to the gods in order to earn their favor. In ancient Canaan men and women practiced *temple prostitution* to gain the gods' blessings. This is the sort of worship the sinful human mind will invent when left to itself. Surely it was not an accident, therefore, that Adam's family practiced a type of worship that was pleasing to God.

Their sacrifices were offered "to the LORD." Adam and Eve had taught their children to know and to love the Savior-God, the God of free and faithful grace. The symbolism behind the offering may have been the same as that behind our offerings: we place a portion of our *possessions* on the LORD's altar in token of the fact that we have first dedicated *ourselves* to him.

Why Abel's offering was acceptable to God but Cain's wasn't the New Testament tells us: "By faith Abel offered God a better sacrifice than Cain did" (Hebrews 11:4). And the Apostle John gives us this significant insight into the goings-on in Cain's heart: "Cain ... belonged to the evil one and murdered his brother ... because his own actions were evil and his brother's were righteous" (1 John 3:12). Cain was angry when his sacrifice was not accepted, thereby showing that his sacrifice had been made from a self-righteous motivation.

In the actions of these two brothers we see that not all the children of Adam and Eve shared their parents' faith in the promised Savior. Cain's sacrifice was displeasing to God because God regarded it as a piece of unbelief. "Without faith it is impossible to please God," the apostle writes (Hebrews 11:6). From the earliest days of the world's history down to the present, there have always been two groups of people — believers and unbelievers. In the two sons of Adam and Eve we can detect the beginnings of these two tendencies, which become more pronounced as the narrative of chapter 4 progresses.

"The LORD looked with favor on Abel and his offering." Note the double object of the LORD's favor. Through faith in God's promise *Abel* was acceptable to God; God looked upon him as his own dear child. Because his sacrifice flowed from that same faith, *Abel's sacrifice* was pleasing to God. Nor could the unbelief in Cain's heart remain secret from God. Although Cain was a member of the family of Adam and Eve and even participated in joint family worship, he was outside the family of God. Outwardly Cain offered his gifts to the true God, but his motivation was impure. He went through the motions of worship, but his motives were selfish and self-seeking.

In some way unknown to us God let Cain know that the attitude of his heart displeased God and that his offering was unacceptable. Cain recognized this, he resented it, and the angry look on his face showed it. When Cain added the sin of anger to his sin of false worship, the LORD, the Savior-God, spoke to him, perhaps face-to-face. He showed his faithful love by warning him: "Cain, you've got no business being angry with me and with your brother! Sin, like a dangerous beast, is crouching at the door of your heart, but with my help you can resist it."

Cain rejected the LORD's warning and his kind offer. He resisted the gentle striving of the Spirit of God. Instead he invited his brother out to the field, where there'd be no witnesses. And then in cold blood he killed his brother. It was clear that Eve's offspring had become Satan's offspring (John 8:44).

⁹Then the LORD said to Cain, "Where is your brother Abel?" "I don't know," he replied. "Am I my brother's keeper?" ¹⁰The LORD said, "What have you done? Listen! Your brother's blood cries out to me from the ground. ¹¹Now you are under a curse and driven from the ground, which opened its mouth to receive your brother's blood from your hand. ¹²When you work the ground, it will no longer yield its crops for you. You will be a restless wanderer on the earth." ¹³Cain said to the LORD, "My punishment is more than I can bear. ¹⁴Today you are driving me from the land, and I will be hidden from your presence; I will be a restless wanderer on the earth, and whoever finds me will kill me." ¹⁵But the LORD said to him, "Not so; if anyone kills Cain, he will suffer vengeance seven time over." Then the LORD put a mark on Cain so that no one who found him would kill him. ¹⁶So Cain went out from the LORD's presence and lived in the land of Nod, east of Eden.

The faithful God of the covenant appeared to Cain again, this time not with an offer of help, but with a crushing message of law for the bold sinner. "Where is your brother? What have you done?" Cain may have thought he had forever silenced his brother's voice, but he learned that Abel's shed blood was continually crying to God for vengeance.

To arouse Cain's conscience and to serve as a lifelong reminder of his crime, God announced a curse on him. This was not an irreversible sentence of damnation. Cain, a farmer, would no longer be permitted to settle in the culti-vated portion of the land but would eke out a living only with the greatest difficulty. Furthermore, he would be com-pelled to spend his life as a restless wanderer.

With those solemn words God had gotten Cain's atten-tion. The bold sinner was terrified by what he had just heard, but his response shows no indication of repentance. His worst fear was for his own life. "Whoever finds me will kill me." It has been estimated that there may have been three or four generations of Adam's descendants on earth at this time, all of them blood relatives of the man whom Cain had murdered. Cain's fear was a very realistic one, that one of Abel's relatives might take blood-revenge on him.

To assure Cain this was not going to happen, the faithful LORD gave Cain a sign. Some have understood this to be a visible mark of identification on his body. The Hebrew seems to suggest it was a miraculous sign God gave to Cain, similar to the signs God gave to Moses (Exodus 4:8,9), to Gideon (Judges 6:17-22), or to Hezekiah (Isaiah 38:5-8). In either case, the sign was a miraculous reassur-ance to Cain that his life would be spared.

The sight of this wretched man — homeless, forever on the move, and managing to survive only with the greatest difficulty — would be a warning to anyone minded to imi-tate the attitude and the behavior of Cain.

¹⁷Cain lay with his wife, and she became pregnant and gave birth to Enoch. Cain was then building a city, and he named it after his son Enoch. ¹⁸To Enoch was born Irad, and Irad was the father of Mehujael, and Mehujael was the father of Methushael, and Methushael was the father of Lamech. ¹⁹Lamech married two women, one named Adah and the other Zillah. ²⁰Adah gave birth to Jabal; he was the father of those who live in tents and raise livestock. ²¹His brother's name was

Jubal; he was the father of all who play the harp and flute.
²²Zillah also had a son, Tubal-Cain, who forged all kinds of
tools out of bronze and iron. Tubal-Cain's sister was Naamah.
²³Lamech said to his wives,

> "Adah and Zillah, listen to me;
> wives of Lamech, hear my words.
> I have killed a man for wounding me,
> a young man for injuring me.
> ²⁴If Cain is avenged seven times,
> then Lamech seventy-seven times."

The Bible says: "A good man leaves an inheritance for
his children's children" (Proverbs 13:22). The heritage Cain
left to his children was a dreadful one. They did not learn
from their father what a precious gift God's mercy is. They
didn't learn that the purpose of life is to glorify God.
Consequently Cain's descendants followed the path their
ancestor had chosen.

Cain married, and his wife followed him into the
wretched existence God had promised him. Since at the
beginning God had created only one family to populate the
earth, Cain's wife must have been a close relative — probably his own sister, possibly a niece. (If Cain didn't marry
his sister, one of his brothers must have.) This was
inevitable, since God had determined that all of earth's
inhabitants were to have a common parentage.

We have quite a detailed description of the Cainite branch
of Adam's family, and we're not impressed. Consider these
specifics:

"Cain was building a city," a fortified settlement. We're
not told that the building project was ever completed, but
Cain apparently tried to neutralize God's curse of banish-
ment.

"Lamech married two women." Lamech, the fifth generation after Cain, introduced polygamy into the human race. By so doing he showed contempt for God's stated purpose for marriage, that a man and a woman glorify God and serve each other by an unconditional commitment of love. Among the Cainites, God's original purpose was perverted by lust.

The occupations followed by the Cainites are listed, and they're impressive. Cain's descendants raised livestock; they made musical instruments; they were skilled in working with metals. All of these point to an advanced culture, in sharp contrast to the picture commonly drawn of the early occupants of our planet. The picture we get here of the Cainites is of a group of people who developed the fine arts and an advanced culture, but whose activities were completely directed toward this earthly existence. Cain's descendants were people who had little use for God.

To this record of cultural advancement Lamech provides an unhappy postscript. The *first poetry* recorded in the Scripture is a song Lamech sang to his two wives which breathes the spirit of revenge. Perhaps at the moment Lamech was holding a sword his son Tubal-Cain had made. To his boasting he adds the blasphemy that, if anybody would dare to harm him, his own hand could do more than God's sevenfold vengeance would do to anyone who would dare to take Cain's life.

From this sacred record it becomes clear that the earliest civilizations made the greatest strides among those who were alienated from God. Perhaps this is not surprising. For one thing, the person divorced from God wants to blunt the curse of sin and tries desperately to anesthetize himself against the dull ache of an accusing conscience. Secondly, the person trying to live independently of God struggles to inject meaning into his life, which is empty without God.

Understandably, all of his efforts will be channeled toward the goal of achieving a pleasant existence.

²⁵Adam lay with his wife again, and she gave birth to a son and named him Seth, saying, "God has granted me another child in place of Abel, since Cain killed him." ²⁶Seth also had a son, and he named him Enosh. At that time men began to call on the name of the LORD.

This brief description of the *Sethite* branch of Adam's family is in sharp contrast to the *Cainite* branch Moses had just sketched. God gave Adam and Eve another son, Seth, to take the place of Abel. In contrast to the boastful, blasphemous Lamech, who claimed credit for what he was, Eve gave God the credit for having blessed her with another son.

Moses supplies very little information about the descendants of Seth, but that little says a lot. The New International Version and the King James Version both say that at the time of Seth's son Enosh ". . . men began to call on the name of the LORD." In our idiom to "call on the name of the LORD" means *to pray.* Surely the sacred writer cannot mean to say that the practice of praying to God started with Adam's grandchildren. A footnote in the NIV offers the alternate translation *"to proclaim"* the name of the LORD, and that surely must be the sense of the passage here. Up to this time worshipping the faithful Savior-God had been done privately, within the family. At the time of Enosh God's children began to proclaim publicly the Savior's name, his marvelous works in the interest of his people. While their Cainite relatives were perfecting their skills in the arts and sciences to enhance their life in this world, the Sethites were making significant cultural advances in matters pertaining to God and to life in his presence.

Genesis 4 begins with the scriptural record of *Cain's* lineage. The record of this branch of Adam's family began with premeditated murder and ended with a song glorifying violence and bloodthirsty revenge. It becomes clear that this would not be the lineage from which God would give the promised Savior to the world. Because of its godlessness this brilliant early civilization was destroyed in the great flood. Genesis 4 closes with the record of the *Sethite* branch of Adam's family, the lineage from which the Savior descended. From this point on the book of Genesis traces the history only of this Sethite branch.

THE SECOND ACCOUNT:
OF ADAM'S LINE
GENESIS 5:1-6:8

This second of Moses' ten mini-histories, the "Account of Adam's Line," provides a list of the Savior's ancestors from Adam to Noah. These are the Sethites, whose loyalty to Jehovah was documented in the closing verses of the previous chapter. This "account" of the Sethite line, however, ends on a tragic note. Moses informs us that even the descendants of Seth, through whom God established the public preaching of his name, gradually came to despise their heritage and joined the Cainites in their ungodliness.

5 **This is the written account of Adam's line. When God created man, he made him in the likeness of God. ²He created them male and female and blessed them. And when they were created, he called them "man."**

Moses speaks of a document, a "written account" that had come down to him, containing information about ten patriarchs from the time of creation to the time of the flood. Under the guidance of the Holy Spirit, and under the umbrella of divine inspiration, Moses incorporated this document into the book of Genesis as the second of his ten accounts.

Moses reaffirms that when Adam and Eve were created they bore the image of their Creator. Their intellect and emotions and will were in perfect harmony with God, and they enjoyed perfect fellowship with him. Three times

Moses refers to conditions as they were at the time of creation. The reason for this will become clear when Moses now contrasts man's original perfect condition with his sad situation after he lost the divine image.

³When Adam had lived 130 years, he had a son in his own likeness, in his own image; and he named him Seth. ⁴After Seth was born, Adam lived 800 years and had other sons and daughters.
⁵Altogether, Adam lived 930 years, and then he died.

In sharp contrast with the preceding, we're told here that when Adam fathered children they bore their father's sinful image. Adam had begun his life in a state of *perfection*. Every one of his descendants, with only one exception, began his or her life in a state of *imperfection*.

In these verses we can observe the three-step pattern Moses followed in describing the ten patriarchs from Adam to Noah. He did so by supplying chronological data about the lifespans of these ten important people.

Moses tells us, first of all, how old the patriarch was when he fathered the next-named link in the Messianic genealogy. He then tells us how long the rest of the patriarch's life lasted and, finally, what the man's total life span was. This three-step pattern is followed throughout the chapter (with only two exceptions, which will be noted).

Genesis 5 does not make for exciting reading. Genealogies are not the sort of thing you pick up for the sheer joy of reading. But there are jewels for the taking in this chapter. The alert reader will note, for example, that with a single exception each segment of the genealogy ends on the same note: "... and he died." Here is the ultimate proof that humans have fallen from the high dignity that was theirs while they still possessed the image of God. In generation after generation God's warning in Eden ("When you eat of it, you will surely die") proved to be true. Like the tolling of a bell at a funeral, the recurring phrase "… and he died" is a forceful reminder of how true the statement is: "Down through the years the death rate has remained the same: one per person."

⁶When Seth had lived 105 years, he became the father of Enosh. ⁷And after he became the father of Enosh, Seth lived 807 years and had other sons and daughters. ⁸Altogether, Seth lived 912 years, and then he died.

⁹When Enosh had lived 90 years, he became the father of Kenan. ¹⁰And after he became the father of Kenan, Enosh lived 815 years and had other sons and daughters. ¹¹Altogether, Enosh lived 905 years, and then he died.

¹²When Kenan had lived 70 years, he became the father of Mahalalel. ¹³And after he became the father of Mahalalel, Kenan lived 840 years and had other sons and daughters. ¹⁴Altogether, Kenan lived 910 years, and then he died.

¹⁵When Mahalalel had lived 65 years, he became the father of Jared. ¹⁶And after he became the father of Jared, Mahalalel lived 830 years and had other sons and daughters. ¹⁷Altogether, Mahalalel lived 895 years, and then he died.

¹⁸When Jared had lived 162 years, he became the father of Enoch. ¹⁹And after he became the father of Enoch, Jared lived 800 years and had other sons and daughters. ²⁰Altogether, Jared lived 962 years, and then he died.

²¹When Enoch had lived 65 years, he became the father of Methuselah. ²²And after he became the father of Methuselah, Enoch walked with God 300 years and had other sons and daughters. ²³Altogether, Enoch lived 365 years. ²⁴Enoch walked with God; then he was no more, because God took him away.

²⁵When Methuselah had lived 187 years, he became the father of Lamech. ²⁶And after he became the father of Lamech,

Methuselah lived 782 years and had other sons and daughters. ²⁷Altogether Methuselah lived 969 years, and then he died.

Recurring *death* was not the only notable factor in this "Account of Adam's Line." The reader will note the uncommonly *long life spans* of these pre-flood patriarchs. Of the ten, seven lived more than 900 years (and an eighth missed it by only five years). In generation after generation the icy hand of death touched Adam's descendants, but not until they had passed on the gift of life to their children. The long life spans attest to the vigor of the human race in those days of the world's prime.

These pre-flood patriarchs passed on life of another kind to their descendants. In each generation God raised up people who passed on his gracious promise of a Savior. Faithful fathers and mothers made sure that their children heard of the promise of the woman's seed who would crush Satan's power and free his slaves.

What are we to say about the tremendously long life spans enumerated in this chapter? The fact that the average life span dropped sharply immediately after the flood has led many to wonder if perhaps climatic conditions on earth were more hospitable in the days before the flood, more conducive to long life. Did people live longer then because the cancer of sin hadn't had as much time to do its dirty work? We can ask the questions, but we lack the solid information to answer them positively. We can be sure that God used these faithful and long-lived descendants of Seth to stem the tide of evil threatening to engulf the world, and to preserve and transmit his word down to our day.

One of two significant variations from the set pattern of this genealogy occurs in verses 21-24, in the case of the patriarch Enoch. His brief biography twice mentions that "Enoch walked with God." In a world which was becoming progressively more wicked, Enoch not only believed God's

71

promise of a Savior but put his faith to work in his life. The Apostle Jude tells us Enoch warned the people of his day about God's judgment on unbelievers (Jude 14,15). The descendants of Adam named in this chapter did what they could to hold back the tide of evil.

God rewarded the faith of this pious man in a striking way: "Enoch ... was no more, because God took him away." Enoch is listed among the heroes of faith named in the epistle to the Hebrews: "By faith Enoch was taken from this life, so that he did not experience death; he could not be found, because God had taken him away. For before he was taken, he was commended as one who pleased God." (Hebrews 11:5,6).

Here is significant evidence that already at the time of the Old Testament God's people were aware of the fact that there is another life beyond the grave. God's taking Enoch (as he did his faithful prophet Elijah centuries later) must surely have strengthened the faith of those Old Testament saints in the resurrection of the body and the life everlasting.

28When Lamech had lived 182 years, he had a son. 29He named him Noah and said, "He will comfort us in the labor and painful toil of our hands caused by the ground the LORD has cursed." 30After Noah was born, Lamech lived 595 years and had other sons and daughters.

31Altogether, Lamech lived 777 years, and then he died. 32After Noah was 500 years old, he became the father of Shem, Ham and Japheth.

The second significant variation from the three-step pattern Moses followed in presenting the patriarchal genealogies occurs in the case of Lamech, father of Noah. As he held his infant son, this godly man explained the name he had chosen for him.

"Noah" sounds like the Hebrew word for "comfort." Speaking under the guidance of the Holy Spirit Lamech prophesied about his son: "He will comfort us in the labor and painful toil of our hands caused by the ground the LORD has cursed." Although we don't know how much of what Lamech said he understood, he sensed that in an unusual way God would use this son to bless the human race. Did he think Noah was the promised Messiah? Luther thought so. Or was Lamech prophesying that through Noah God would preserve a godly remnant from the curse of the flood?

Noah stood in the Messianic line. From that lineage would come the One who would bring final deliverance from the curse of sin. Regardless of how much of what he was saying Lamech understood, his prophecy is nonetheless valid.

Moses begins the next link in his genealogy with a reference to Noah and his three sons. At this point he interrupts the genealogy. Mention of Noah, Shem, Ham and Japheth calls for a more detailed description of the catastrophe which during their lifetimes God sent as a judgment upon earth. Moses will resume the genealogy in Genesis 9:28.

Conditions Which Called For The Judgment Of The Flood

6 **When men began to increase in number on the earth and daughters were born to them, ²the sons of God saw that the daughters of men were beautiful, and they married any of them they chose. ³Then the LORD said, "My Spirit will not contend with man forever, for he is mortal; his days will be a hundred and twenty years." ⁴The Nephilim were on the earth in those days — and also afterward — when the sons of God went to the daughters of men and had children by them. They were the heroes of old, men of renown. ⁵The LORD saw how great man's wickedness on the earth had become, and that every inclination**

73

of the thoughts of his heart was only evil all the time. ⁶The LORD was grieved that he had made man on the earth, and his heart was filled with pain. ⁷So the LORD said, "I will wipe mankind, whom I have created, from the face of the earth — men and animals, and creatures that move along the ground, and birds of the air — for I am grieved that I have made them." ⁸But Noah found favor in the eyes of the LORD.

Moses had interrupted his genealogy of Adam's descendants in order to describe the awesome catastrophe God sent on earth's inhabitants during the life of Noah. Here he traces the developments which led to God's decision to send the flood.

This closing episode in Moses' "Account of Adam's Line" is not a happy one. The Sethites, the people of God who had up to now remained separate from the unbelieving Cainites, began to drift from their loyalty to the true God and to draw closer to their heathen neighbors. The "sons of God," God's believing children, saw that the "daughters of men were beautiful, and they married any of them they chose." If the "sons of God" were Sethite men, then by contrast the "daughters of men" were unbelieving women. When contemplating marriage, the most important of human relationships, the Sethites pushed their faith and their godly heritage into the background. When looking for a prospective wife, they didn't ask: "Will this woman help to make my home a place of godly instruction?" They asked only the question which to them was the most important: "Is she good-looking?"

These mixed marriages led to still further degeneration of the Sethites, until it was no longer possible to distinguish them from the Cainites. God warned: "My Spirit will not contend with man forever." The Spirit of God had been active then as now through the word of God that was still being preached — for example, by Noah (2 Peter 2:5). But the Spirit cannot continue to rebuke and correct people if they reject his gracious work. As God saw it, his human creatures were nothing but sinful flesh, totally under the control of sin. In an amazing display of his patient love the LORD, the Savior-God, granted the human race another 120 years. For more than another century he would continue to speak through his spokesmen, seeking to reverse the deadly drift toward evil, seeking to stop people from plunging headlong into judgment.

One of the characteristics of life on earth that was displeasing to God was violence. When love *for God* is absent from the life of a person or a nation, love *for people* will also be absent. Prodigal sons don't make very good brothers. There were violent men on earth in those days before the flood: Moses calls them "Nephilim," a word which seems to come from a Hebrew word meaning "to fall upon," "to attack." Even before Sethite-Cainite intermarriages became common, there were violent men who trampled on the rights of others; those mixed marriages spawned more of them. And the ultimate irony was that in that topsy-turvy world this sort of self-centered, strong-armed individual was looked up to as role model, the type of person to be admired.

It was then that God announced a change of course in his world government. His purpose remained constant. (Thank God, that cannot change!) He wanted — and still wants — all people to be saved, but he realized that unless he intervened, even his own believing children might be swept away by the rampant evil everywhere on earth. The God who had once looked at his highest creatures and said: "Very good!" now looked at them and said, in dismay and disgust: "That isn't the human race I created! Why, their heart is only evil all the time. I must destroy them and start over!" Even

God's non-human creation had been contaminated and dese-crated and fell under God's decree of judgment.

It is significant to note that the One who announced the destruction of the world is the LORD (verse 7), the God of loyal love. His action has been seen by some as heartless and vindictive; actually it's the very opposite. He took this drastic action because he didn't want his plan for gathering his family of believers to be frustrated.

The "Account of Adam's Line," which began at 5:1, clos-es with the significant statement: "But Noah found favor in the eyes of the LORD." God's favor is his grace, his unmerit-ed love, which is accepted by faith. This grace not only gave Noah *something he did not deserve*, but actually gave him *the very opposite of what he deserved*. God not only delivered Noah and his family from the waters of the flood, but actually used them to continue the line of Adam and Seth. It was from that slender thread that God's promise of the woman's offspring hung. It was through Noah's descen-dants that a merciful God kept that important promise.

It is important to note that the condition described in verse 5 is still the condition of every person from birth. The Bible teaches the total depravity of the human race. The only remedy today is the same one Noah found at the time of the flood: the grace of God, that amazing love which reaches out to rescue sinners who deserve to be rejected by God.

THE THIRD ACCOUNT:
OF NOAH
GENESIS 6:9-9:28

Genesis 6-8 tells the story of the great flood. It's interesting to note the name Moses gives to this section of his book. He doesn't call it "The Disaster of the Flood," but "The Account of Noah." Moses' emphasis is not on the nightmare of judgment, the global catastrophe which destroyed a world population estimated at three billion people and permanently altered the face of the earth. Instead Moses emphasizes the deliverance God accomplished through Noah, the man who found favor in the eyes of the LORD. As Moses described it, this is not the *story of the flood*. This is *Noah's story* — including his faith, his obedience, his deliverance, his sin, and the solemn covenant God made with him.

⁹**This is the account of Noah. Noah was a righteous man, blameless among the people of his time, and he walked with God. ¹⁰Noah had three sons: Shem, Ham and Japheth. ¹¹Now the earth was corrupt in God's sight and was full of violence. ¹²God saw how corrupt the earth had become, for all the people on earth had corrupted their ways. ¹³So God said to Noah, "I am going to put an end to all people, for the earth is filled with violence because of them. I am surely going to destroy both them and the earth. ¹⁴So make yourself an ark of cypress wood; make rooms in it and coat it with pitch inside and out. ¹⁵This is how you are to build it: the ark is to be 450 feet long, 75 feet wide and 45 feet high. ¹⁶Make a roof for it and finish the ark to**

within 18 inches of the top. Put a door in the side of the ark and make lower, middle and upper decks.

The account begins with a capsule description of Noah. He was, first of all, *righteous*. In the Bible this is a courtroom term. Noah, a sinner, had been pronounced innocent by God. God wanted Noah, as he wants us, to believe him, to trust his promise of help and forgiveness through the promised Savior. "By faith Noah ... became heir of the righteousness that comes by faith" (Hebrews 11:7).

Noah is further described as "blameless" (King James Version: "perfect"). Both of those translations are unsatisfactory. Noah was a sinner, neither blameless nor perfect. The adjective Moses uses to describe Noah comes from a verb meaning "to be complete." Noah was "righteous-complete." Noah was a *devout* man. His saving faith in the promised Messiah was not confined to his heart, but showed itself in every phase of his life. This devout child of God practiced his faith also by fathering and rearing three sons.

God-fearing parents have always had a tough job training children in the fear of the Lord in an ungodly world. Noah's job of parenting, however, was infinitely tougher than any other parent has ever faced, because he and his wife stood absolutely alone in a world which had turned against God. Noah's contemporaries showed contempt for God and selfishness, even violence, toward one another. God saw that the ailment afflicting Noah's world was not a light case of the spiritual measles, but terminal cancer.

It was then that God spoke to Noah. He took Noah into his confidence and informed him of the judgment that lay just ahead. He took this action as the Creator whose creatures had forfeited their right to live by refusing to acknowledge their Creator and Master. But God assured Noah also that the well-deserved judgment he was about to bring on the world would serve his great good plan to deliver his people, to keep them from being swept along in the rampant unbelief and godlessness of the time.

God did not immediately reveal to Noah exactly how he was going to destroy the world; those details would come later. From the building project God outlined for him, however, Noah could draw his own conclusions. He was to build a large seagoing barge — 450 feet long (as long as a football field and a half), 75 feet wide, and as tall as a four-story building. The storage capacity of this vessel would be a million and a half cubic feet — approximately the equivalent of a 14-ton vessel. This was not a ship, whose purpose it would be to sail from point A to point B; this was a barge, a huge box, whose only purpose was to float, thereby preserving the lives of its precious cargo.

To accommodate a vast variety of passengers, the ark was to have three decks. To allow for light and exchange of air, there was to be an 18-inch opening all around the ark immediately below the overhang of the roof.

¹⁷"I am going to bring floodwaters on the earth to destroy all life under the heavens, every creature that has the breath of life in it. Everything on earth will perish. ¹⁸But I will establish my covenant with you, and you will enter the ark — you and your sons and your wife and your sons' wives with you. ¹⁹You are to bring into the ark two of all living creatures, male and female, to keep them alive with you. ²⁰Two of every kind of bird, of every kind of animal and of every kind of creature that moves along the ground will come to you to be kept alive. ²¹You are to take every kind of food that is to be eaten and store it away as food for you and for them." Noah did everything just as God commanded him.

Now God revealed the specifics of his awesome plan: he was going to use water to destroy the earth. Noah's ears must have tingled as God spelled out the details: "I am going ... to destroy all life under the heavens. ... But I will establish my covenant with you." God referred to "my covenant" as though it were a known quantity to Noah. One gets the impression God had previously made a solemn agreement with Noah (perhaps at the beginning of the 120-year grace period) and here promised to implement the provisions of that covenant — to preserve in the ark a tiny remnant of his creation.

God specified who the occupants of the ark were to be. Most important, of course, were the eight members of Noah's family. Noah was also to take a wide variety of animals and birds into the ark, so that the earth could again be populated with them after the flood. Initially God instructed Noah to take on board one mated pair of each kind; later on God modified these instructions.

To reassure Noah that he wouldn't have to conduct extensive trapping expeditions, God informed him that the animal passengers would come to him. Noah would otherwise have been unable to select the precise mated pairs with the genes present in their reproductive cells to provide for all the variations in size and color we see in their offspring today.

God's final instructions to Noah concerned the feeding of the ark's occupants during the months they would spend aboard the ark. Noah was not to rely on God to feed them miraculously, but was to assemble food supplies sufficient to last for more than a year. Noah and his seven relatives were going to have plenty to do aboard the ark. They would have little time to feel sorry for themselves or, for that matter, to be bored. In this we can again see the wisdom of a loving Creator.

The Bible record does not tell us whether God used any other means to make Noah's work of feeding the animals easier. Were all the animals aboard the ark *full-grown*, or could there have been *younger* animals with smaller appetites? It might seem reasonable that during their lengthy stay in a confined area some of the animals *hibernated.* The closing verse of the chapter records the fact that Noah responded to God's commands with glad obedience. The statement reminds us of God's description of Noah earlier in the chapter: he was devout. His life matched his faith. Noah can teach us something here. If our goal in life is to live to the glory of God, then, like Noah, we will seek to learn what God's will is and to get in line with it.

7 **The LORD then said to Noah, "Go into the ark, you and your whole family, because I have found you righteous in this generation. ²Take with you seven of every kind of clean animal, a male and its mate, and two of every kind of unclean animal, a male and its mate, ³ and also seven of every kind of bird, male and female, to keep their various kinds alive throughout the earth. ⁴Seven days from now I will send rain on the earth for forty days and forty nights, and I will wipe from the face of the earth every living creature I have made." ⁵And Noah did all that the LORD commanded him.**

The 120 years of grace God had mercifully granted the unbelieving world were over. Only seven days remained before the great flood, and God had some final instructions for his faithful son and servant. Some of these instructions were a *repetition* of things God had said earlier, to reassure Noah that he was on the right track, and that he was not acting on his own. God reassured him also that through faith in the coming Messiah Noah was acceptable in his sight.

Some of the things God told Noah were *modifications* of what he had said earlier. A literal translation of what God said is: "Of every kind of clean animal take to yourself by sevens, a male and his mate." The words cause a bit of a problem for the reader. Does the expression *"by sevens"* modify "*every kind of clean animal*?" (Then Noah was to take seven of each clean animal.) Or does "by sevens" modify "*a male and his mate*?" (In that case Noah was to take seven mated pairs, a total of fourteen.) Interpreters are divided on the question. The NIV puts one translation in the text, the other in a footnote. Unclean animals were to be taken "by twos."

In the law announced centuries later from Mt. Sinai, God clarified the distinction between clean and unclean animals. The former were acceptable for food and for sacrifice, the latter were not. Remember that Moses wrote Genesis for people who had been at Mt. Sinai. They knew the difference between clean and unclean animals, and we assume Noah did, too — at least after God led the proper numbers of animals to him in the ark. The Lord preserved a larger number of those land animals which he knew would be in greater demand for food and for sacrifice after the flood. Even those animals and birds which by nature fear humans and avoid them were led by God to come to Noah and to enter the ark willingly.

⁶Noah was six hundred years old when the floodwaters came on the earth. ⁷And Noah and his sons and his wife and his sons' wives entered the ark to escape the waters of the flood. ⁸Pairs of clean and unclean animals, of birds and of all creatures that move along the ground, ⁹ male and female, came to Noah and entered the ark, as God had commanded Noah. ¹⁰And after the seven days the floodwaters came to the earth. ¹¹In the six hundredth year of Noah's life, on the seventeenth day of the second month — on that day all the springs of the great deep burst forth, and the floodgates of the heavens were opened. ¹²And rain fell on the earth forty days and forty nights.

¹³On that very day Noah and his sons, Shem, Ham and Japheth, together with his wife and the wives of his three sons, entered the ark.

¹⁴**They had with them every wild animal according to its kind, all livestock according to their kinds, every creature that moves along the ground according to its kind and every bird according to its kind, everything with wings. ¹⁵Pairs of all creatures that have the breath of life in them came to Noah and entered the ark. ¹⁶The animals going in were male and female of every living thing, as God had commanded Noah. Then the LORD shut him in.**

Many Bible students today treat Genesis 1-11 as symbolic, as a *sort of parable*. But as you read the flood narrative, you recognize at once that this does not read like a parable. The precise dating of events by year, month and day of Noah's life, for example, convinces us that this is *historical narrative*. To call this a parable is to import a foreign element into Genesis, and to force an interpretation on it which does not arise out of the sacred text. If I am free to call the flood narrative a parable, what's to stop me from calling the teaching of Christ's virgin birth a parable, and the account of Christ's bodily resurrection, and the prophecy of his second coming? And yet we must recognize that all these things are being taught in the Christian church today.

In the absence of any other chronological reference point, the onset of the flood is dated according to Noah's life: the 600th year, the second month, the seventeenth day. This precise dating will later help us to determine exactly how long the flood lasted.

Moses carefully lists the occupants of the ark. In the creation account five different categories of animal life were listed (Genesis 1:21-25): sea creatures, wild animals, domestic animals, those that creep along the ground, and birds. Four of these five categories are mentioned as being aboard the ark. The sea creatures, including amphibians, could have survived outside of the ark. As a special act of love to safeguard his children, and to bar entrance to anyone else, the LORD, the Savior-God, closed the door of the ark.

At precisely the time God had predicted, the floodwaters came on earth. Two sources are listed. "The springs of the great deep burst forth, and the floodgates of the heavens were opened." We know what the *first* source was: we're not so sure about the *second*. In a series of gigantic convulsions the huge reservoirs of water beneath the ground and all the surface waters exploded from behind the boundaries the Creator had originally set for them and flooded the earth. This may very well have provided the bulk of the floodwaters.

The second source of the floodwaters is more difficult to define. It is possible to think of the "floodgates of the heavens" as the cloud waters, the huge mass of atmospheric vapor held in suspension above the earth and periodically released in the form of rain or snow, only to evaporate and start the process all over again. This is the hydrologic system under which we live today.

In our comment on Genesis 1 the possibility was discussed that the world from the time of creation to the time of the flood may have had a different hydrologic system. Many Bible students see evidence in the Old and New Testament that in the pre-flood world there was an immense vapor canopy arched above the earth, providing a sheltered climatic environment for every living thing on earth. In that case, at the time of the flood God released those vast quantities of water, so that for almost six weeks water gushed from the heavens. This uninterrupted downpour, added to the waters coming from below, brought the floodwaters on earth.

According to Genesis 7:24 and 8:3, the two sources of water were shut off at the end of 150 days. Some have seen a conflict between these two passages and 7:12, which speaks of a 40-day period. We conclude that the waters reached their maximum height after 40 days, and that intermittent rains maintained the level of the waters at flood stage for another 110 days.

[17]**For forty days the flood kept coming on the earth, and as the waters increased they lifted the ark high above the earth. [18]The waters rose and increased greatly on the earth, and the ark floated on the surface of the water. [19]They rose greatly on the earth, and all the high mountains under the entire heavens were covered. [20]The waters rose and covered the mountains to a depth of more than twenty feet. [21]Every living thing that moved on the earth perished — birds, livestock, wild animals, all the creatures that swarm over the earth, and all mankind. [22]Everything on dry land that had the breath of life in its nostrils died. [23]Every living thing on the face of the earth was wiped out; men and animals and the creatures that move along the ground and the birds of the air were wiped from the earth. Only Noah was left, and those with him in the ark. [24]The waters flooded the earth for a hundred and fifty days.**

When you read these verses you sense that the author was struggling to find words that would adequately describe the awesome catastrophe that took place on earth. He tells us: "... the flood kept coming ... the waters increased ... the waters rose and increased greatly ... ." The picture we get is that of huge masses of water, tidal waves on a rampage, carrying rocks and uprooted trees, raging and tearing away at the earth for almost half a year. Add to this the fact that the interior of the earth had been split open, perhaps by earthquakes and volcanic eruptions, totally rearranging water and land masses. The tremendous weight of this massive layer of water, which covered even the highest mountains, would have compacted whatever lay beneath.

There were two immediate results of the flood, and they are stated very simply. "Everything on dry land that had the breath of life in its nostrils died. Every living thing on the face of the earth was wiped out." The second effect of the floodwaters was the exact opposite of the first. As the waters increased, they lifted the ark high above the earth, "... and the ark floated on the surface of the water." We usually think of the flood as an awesome act of *destruction*. Now, to be sure, it was that. But it was more than that; it was also a marvelous and mighty act of *deliverance*. The same water which drowned billions of screaming, blaspheming unbelievers lifted the ark with its precious cargo high above all of the death and destruction.

The account of the flood occupies a prominent place also on the pages of the New Testament. Christ uses it as *a type of the end of the world* (Matthew 24:37-39; Luke 17:26,27). The days leading up to Judgment Day will be deceptively normal, and God's great judgment will come unexpectedly, just as did the judgment of the flood. Christ's apostles describe the flood also as *a type of baptism* (1 Peter 3:20,21; Romans 6:4).

8 **But God remembered Noah and all the wild animals and the livestock that were with him in the ark, and he sent a wind over the earth, and the waters receded. ²Now the springs of the deep and the floodgates of the heavens had been closed, and the rain had stopped falling from the sky. ³The water receded steadily from the earth. At the end of the hundred and fifty days the water had gone down, ⁴and on the seventeenth day of the seventh month the ark came to rest on the mountains of Ararat.**

For almost half a year, from his window in the ark, Noah had watched the total destruction of the world as he knew it. As he looked out, all he could see were angry waves carrying out the Creator's judgment on a creation that had rebelled against him. God had promised Noah that after *destroying* the world he would *restore* it, but up to this time Noah could only take that statement on faith. As he looked out of the ark all he could see was evidence of God's *anger*.

Now that was about to change. Moses signals the change with an uncommon expression: *"God remembered Noah."* We dare not interpret this to mean that for a time God had forgotten about his righteous and devout servant. The Scripture uses the expression "to remember" in the sense of *"to show kindness to."* Centuries later, for example, when Jacob's wife Rachel was unhappy about her inability to bear children, we're told "God remembered Rachel ... and she gave birth to a son" (Genesis 30:22). Several centuries after that, when God stepped in to rescue his people from Egyptian slavery, "God remembered his covenant" (Exodus 2:24). When he "remembered" Noah and the other occupants of the ark, therefore, the Creator *made his loving care evident*. From that moment on Noah could observe that the floodwaters were receding.

God accomplished this in several ways. He used natural processes of evaporation and absorption, but accentuated them miraculously. A wind from the Creator speeded up evaporation of the floodwaters. It appears that ocean basins were lowered, bringing about corresponding shifts of huge land masses. This may very well account for the formation of our highest mountains, most of which are fossil-bearing, strong evidence that they were formed by the action of water. The writer of Psalm 104 points to the majestic miracle God performed here:

At your rebuke the waters fled,
> at the sound of your thunder they took to flight;
they flowed over the mountains,
> they went down into the valleys,

> to the place you assigned for them.
> You set a boundary they cannot cross;
> never again will they cover the earth.
> (Psalm 104:7-9)

The waters continued to recede rapidly month after month, and in the seventh month Noah and his family could feel the ark was no longer moving. It had come to rest on one of the mountains of the Ararat range, in what is today Armenia.

We can see the Creator's marvelous provision here, too. For a vessel as big as the ark to come to rest on an even keel in mountainous country is nothing short of a miracle. And the site God selected — near where three continents come together — could hardly have been a more strategic spot for Noah's descendants to disperse to the east and west, to the north and south.

⁵The waters continued to recede until the tenth month, and on the first day of the tenth month the tops of the mountains became visible. ⁶After forty days Noah opened the window he had made in the ark ⁷ and sent out a raven, and it kept flying back and forth until the water had dried up from the earth. ⁸Then he sent out a dove to see if the water had receded from the surface of the ground. ⁹But the dove could find no place to set its feet because there was water over all the surface of the earth; so it returned to Noah in the ark. He reached out his hand and took the dove and brought it back to himself in the ark. ¹⁰He waited seven more days and again sent out the dove from the ark. ¹¹When the dove returned to him in the evening, there in its beak was a freshly plucked olive leaf! Then Noah knew that the water had receded from the earth. ¹²He waited seven more days and sent the dove out again, but this time it did not return to him. ¹³By the first day of the first month of Noah's six hundred and first year, the water had dried up from

the earth. Noah then removed the covering from the ark and saw that the surface of the ground was dry. ¹⁴By the twenty-seventh day of the second month the earth was completely dry.

More than a century ago a German pastor made the interesting comment: "In this chapter Noah's diary lies open before us." Two and a half months after the ark came to rest, the waters had receded to the point where Noah could see the tops of mountains. He patiently waited another six weeks and then opened a window and released a raven. When it didn't return Noah concluded that the debris of the flood must have provided this scavenger bird enough to survive outside the ark.

Noah waited a week and released a dove. Its return signaled that because water was still covering the earth the dove hadn't found a place to land. Seven days later Noah again released the dove. When it returned this time with a freshly plucked olive leaf, Noah knew trees were growing. A week later the dove did not return when it was released — evidence that the water had subsided almost completely.

We must marvel at Noah's patience of faith. Although he and his family had been confined in the ark for 285 days, he waited still another month before removing a portion of the ark's covering, to get a better view of the situation from his mountain lookout. Now he could see that the ground was no longer covered with water. Another two months passed before the ground was dry enough, so that God could say the words eight people had been waiting to hear: "You may leave the ark!" The flood had lasted a year and ten days.

¹⁵Then God said to Noah, ¹⁶ "Come out of the ark, you and your wife and your sons and their wives. ¹⁷Bring out every kind of living creature that is with you — the birds, the animals, and all the creatures that move along the ground — so they can

The dove returns to Noah

multiply on the earth and be fruitful and increase in number upon it." ¹⁸So Noah came out, together with his sons and his wife and his sons' wives. ¹⁹All the animals and all the creatures that move along the ground and all the birds — everything that moves on the earth — came out of the ark, one kind after another.

Noah and his family had *entered* the ark at God's command, and now they *left* it at God's command. The detailed listing of all the animals and birds that left the ark once again shows the detailed concern the Creator has for all his creatures. It also serves to reassure us that despite less than ideal living conditions aboard the ark no species was lost. God restated his creative blessing on the animals, just as he had during the creation week. The flood had not changed his purpose for them, "to be fruitful and increase in number" on the earth.

²⁰Then Noah built an altar to the Lord and, taking some of all the clean animals and clean birds, he sacrificed burnt offerings on it.

²¹The LORD smelled the pleasing aroma and said in his heart: "Never again will I curse the ground because of man, even though every inclination of his heart is evil from childhood. And never again will I destroy all living creatures, as I have done.

> ²²"As long as the earth endures,
>   seedtime and harvest,
>   cold and heat,
>   summer and winter,
>   day and night
>   will never cease."

The great flood was over, the animals had begun to disperse, and Noah and his family were eager to resume their normal lives. But there was something Noah wanted to do first. He built an altar and offered some of each of the clean animals and birds as an offering to the Savior-God.

Moses describes Noah's offering as a *burnt offering*. Since Moses wrote the book of Genesis for the people of Israel, it seems reasonable to assume that *Noah* was expressing with his offering what *the Israelites* expressed when they brought this particular offering to the LORD. Of the different types of Old Testament blood sacrifices, the burnt offering was the only one in which the entire sacrificial animal went up in smoke. This offering, therefore, symbolized the worshiper's *complete dedication* to the LORD.

No wonder God was pleased with Noah's offering and responded to it "in his heart." Moses shares God's thoughts with us. God resolved never again to curse the earth because of man. God's decision was, however, not prompted by a basic change in human nature. "Every inclination of man's heart is evil from childhood." Sinful human beings would therefore need, and God would mercifully grant them, ample time for repentance.

While the waters of the flood were on earth, the normal succession of times and seasons on earth was interrupted. Now God promised that this would never happen again. As long as the earth exists, we can depend on the regular rotation of the seasons that are essential to our continued existence and wellbeing. The words "as long as the earth endures ..." remind us that this earth will not last forever. As there was for Noah's contemporaries, so there will be for us a day of judgment, a day of final accounting.

9 **Then God blessed Noah and his sons, saying to them, "Be fruitful and increase in number and fill the earth. ²The fear and dread of you will fall upon all the beasts of the earth and all the birds of the air, upon every creature that moves along**

the ground, and upon all the fish of the sea; they are given into your hands. ³Everything that lives and moves will be food for you. Just as I gave you the green plants, I now give you everything. ⁴But you must not eat meat that has its lifeblood still in it. ⁵And for your lifeblood I will surely demand on accounting. I will demand an accounting from every animal. And from each man, too, I will demand an accounting for the life of his fellow man.

⁶"Whoever sheds the blood of man,
by man shall his blood be shed;
for in the image of God
has God made man.

⁷As for you, be fruitful and increase in number; multiply on the earth and increase upon it."

Can you imagine the hesitation and uncertainty in which Noah's little family group approached its new life ahead in a world totally strange to them? God addressed this problem by giving Noah a blessing similar to the one he had once spoken in Paradise.

Perhaps while Noah was still sacrificing his burnt offering the Creator said: "Be fruitful and increase in number and fill the earth." This blessing of God was more than just a pious *wish*. As was the case with God's blessing in paradise, God's blessing actually *enabled* Noah's family to carry out God's plan to repopulate the earth.

Human reproductive capability is a distinct blessing from God, and it is his will that we use it with a sense of accountability to him. Although we live in a society where children are often unwanted (in the United States there are presently a million and a half abortions each year), God has made it very clear that he wants the human race to reproduce itself. The begetting and rearing of children for God is not only a high privilege but also a solemn responsibility of people who enter marriage.

One stipulation of the blessing in Eden is missing here. Adam and Eve had once been given the divine mandate to *subdue the earth*, to rule over every living creature (1:28). In the fall Adam and Eve had lost the divine image, and God knew that to give imperfect creatures complete control of the created world could lead to all sorts of abuse. This lack of dominion over God's creation did, however, put the human family in jeopardy. The animals were no longer subject to man, and they vastly outnumbered him. To make sure they would not exterminate the human race, God announced: "The fear and dread of you will fall upon all the beasts of the earth."

God added: "Everything that lives and moves will be food for you." At creation God had directed Adam and Eve to the green plants for their food supply (1:29). Here God gave Noah explicit permission to add animals, birds and fish to his diet. Does this mean that until the time of Noah all humans were vegetarians? Although this might seem to be the case, the Scripture stops short of saying that (and what we're told in Genesis 3:21 and 4:2-4 even seems to argue against that).

There was one string attached to God's broad permission: "You must not eat meat that has its lifeblood still in it." The blood of any living creature is its life. To train the people of Israel to have reverence for life, God later forbade them to eat blood. Centuries later at Mt. Sinai God would tell them: "The life of a creature is in the blood, and I have given it to you to make atonement for yourselves on the altar; it is the blood that makes atonement for one's life. Therefore I say to the Israelites, 'None of you may eat blood'" (Leviticus 17:11,12).

More frequent killing of animals was not to make people indifferent to the shedding of human blood. God therefore added a special warning. He will demand an accounting for the life of a person who is murdered. What an earnest reminder in an age when life is cheap! In ancient Israel even a beast responsible for the death of a person had to be put to death (Exodus 21:28).

God therefore announced the general rule: "Whoever sheds the blood of man, by man shall his blood be shed." The verb "sheds" is the translation of a Hebrew verb form which indicates continuous or characteristic action. God was not referring here to accidental manslaughter, but to intentional, premeditated murder, murder in the first degree. The murderer, God says, is to forfeit his life for willfully cutting off the life of another.

Who is to avenge the life of the victim? Some self-appointed vigilante? Luther commented: "In the words '... by man shall his blood be shed' we have the institution of government." In his letter to the Christians in ancient Rome the Apostle Paul added this commentary on the role of the government: "He does not bear the sword for nothing. He is God's servant, an agent of wrath to bring punishment on the wrongdoer" (Romans 13:4). With a total world population of only eight people there were no government authorities at Noah's time, but the germ of the concept of civil government was already then established by God.

God's reason for demanding that the murderer be made to forfeit his life is clear from the words: "... for in the image of God has God made man." The first two human beings were originally created in the very image of God. Murder strikes at the majesty of God. And since the divine image, lost in the fall, can be regained only during a person's lifetime, to end his life means to cut off his time of grace and, if he has not regained God's image, to doom him to an eternity of separation from God.

After reaffirming the sanctity of life, God restated his will that the human race multiply and spread abroad on the earth.

[8]Then God said to Noah and to his sons with him: [9]"I now establish my covenant with you and with your descendants after you [10]and with every living creature that was with you — the birds, the livestock and all the wild animals, all those that came out of the ark with you — every living creature on earth. [11]I establish my covenant with you: Never again will all life be cut off by the waters of a flood; never again will there be a flood to destroy the earth." [12]And God said, "This is the sign of the covenant I am making between me and you and every living creature with you, a covenant for all generations to come: [13]I have set my rainbow in the clouds, and it will be the sign of the covenant between me and the earth. [14]Whenever I bring clouds over the earth and the rainbow appears in the clouds, [15]I will remember my covenant between me and you and all living creatures of every kind. Never again will the waters become a flood to destroy all life. [16]Whenever the rainbow appears in the clouds, I will see it and remember the everlasting covenant between God and all living creatures of every kind on the earth." [17]So God said to Noah, "This is the sign of the covenant I have established between me and all life on the earth."

God had one more word of assurance for the eight people who were about to set out on their new life. God gave them that assurance in the most solemn and binding form of divine promise — by means of a *covenant*. Think of it! *God actually obligated himself* to observe the terms of a solemn contract: "Never again a flood!"

But hadn't God said that to Noah when he first came out of the ark? (See 8:21.) Why should he repeat his promise? Luther points out that Noah and the members of this family must have lived in great trembling. The sense of the awesomeness of the year-long experience they had just gone through hadn't left them. All around them was evidence of fearful destruction. God saw that these frail creatures of dust needed all the assurance he could give them.

In addition to assuring them *with words* that he would never send another flood, God gave them *a visible sign* as a seal of the truthfulness of his promise. "I have set my rainbow in the clouds." Whenever the rainbow appears, God remembers his covenant. And whenever the rainbow appears, all of Noah's descendants are reminded that God is faithful to his promise.

[18]The sons of Noah who came out of the ark were Shem, Ham and Japheth. (Ham was the father of Canaan). [19]These were the three sons of Noah, and from them came the people who were scattered over the earth. [20]Noah, a man of the soil, proceeded to plant a vineyard.

[21]When he drank some of its wine, he became drunk and lay uncovered inside his tent. [22]Ham, the father of Canaan, saw his father's nakedness and told his two brothers outside. [23]But Shem and Japheth took a garment and laid it across their shoulders; then they walked in backward and covered their father's nakedness. Their faces were turned the other way so that they would not see their father's nakedness.

[24]When Noah awoke from his wine and found out what his youngest son had done to him, [25] he said,

> **"Cursed be Canaan!**
> **The lowest of slaves**
> **will he be to his brothers."**

[26]He also said,

> **"Blessed be the LORD, the God of Shem!**
> **May Canaan be the slave of Shem.**
> **[27]May God extend the territory of Japheth;**
> **may Japheth live in the tents of Shem,**
> **and may Canaan be his slave."**

²⁸**After the flood Noah lived 350 years.** ²⁹**Altogether, Noah lived 950 years, and then he died.**

The "Account of Noah" (6:9-9:29) ends on an unhappy note. Noah, a pious, mature child of God, stumbled and fell into sin. In unblinking honesty, the Bible makes no attempt to hide the sinful weakness of famous people of faith. We need to be reminded that they were not gold-plated saints, but sinful men and women who, like us, lived *by faith in God's forgiveness.* God tells us these things to comfort us, but also to warn us.

Before spelling out the sordid details, Moses reaffirms that God's way of repopulating the earth after the flood was through the normal process of human reproduction. According to Genesis 10, Japheth had seven sons, Shem five, and Ham four.

Noah had apparently been a farmer before the flood and now took up that work again. God blessed his labors and granted his vineyard a harvest, and Noah turned some of it to wine — also a gift of God. But Noah abused God's gift, drank to excess and — in his drunken stupor — dishonored God and himself by lying naked.

Among the sons of Noah, as among the sons of Adam, there was a difference of attitude and spirit. Ham saw his father's nakedness and told his brothers. (It's important for what follows to note that Ham is twice described as "the father of Canaan"). Ham seemed to enjoy looking at his father's shame and thought his brothers would enjoy it, too. Shem and Japheth, however, charitably sought to cover the sin of their father.

Noah returned not only to sobriety, but in repentance and faith he returned to the Lord whom he had offended. And, filled with the Spirit of God, he spoke one of the most remarkable predictions found anywhere in the Scripture. He pointed out what the future would hold for each of his three sons and their descendants.

"Cursed be *Canaan.*" Noah foresaw that the coarse sensuality, the tendency toward immorality which his son Ham had displayed would be developed more fully in Canaan, one of Ham's four sons. Canaan was the ancestor of that branch of Ham's family which occupied the promised land before the Israelites conquered and occupied it. Wherever we meet Canaanite culture, we note that its outstanding characteristic was its moral depravity. Canaanite religion, for example, was a combination of idolatry and adultery. Temple prostitution — heterosexual and homosexual — was a Canaanite way of honoring the gods. Noah predicted that for this reason a curse would fall upon the Canaanites; they would be slaves to their brothers. History records that in subsequent centuries the Canaanites were enslaved, in turn, by their fellow Hamites, as well as by the Shemites and the Japhethites.

From that distasteful segment of prophecy Noah burst out in a hymn of praise to the LORD, the God of *Shem.* The Holy Spirit had revealed to Noah that the line of Shem would be the cradle of the promised Messiah. In contrast to the bleak future ahead for the Hamites, the Shemites would become God's chosen people. He would reveal himself to them, and they would worship Jehovah as the true God, the God of free and faithful grace. Throughout the Old Testament we can trace the fulfillment of what Noah prophesied about the blessedness of Shem's line, the Hebrew people.

Even though the Canaanites later became slaves of the Hebrews, this slavery became a blessing for them, for through it they came in contact with the true God (see Joshua 6:25; 9:27). It should, therefore, be emphasized that Noah spoke in generalities. His prophecy does not predict the unalterable fate of every Canaanite or of every Israelite. The Bible records instances of Canaanites who were saved (1 Kings 17:24; Matthew 15:21-28), as well as of Shemites who were lost (Matthew 23:13).

Noah now addressed the third of his sons. "May God extend the territory of *Japheth*: may *Japheth* live in the tents of Shem. ..." Noah first mentioned an earthly blessing which the descendants of Japheth would enjoy. He would have numerous descendants. Genesis 10 informs us that Japheth was the ancestor of the Indo-Europeans, who later occupied vast stretches of land in Asia and Europe and points north and west. The choicest blessings Noah foretold for the Japhethites, however, were not earthly, physical ones, but the spiritual blessings they would enjoy. They would "live in the tents of Shem," sharing in the blessed inheritance given to Shem — the truth of God as we have it in the gospel of Jesus Christ. Noah prophesied that Gentiles would share in all the blessings Christ came to bring.

The "Account of Noah" closes with the brief note that Noah, sinner and saint, lived a long and eventful life of 950 years and died.

THE FOURTH ACCOUNT:
OF THE SONS OF NOAH
GENESIS 10:1-11:9

The Table of Nations

10 This is the account of Shem, Ham and Japheth, Noah's sons, who themselves had sons after the flood.

A question everyone wants to know the answer to is the question: "*Where did I come from*? What is the origin of the human race?" The very first chapter of Genesis answers that question conclusively.

A question every student of history wants answered is the question: "*Where did the many nations of the world come from*? If the world's billions have a common ancestor, why are there so many different national groupings?" Moses answers this question before focusing in on the history of God's chosen people of Israel. We have his answer in Genesis 10.

This chapter is often referred to as the "Table of Nations." It's part of what Moses calls the "Account of the Sons of Noah," the fourth of the ten "accounts" that make up the book of Genesis. Moses had previously introduced us to Noah's three sons; here he gives us the subsequent history of these three branches of Noah's family.

A word of warning before we begin to read the chapter. Genesis 10 does not make for easy or interesting reading. There are many names, and we can't identify them all. You may very well be tempted simply to skip over a chapter like this. But before you do so, remember two things;

1. *God wanted you to have this document.*
2. In all of literature, *this is the only document of its kind,* listing the geographical distribution of the human race by nation. Israel is the only nation of antiquity that preserved this information.

The Table of Nations has been criticized for not being complete. Not all nations are described with the same degree of detail, nor should we expect this. Moses devotes more attention to those nations that stood in close relationship to the people of Israel. Since the Table is inserted in Genesis just prior to the story of Abraham, we conclude that it represents the state of nations at that time. Chronologically it follows the dispersion of people at the Tower of Babel (see Genesis 10:25).

The Japhethites

²**The sons of Japheth: Gomer, Magog, Madai, Javan, Tubal, Meshech and Tiras. ³The sons of Gomer: Ashkenaz, Riphath and Togarmah. ⁴The sons of Javan: Elishah, Tarshish, the Kittim and the Rodanim. ⁵ (From these the maritime peoples spread out into their territories by their clans within their nations, each with its own language.)**

The descendants of *Japheth* are listed first, because in the centuries to come, the Israelites would have the *least amount of contact* with them. The Japhethites settled in areas farthest removed from the Promised Land. Fourteen descendants of Japheth are named, seven sons and seven grandsons, and they form a group known as the Indo-European family of nations.

They're called "the maritime peoples" because they inhabited countries bordering on the Mediterranean and the

Shem, Ham and Japheth

coasts of the Black and Caspian seas. Each Japhethite group had its own *country* and its own *language*. Each lived in tribal divisions or *clans*, and in its own *nation*. These four are the only points of difference Moses listed in compiling this Table. The Bible is quite silent about the origin of *differences in race*.

The Hamites

⁶The sons of Ham: Cush, Mizraim, Put and Canaan. ⁷The sons of Cush: Seba, Havilah, Sabtah, Raamah and Sabteca. The sons of Raamah: Sheba and Dedan. ⁸Cush was the father of Nimrod, who grew to be a mighty warrior on the earth. ⁹He was a mighty hunter before the LORD; that is why it is said, "Like Nimrod, a mighty hunter before the LORD." ¹⁰The first centers of his kingdom were Babylon, Erech, Akkad and Calneh, in Shinar. ¹¹From that land he went to Assyria, where he built Nineveh, Rehoboth Ir, Calah ¹² and Resen, which is between Nineveh and Calah; that is the great city.

¹³Mizraim was the father of the Ludites, Anamites, Lehabites, Naphtuhites, ¹⁴Pathrusites, Casluhites (from whom the Philistines came) and Caphtorites. ¹⁵Canaan was the father of Sidon his firstborn, and of the Hittites, ¹⁶Jebusites, Amorites, Girgashites, ¹⁷Hivites, Arkites, Sinites, ¹⁸Arvadites, Zemarites and Hamathites. Later the Canaanite clans scattered ¹⁹and the borders of Canaan reached from Sidon toward Gerar as far as Gaza, and then toward Sodom, Gomorrah, Admah and Zeboiim, as far as Lasha. ²⁰These are the sons of Ham by their clans and languages, in their territories and nations.

Listed next are the *sons of Ham*: Cush, Mizraim, Put and Canaan. We learn that they settled in north Africa and Canaan, or Palestine. Mizraim is the Hebrew name for Egypt. In Bible times Cush was a country south of Egypt, perhaps present-day Sudan. It is clear that at certain points in the Table of Nations we don't know if the name Moses preserved is that of the actual *ancestor*, or that of a *tribe*, or even of an entire *nation*.

Special mention is made of a famous grandson of Ham: Nimrod. He is described as "a mighty warrior in the earth." Nimrod was a *ruler* who was also the *founder of empire*. The first step in his empire-building was to gain control over the four cities of Babylon, Erech, Akkad and Calneh (north and west of the Persian Gulf, on the Tigris and Euphrates rivers). From there Nimrod moved northwest and established a *second center of empire* around the four cities of Nineveh, Rehoboth Ir, Calah and Resen. This famous ruler is called "a mighty hunter before the LORD," the very opposite of God's ideal of a king. God's ideal of a king is a shepherd, a man who seeks the welfare of the flock entrusted to his care. A hunter, by contrast, gratifies himself at the expense of his victim.

A number of verses are devoted to describing *the Canaanites*. In years to come God's people were going to have a lot of contact with them. God later instructed the Israelites to dispossess the Canaanites, to occupy their homeland, and to exterminate them because of their vile idolatry. We can therefore understand why Moses not only includes them in the Table of Nations but describes them in such detail.

The Shemites

²¹Sons were also born to Shem, whose older brother was Japheth; Shem was the ancestor of all the sons of Eber. ²²The sons of Shem: Elam, Asshur, Arphaxad, Lud and Aram. ²³The sons of Aram: Uz, Hul, Gether and Meshech. ²⁴Arphaxad was the father of Shelah, and Shelah the father of Eber. ²⁵Two sons were born to Eber: One was named Peleg, because in his time the earth was divided; his brother was named Joktan. ²⁶Joktan was the father of Almodad, Sheleph, Hazarmaveth, Jerah,

²⁷Hadoram, Uzal, Diklah, ²⁸ Obal, Abimael, Sheba, ²⁹ Ophir, Havilah and Jobab. All these were sons of Joktan. ³⁰The region where they lived stretched from Mesha toward Sephar, in the eastern hill country. ³¹These are the sons of Shem by their clans and languages, in their territories and nations.

³²These are the clans of Noah's sons, according to their lines of descent, within their nations. From these the nations spread out over the earth after the flood.

Five sons of *Shem* are named, but the sons of only two are listed. Apparently the other three were too far removed from Israel to be of special interest.

Shem's son *Aram* gave his name to the country immediately north of Palestine. Four sons are named, indicating that this branch of the family was important to God's ancient people. Rebekah, wife of Isaac, was an Aramean, as were Leah and Rachel, wives of Jacob and mothers of the heads of the twelve tribes of Israel.

Arphaxad was the ancestor of the most important branch of Shem's family tree. The line of Arphaxad became *the Messianic line*. After two generations, this line divided into two branches. The first was that of Joktan, thirteen of whose descendants are named, all in eastern Arabia. The more important branch was that of *Peleg*, whose line is the Messianic one, leading to Abraham (11:10-26), and ultimately to Christ.

Genesis 10 is a one-of-a-kind document on the pages of the Scripture. It teaches the unity of post-flood humanity, showing that every person on earth today is a descendant not only of Adam but of Noah. It describes the rise of states and identifies the first founder of empires. It shows that God had a hand in distributing the nations. It helped ancient Israel to determine its relationship to the surrounding nations. And — most important — it shows the develop-

ment through six generations of the family which gave us
our Savior.

Relapse into Heathenism

11 Now the whole world had one language and a common
speech. ²As men moved eastward, they found a plain in
Shinar and settled there. ³They said to each other, "Come, let's
make bricks and bake them thoroughly." They used brick
instead of stone, and tar for mortar.

⁴Then they said, "Come, let us build ourselves a city, with a
tower that reaches to the heavens, so that we may make a name
for ourselves and not be scattered over the face of the whole
earth."

In the preceding chapters Moses has given us a history of
God's first universal judgment, and a brief survey of the
dispersion of nations after the flood. Now he provides an
explanation for the puzzling fact that nations which trace
their origin to a common ancestor today speak more than
5000 different languages. The great variety of languages in
the world today has been called a monument to the cleverness of the human mind. Genesis 11 shows us that it's more
a monument to the rebelliousness of the human heart.

It's understandable that in the first centuries after the
flood the whole world had a single language. Since all people came from the family of Noah the vocabulary they used
was the same, and the way they spoke was the same. It soon
became obvious, however, that although their *language* had
not changed, the *attitude* of these descendants of Noah had
changed — and not for the better. We see a development
similar to the one we have observed in the family of Adam
after the fall, when the godly Sethites gradually patterned
their lives after the unbelieving Cainites. This brought down
on the whole race God's judgment of the flood.

Here we see the Shemites, the line which had received Noah's special blessing, *rebelling against God's expressed will* for them. After Noah's family left the ark God had commanded them: *"Fill the earth!"* It was God's good will that in time the whole earth should be filled with people who would *live for his glory*, so that from east to west his reputation as Savior would be magnified.

Noah's descendants started out well. From Armenia, where the ark had come to rest, they journeyed down into the Tigris-Euphrates valley, often referred to as Mesopotamia (present-day Iraq). The direction of their migration was to the southeast; here it's described as "eastward," because the Hebrew language has expressions only for the four points of the compass; it has none for the oblique directions.

"They found a plain in Shinar and settled there." A well-watered plain would naturally look good to farmers and, in disobedience to God, they decided to *stop their migration* and settle down. It didn't matter to them that God had said: "Fill the earth!" They answered: "Why should we? It doesn't get any better than this!"

The settlement they planned to establish was not a temporary one, either. "Let us build us a city," they said — a fortified settlement. The materials they chose also indicate that this settlement was to be permanent. Instead of sun-dried clay or stone, they chose fire-hardened brick for their building project, with tar for mortar instead of the customary mud. And look at the stated purpose of their building project: "... so that we may *make a name for ourselves.*"

"Glory to man in the highest!" That's turning God's plan for us topsy-turvy. That's rejecting his goal for life and substituting a goal of our own. Sustenance (food and shelter), security, status — these were the life goals the descendants of Noah had adopted. Satan doesn't have to persuade us to kneel down in front of an idol, if he can only get us to look at life *in terms of ourselves.*

⁵But the LORD came down to see the city and the tower that the men were building. ⁶The LORD said, "If as one people speaking the same language they have begun to do this, then nothing they plan to do will be impossible for them. ⁷Come, let us go down and confuse their language so they will not understand each other." ⁸So the LORD scattered them from there over all the earth, and they stopped building the city. ⁹That is why it was called Babel — because there the LORD confused the language of the whole world. From there the LORD scattered them over the face of the whole earth.

It does not surprise us that the LORD intervened in judgment to stop that building project. "I am the LORD," he has told us. "I will not give my glory to another" (Isaiah 42:8). Moses tells us that "the LORD came down to see the city and the tower that the men were building." The statement that the LORD "came down" is not to be understood literally, as though the LORD had to travel to the building site to learn what the builders were up to. God does want to emphasize, however, that whenever he intervenes in judgment *he has carefully evaluated all the facts*; his judgment is never impulsive or arbitrary.

God's judgment here, unlike at the time of the flood, wasn't even visible. God simply made some changes inside the minds of the builders. They could no longer understand one another's language. For one thing, that meant that they could *no longer work together.* Worse yet, they *no longer trusted one another.* The spirit of friendliness and confidence was replaced by ugly suspicion, and they had to move away from their dream home. The settlement they had hoped would bring them fame became known as Babel ("confusion"). It is significant that this judgment of scattering the descendants of Noah is ascribed *to the* LORD, Jehovah, the Savior-God. It is *the Savior* who says: "Do not be deceived: I will not be mocked." He is absolutely unwilling to let people wipe their feet on his great good plan for this world.

Martin Luther called God's action at Babel a much more horrible judgment than the flood. That divine judgment wiped out only a single generation of humanity. Confusing the languages at Babel, however, has bred confusion and suspicion and hatred in every generation since then, down to our broken, disorderly world. Why is nation pitted against nation, social element against social element, individual against individual? We have an answer here.

The narrative of Babel brings the "Account of the Sons of Noah" to a close, and it ends on a sour note. The descendants of Noah were *running away from God* — some of them no doubt ignorantly, but most of them maliciously.

The unanswered question at this point is: what would God's relationship be to this disorderly and rebellious human race? Would his patience finally be exhausted? If people wanted to run away from him, would he finally say: "All right! If you want to go to hell so badly, have it your way! See if I care"? If the God of grace had not once again intervened, the history of mankind would have ended in the darkness of heathenism.

THE FIFTH ACCOUNT:
OF SHEM
GENESIS 11:10-26

God has promised that his plans for his people will not end in the darkness of ignorance and of false religion — and of damnation. The fourth of Moses' ten "accounts," the "Account of the Sons of Noah," had closed on a dismal and disappointing note. The descendants of pious Noah had rebelled against God and had been forcibly dispersed by an act of God's judgment. Was this, then, to be the end of God's great good plan for his people?

Moses' fifth "account," the "Account of Shem," assures us that the Savior-God had not lost control of the situation. Although Satan had won a *victory* at Babel, he had not won the *war* against God and his people. He had not succeeded in destroying the Church, the family of God.

The "Account of Shem" is a brief and not very exciting passage of the Scripture to read. It's a ten-link genealogy that *traces the line of the Messiah from Shem to Abraham.* Of Shem's five sons (10:22) Arphaxad is singled out as the one who carried forward the Messianic line.

[10]This is the account of Shem. Two years after the flood, when Shem was 100 years old, he became the father of Arphaxad. [11]And after he became the father of Arphaxad, Shem lived 500 years and had other sons and daughters. [12]When Arphaxad had lived 35 years, he became the father of Shelah. [13]And after he became the father of Shelah, Arphaxad lived 403 years and had other sons and daughters. [14]When

111

Shelah had lived 30 years, he became the father of Eber. [15]And after he became the father of Eber, Shelah lived 403 years and had other sons and daughters. [16]When Eber had lived 34 years, he became the father of Peleg. [17]And after he became the father of Peleg, Eber lived 430 years and had others sons and daughters. [18]When Peleg had lived 30 years, he became the father of Reu. [19]And after he became the father of Reu, Peleg lived 209 years and had other sons and daughters. [20]When Reu lived 32 years, he became the father of Serug. [21]And after he became the father of Serug, Reu lived 207 years and had other sons and daughters. [22]When Serug had lived 30 years, he became the father of Nahor. [23]And after he became the father of Nahor, Serug lived 200 years and had other sons and daughters. [24]When Nahor had lived 29 years, he became the father of Terah. [25]And after he became the father of Terah, Nahor lived 119 years and had other sons and daughters. [26]After Terah had lived 70 years, he became the father of Abram, Nahor and Haran.

The seventeen verses of this "account" cover centuries of history. Moses supplies few details about the men whose names are listed here.

The first detail to catch our eye is the *shortened life spans* of the patriarchs who lived after the flood. The reader may remember that in the centuries before the flood the majority of the Savior's ancestors lived 900 years and more. Contrast that with what you read here. Shem, the first and longest-lived of the post-flood patriarchs, lived only 600 years; his son lived only 430. At Peleg's time (the time of the Tower of Babel, 10:25), the life span had dropped to half of that. Abram, the tenth on the list, lived to be a mere 175.

We don't know the reasons for the sharp drop in the span of human life. It's enough for us to know that God knows. He has told us: "My sheep listen to my voice; I know them ..." (John 10:27). He knows their names, the number of years they live and the children they leave behind.

What we do know — and this is the important thing about the "Account of Shem" — is that *twenty generations had come and gone, and God's promises were not forgotten.* The family of the Messiah was not extinct. The Savior had found a seed to serve him. His name? Abram, later changed to Abraham.

PART II

THE HISTORY OF GOD'S GRACIOUS DEALINGS AMONG THE PATRIARCHS

GENESIS 11:27-50:26

THE SIXTH ACCOUNT: OF TERAH
GENESIS 11:27-25:11

With the first five of the ten "accounts" which make up the book of Genesis Moses has sketched God's saving activity *among the families of the original world.* Genesis 1:1 to 11:26 form Part I of Genesis.

In the remaining five "accounts" Moses again sketches God's saving activity, but this time only *in one single family — the family of the patriarchs* Abraham, Isaac and Jacob. With 11:27, then, Part II of Genesis begins. (Logically a new chapter ought to begin here. Some of the chapter divisions in our English Bibles are unfortunate and unhelpful. The reader is asked to remember that the chapter divisions are not inspired.)

God Calls Abram, Giving Him a Whole Cluster of Promises

²⁷**This is the account of Terah. Terah became the father of Abram, Nahor and Haran. And Haran became the father of**

Lot. ²⁸While his father Terah was still alive, Haran died in Ur of the Chaldeans, in the land of his birth. ²⁹Abram and Nahor both married. The name of Abram's wife was Sarai, and the name of Nahor's wife was Milcah; she was the daughter of Haran, the father of both Milcah and Iscah.

³⁰Now Sarai was barren; she had no children. ³¹Terah took his son Abram, his grandson Lot son of Haran, and his daughter-in-law Sarai, the wife of his son Abram, and together they set out from Ur of the Chaldeans to go to Canaan. But when they came to Haran, they settled there. ³²Terah lived 205 years, and he died in Haran.

The "Account of Terah" traces the life of Abraham and occupies more than a dozen chapters. The reader may wonder why Moses didn't name this "account" *after Abraham*, since he's its most prominent character. There are several reasons. For one, Abraham's father *Terah was the head of this important family* when we meet them here. Then, too, this "account" will introduce us to a number of *members of Terah's family who were not descendants of Abraham* — people like Lot and Rebekah and Rachel and Leah. We see once again that in determining the outline of the book of Genesis, Moses chose and used his terms carefully.

The "Account of Terah" helps us to see how, after the human race had again turned away from God in unbelief, God chose the family of Abram, from the line of Shem, as the Messianic line. In the interest of his magnificent plan for the human race God gave Abram a whole cluster of promises centering in the Savior, and trained him to trust those promises.

We first meet Terah's important clan in the city of Ur, west and north of the Persian Gulf. The time is about 2100 B.C. Ur was the busy and prosperous capital of the ancient Sumerian people. Clay documents uncovered in the archeological excavation of Ur paint a picture of an advanced and sophisticated culture. Unfortunately they also document the existence of a number of heathen temples. Centuries later Joshua told the Israelites: "Your forefathers, including Terah the father of Abraham and Nahor...worshiped other gods" (Joshua 24:2).

It would be overstating the case to say that Terah and his family knew nothing at all of the true God. That would clash with Abraham's words when years later he was seeking a wife for his son Isaac. He commanded his servant not to look for Isaac's wife among the Canaanites, but instead to go to his relatives (24:3-4) to find a God-fearing wife for his son. One would like to think that Terah knew and worshiped the true God. Yet his faith was not completely free from elements of heathen superstition.

God called Abram to leave Ur. In obedience to God Abram and his wife Sarai, together with his father Terah and his brother Nahor, left Ur and traveled about 500 miles northwest to the city of Haran (in present-day Syria). After the death of Terah (Acts 7:2-4) God called Abram a second time. In response to God's call Abram left Haran at the age of 75 and migrated south to the land of Canaan, accompanied by his wife Sarai and his nephew Lot. A significant fact about Sarai is mentioned here which will later become an important factor in God's training program for Abram. Sarai (whose name would later be changed to Sarah) was barren.

12 The LORD had said to Abram, "Leave your country, your people and your father's household and go to the land I will show you.

²ᵇ"I will make you into a great nation
    and I will bless you;
I will make your name great,

> **and you will be a blessing.**
> **³I will bless those who bless you,**
> **and whoever curses you I will curse;**
> **and all peoples on earth**
> **will be blessed through you."**

"The LORD...said to Abram...." With these simple words the book of Genesis begins its narrative of the life of Abram (whose name God would later change to Abraham). Moses devoted more than a dozen chapters to the life of this man (more precisely, to the last half of the life of this man). Why should one man rate so much space in the sacred record?

There are two reasons. *God chose Abram*, first of all, *to become the father of a new nation*, the nation of Israel, the nation which would be the cradle of the Savior. But there is a second reason why Abram gets so much attention in both Old and New Testaments. *The way God dealt with Abram is typical of the way God deals with every sinner.* The better we understand how God spoke to Abram the better we will understand what God has to say to a world of sinners today.

Note also that it was the LORD, the Savior-God, who spoke to Abram. We don't know how he chose to speak to Abram, but we do know it was a miraculous conversation, which would never have taken place if God had not intervened in Abram's life.

Many biblical scholars today have little sympathy with the idea that *God intervenes in human history.* But Christianity asks you to believe the miraculous, and it does so without apology. During the centuries after the flood unbelief had made such progress among the descendants of Shem that the faithful covenant God felt constrained to intervene, if the knowledge of his great plan were not to perish from the earth. Note also *the direction* of this supernatural conversation: God spoke to Abram, not vice versa.

It's important to note that if contact is to be established between God and the sinner, *the initiative must start on God's end*, not on ours.

"Abram, leave your country." Abram heard God say those words twice in his lifetime. This first time was *in Ur*, in southern Mesopotamia, when he, together with his father's and brothers' families left their homes. Following established trade routes of the day, they moved north to Haran. It was *in Haran* that Abram heard God speak those words a second time. Humanly speaking, it must have been more difficult for Abram to obey them the second time. When Abram left Haran God not only asked him to leave his country and his people; he added: "Leave...your father's household." The only relatives who accompanied Abram from Haran were his wife Sarai and his nephew Lot.

It might seem almost unreasonable for God to ask a 75-year old man to leave his home and his relatives and to travel to an unknown destination. To build in Abram a willingness to follow his call, God gave Abram a promise or, more accurately, a whole cluster of promises. And that is a truth which is in itself worth noting. *God deals with us*, as he dealt with Abram, *not in terms of demand but primarily in terms of promise.*

We can isolate various individual jewels in the gem cluster of promises God gave Abram. The childless 75-year old husband of a barren 65-year old woman heard God say: "I will make you *into a great nation*." To drive out the thought "A man my age should pull up all his roots and start a new life?" God assured Abram: "*I will bless you*." God would not only pour blessings into Abram's personal life; he would use him to bless countless other people. "*You will be a blessing*."

"*I will make your name great*." At the time of his call Abram had the reputation of being a well-to-do cattleman.

But that isn't the reputation Abram has on the pages of the Scriptures. He is a man with whom God shared some of his sacred secrets. He is called the friend of God; he is the father of believers; he is the father of the Israelite nation; he is an ancestor of the Messiah. Blessings would be identified with Abram. Throughout history happiness (or the lack of it) would flow from the relationship people have with Abram.

Abram would experience opposition as, for the last century of his life, he lived a nomad in lands belonging to others. But God promised him he would be so closely identified with the work of God that to curse him, to despise him, would be tantamount to opposing God.

The greatest blessing God held out to Abram when he called him was: "*All peoples on earth will be blessed through you.*" The unfaithfulness of the Shemites could threaten once again to plunge the whole race into spiritual darkness, but the love of God took the initiative to guarantee that would not happen. God promised Abram that a great Descendant would be born to his family who would bring blessings to every member of the human race.

We can isolate individual components of this cluster of divine promises to Abram, but the important thing to remember is that *they all centered in Christ*. Everything that God told Abram about his large family of descendants or about the new homeland they would inherit gets its real purpose and meaning from God's revelation centering in Christ. Abram understood this from what God told him. Jesus made this clear when he said: "Abraham rejoiced at the thought of seeing my day; he saw it and was glad" (John 8:58).

Abram was saved not by a generic faith in a merciful God. He was saved by *faith in a Person*, and *only by faith* in a Person, and only by *faith in one Person*. And that's what makes the scriptural record of Abram's faith and life so important. The way Abram was saved is the same way sinners are saved today. God didn't have one way for people of Old Testament times to enter his family and a different way for us of the New Testament period. There has always been *only one way*: to trust God's promises as these center in Jesus Christ.

God Trains Abram to Believe the Promise of the Land

⁴So Abram left, as the LORD had told him; and Lot went with him. Abram was seventy-five years old when he set out from Haran. ⁵He took his wife Sarai, his nephew Lot, all the possessions they had accumulated and the people they had acquired in Haran, and they set out for the land of Canaan, and they arrived there. ⁶Abram traveled through the land as far as the site of the great tree of Moreh at Shechem. At that time the Canaanites were in the land. ⁷The LORD appeared to Abram and said, "To your offspring I will give this land." So he built an altar there to the LORD, who had appeared to him.

⁸From there he went on toward the hills east of Bethel and pitched his tent, with Bethel on the west and Ai on the east. There he built an altar to the Lord and called on the name of the LORD. ⁹Then Abram set out and continued toward the Negev.

In his marvelous conversation with Abram, God had really said all that there was to say. All Abram could do was to speak the "Amen" to what God had promised. The Bible calls this "faith." *Faith*, then, is the hand which takes God's promises and makes them our own. By contrast, *unbelief* closes its hand into a fist and makes it impossible for God to give us his blessings.

Abram's trust in God's promises didn't simply lie in his heart "like foam on beer," to use Luther's earthy comparison. Abram's trust in what God had promised *powered him to respond* to God's call. He took his wife and his nephew, together with their households of servants and their flocks, said good-bye to relatives and friends in Haran and set out on the hot and dusty journey to Canaan, the land God had promised, a narrow land bridge between three continents. Abram committed himself and his future completely into God's hands. There's a time to pray for God's guidance, but there's also a time to stop praying and to start moving. Abram followed God in glad obedience.

Abram traveled south to the center of Canaan, to the ancient city of Shechem. Moses mentions specifically that the Canaanites were in the land. From this Abram realized he would not be able to homestead the land; it was already occupied. Before his descendants could live here as their home, they would have to dispossess the Canaanites. This had to be a sobering realization for Abram. *God was training Abram to believe what God had said*, first of all, *about the promised land.*

At this critical moment for Abram, the LORD, the Savior-God, appeared to him, to reaffirm and clarify his promise and to bolster Abram's faith. He made it clear that Abram was not to try to take immediate possession of the land. It was only for Abram's descendants that the land of Canaan would become a new homeland. Each new promise of God nourished and exercised Abram's faith.

Now look at Abram's response to the LORD's appearance. In a land full of Canaanites and Canaanite religion, he *built an altar* to the LORD, the true God, the God who had appeared to him and restated his promise. Abram traveled south another twenty-five miles, to the city of Bethel. There he built another altar and "called on the name of the LORD," or more precisely, *"proclaimed the name of the LORD."* In a land lying in the darkness of false religion, rays of light streamed from Abram's worship. To the heathen Canaanites, as well as to the men and women of his own household,

Abram's worship announced: "I don't know whom you're going to worship, but I want you to know that the only God deserving of your worship is the God who has appeared to me with all his grace and his favor."

Abram continued to journey south along the spine of mountains that bisects the land of Canaan, the "continental divide" along which most of Canaan's chief cities were built. At the south end of the country was the city of Beersheba, in the region known as the Negev, the hot, dry southland.

Remember that Moses originally wrote the book of Genesis for the ancient people of Israel, who at the time had not yet entered the land. Can you imagine how mentioning the names of cities which they would one day inhabit would awaken anticipation for their new home? Each of the historic spots Abram visited and where he worshiped would have special meaning for his descendants when they one day occupied the homeland God had picked out for them.

Abram was an important person in God's plans for saving the world. Since he was, as the New Testament calls him, the father of believers, God had to train him to trust the promises of God implicitly. The only safe foundation for faith is not what we see and feel but what God has said. That's what God was after with Abram, and that's what he's after with us.

[10]Now there was a famine in the land, and Abram went down to Egypt to live there for a while because the famine was severe. [11]As he was about to enter Egypt, he said to his wife Sarai, "I know what a beautiful woman you are. [12]When the Egyptians see you, they will say, 'This is his wife.' Then they will kill me but will let you live. [13]Say you are my sister, so that I will be treated well for your sake and my life will be spared because of you." [14]When Abram came to Egypt, the Egyptians

saw that she was a very beautiful woman. ¹⁵And when Pharaoh's officials saw her, they praised her to Pharaoh, and she was taken into his palace. ¹⁶He treated Abram well for her sake, and Abram acquired sheep and cattle, male and female donkeys, menservants and maidservants, and camels. ¹⁷But the LORD inflicted serious diseases on Pharaoh and his household because of Abram's wife Sarai. ¹⁸So Pharaoh summoned Abram. "What have you done to me?" he said. "Why didn't you tell me she was your wife? ¹⁹Why did you say, 'She is my sister,' so that I took her to be my wife? Now then, here is your wife. Take her and go!" ²⁰Then Pharaoh gave orders about Abram to his men, and they sent him on his way, with his wife and everything he had.

We call God's grace "*free* grace." By that we mean not only that you get it for nothing, but that *it's independent of our behavior.* God's mercy doesn't need an excuse; it's its own reason for existence. The narrative of Abram's life gives us abundant evidence of how God's mercy reached out for Abram in spite of his sinful shortcomings. We see an example of this in the closing verses of chapter 12.

Canaan has always been a land of what we would call minimal rainfall. Since ancient Canaan's agriculture was rain-fed, drought was a recurring problem. One could guess that this would be especially hard on a non-resident like Abram, who didn't own a square inch of land but depended on the good will of landowners for water and grazing rights for his cattle. Egypt, by contrast, practiced irrigation agriculture. In ancient times the Nile River, swollen by snowmelt from the interior of Africa, each year brought life-giving water and nutrients down through the valley of the Nile, that green five percent of Egypt's territory that supported the other ninety-five percent, and made Egypt the breadbasket of the Mediterranean world. It's not hard to understand why, in a time of drought, Abram would take his household and his flocks and head south for Egypt.

It was in this foreign land that Abram's faith buckled under temptation. Afraid that the Egyptians would be impressed by Sarai's beauty and would kill him to get her, he asked her to demonstrate her love by deceiving the Egyptians into thinking she was Abram's sister, not his wife.

This was a piece of unbelief. When Abram suggested this he was not demonstrating his trust in God's promise but his reliance on his own cleverness to get him out of a potentially dangerous situation. And where the *root* of faith is defective, the *fruits* of faith will also be defective. Instead of loving God above all and his fellow human being (in this case, his wife) as himself, Abram was most concerned about his own safety. He explained to Sarai: "If the Egyptians think you're my sister, not only will they have no thought of killing me, they will probably treat me very well for your sake."

We learn later that there was a grain of truth in what Abram had told the Egyptians. Sarai actually was his half-sister. But that doesn't change the fact that his behavior here was a lie; he was trying to deceive his Egyptian hosts. He was enjoying their hospitality; surely he owed them the truth. Abram could have been confident that the LORD would not let anything happen to him and his wife that would cancel out his great promises about numerous descendants and about one great Descendant.

God let Abram learn the hard way. Part of what Abram had predicted came true; he was treated royally. But what Abraham did not foresee was that Egypt's pharaoh would take Sarai into the royal harem for himself. And she very likely would have stayed there, too, if God had not intervened.

Sarai had an important role in the promise God had solemnly announced to Abram, and God wasn't going to let anything block the fulfillment of that promise — not the frailty of Abram's faith, not even the power of the Egyptian king. Abram's scheme to protect himself had placed God's promise into jeopardy, but God's faithful love preserved the purity of the Savior's ancestress. The LORD, the God of the covenant, inflicted diseases on the royal household. We don't know how Pharaoh came to the conclusion that *God* was warning him, but he surely got the message. He understood that his taking Sarai was the cause of the disaster that had overtaken the palace.

It isn't a pretty sight that we see here. The father of believers was raked over the coals by a heathen king, who then forcibly escorted him to the border as an undesirable alien.

This episode has a familiar ring to it. Like Abram, we are often strong in faith when it comes to *the big things in life* — like accepting God's pardon, or trusting in Christ's merit to make us members of God's family. But then in *some earthly matter* we stumble in doubt and unbelief, and we fall. Perhaps it's a problem with earning our daily bread that trips us up. Maybe our particular problem is learning to face life one day at a time without running to the medicine cabinet or reaching for a bottle. "Satan will climb the fence where it's lowest," Martin Luther once remarked. Fortunately for us, Satan is not the only one who knows what frail creatures of clay we are. It was only the loyal love of God that rescued Abram. If you and I are to be kept from falling and preserved to inherit God's promised blessing, God's free and faithful love is our only hope.

13 So Abram went up from Egypt to the Negev, with his wife and everything he had, and Lot went with him.

²Abram had become very wealthy in livestock and in silver and gold. ³From the Negev he went from place to place until he came to Bethel, to the place between Bethel and Ai where his tent had been earlier ⁴ and where he had first built an altar. There Abram called on the name of the LORD. ⁵Now Lot, who was moving about with Abram, also had flocks and herds and tents. ⁶But the land could not support them while they stayed together, for their possessions were so great that they were not able to stay together. ⁷And quarreling arose between Abram's herdsmen and the herdsmen of Lot. The Canaanites and Perizzites were also living in the land at that time. ⁸So Abram said to Lot, "Let's not have any quarreling between you and me, or between your herdsmen and mine, for we are brothers. ⁹Is not the the whole land before you? Let's part company. If you go to the left, I'll go to the right; if you go to the right, I'll go to the left."

We can imagine how happy Abram was to leave Egypt and to set foot on the soil of Canaan again. He had embarrassed himself and his household with his shameful dishonesty. He must have been especially thankful that his beloved Sarai was still at his side. Abram knew he'd almost lost her; it was only the LORD's hand that had safeguarded the family of promise.

The first thing Abram did upon returning to Canaan was to head for Bethel. At the time he had first entered the land years earlier, Bethel was one of the places where he had built an altar to the LORD and conducted public worship (12:8). There may have been more than one reason why Abram made this special trip to the altar at Bethel. One reason was surely *his own personal need*. Abram needed to express his penitence over his sorry performance in Egypt and his gratitude to God for mercifully undoing any potential damage he could have caused.

There may have been an additional reason. Abram had just experienced the grace of God as it appeared on the dark background of his sin, and he wanted to *give public testimony to God's amazing grace*. Abram may have realized, furthermore, that it was not only the heathen inhabitants around Bethel who needed to hear that testimony. He knew that he owed a clear witness to the many members of his own household, who must have numbered in the hundreds (see Genesis 14:14). There was no way they could have been impressed with their master's dishonesty. Some of them may even have wondered: "Is this what it means to be a follower of the true God?" Abram's worship at Bethel gave them a clear and correct answer.

Now that the important spiritual business had been attended to, Abram could give his attention to another problem that demanded his attention. He was surrounded by all sorts of evidence that the LORD had blessed him and his nephew Lot. In Mesopotamia, in Canaan, and most recently in Egypt the LORD had blessed him with earthly wealth — most of which had four legs. The LORD who had promised Abram "I will bless you" had kept his promise so abundantly that "the land could not support them while they stayed together." There simply weren't enough grazing areas and waterholes to satisfy the needs of the two flocks, and this led to arguments between Abram's and Lot's herdsmen.

Here the question might arise: "Was this the land the Bible later described as 'flowing with milk and honey'?" We need to remember that the best portions of Canaan were not available to Abram and Lot. They were only strangers, temporary residents, who had to be satisfied with what range land was available. Here again we can see part of God's training program for Abram. God was training him to believe what God had promised about the land, despite all evidence to the contrary.

Abram saw in the herdsmen's quarreling something that could not be allowed to continue. "There simply must be no quarreling between you and me," he told Lot. Surrounded as they were by heathen occupants of the land, it would simply not do for two of the LORD's sons to be seen quarreling. Abram saw clearly that not only was *their fellowship of faith endangered*, but the *testimony of their faith was being blunted* by the continual bickering.

Abram not only pointed out the problem, he offered the solution. "Better that there be an *outward* separation between us than an *inner* one, Lot, and I'll make the parting of our ways as pleasant for you as I can. You choose where you want to live, and I'll go in the opposite direction."

By making this generous offer Abram was putting his faith in God's promise to work. God had promised the land to his descendants. Since he had God's promise he did not have to guard his future possessions jealously. Abram's attitude toward earthly possessions gives us a good illustration of living to the glory of God. How easy it is to say: "I trust in Christ as my *Savior!*" But how hard it often seems to say: "I trust in him as my *Provider!*" Those who have learned to trust God's promise to provide can be generous with their possessions. Like Abram, they know they have the Savior's promise: "Christian, you put me first, and I promise you will lack for nothing you need for body and soul!"

¹⁰Lot looked up and saw that the whole plain of the Jordan was well watered, like the garden of the Lord, like the land of Egypt, toward Zoar. (This was before the Lord destroyed Sodom and Gomorrah.) ¹¹So Lot chose for himself the whole plain of the Jordan and set out toward the east. The two men parted company: ¹²Abram lived in the land of Canaan, while Lot lived among the cities of the plain and pitched his tents

near Sodom. ¹³Now the men of Sodom were wicked and were
sinning greatly against the LORD. ¹⁴The LORD said to Abram
after Lot had parted from him, "Lift up your eyes from where
you are and look north and south, east and west. ¹⁵All the land
that you see I will give to you and your offspring forever. ¹⁶I will
make your offspring like the dust of the earth, so that if anyone
could count the dust, then your offspring could be counted.
¹⁷Go, walk through the length and breadth of the land, for I am
giving it to you." ¹⁸So Abram moved his tents and went to live
near the great trees of Mamre at Hebron, where he built an
altar to the LORD.

Lot took advantage of his uncle's generous offer. He
thought back to the time, years earlier, when he and Abram
had traveled south along Canaan's central ridge. At that
time Lot had noted that the area through which the Jordan
River flowed on its way to the Dead Sea was an attractive
place to raise cattle. Now he chose to settle there, and
"pitched his tents near Sodom." It was a terribly unwise
choice, and Lot was going to pay dearly for it, in heartache
and heartbreak.

One can imagine the loneliness Abram must have felt,
separated from the only blood relative he had in the land.
And right there the LORD, the God of the covenant, intervened. Once again Moses inverts the customary word order
of the Hebrew sentence, to emphasize the fact that after
Abram said good-bye to Lot *the Savior-God* spoke to him.
To indicate his approval of what Abram had done and to
compensate him for what he had given up, the LORD first of
all reaffirmed the promise of blessing to him. "All the land
that you see I will give to you and your offspring forever."
Abram had yielded grazing and water rights to his nephew,
but God reserved the right of ownership for Abram and his
descendants.

God did still more to reward Abram for the splendid demonstration of his faith. He not only *restated* the promise but *enlarged* it by promising to give the entire land, including the land to the east which Lot had chosen, to Abram's descendants "forever." That last word calls for explanation, since some have interpreted it to mean that the descendants of Abram hold title to the land of Canaan for all time. The word Moses originally used means "for the indefinite future." God later warned the Israelites that if they turned from him they would forfeit the good land he had given them (Deuteronomy 28:63f; 30:17f). Twenty-five centuries of history have documented the fact that this actually happened.

God also enlarged his promise of descendants for Abram. This childless old man heard God say: "I will make your offspring like the dust of the earth." Apart from God's special promise, Abram and Sarai could only have expected that their family line would die out with them. But by faith they knew otherwise, and now God had bolstered their faith with a special promise.

God also instructed Abram to give evidence of this strengthened faith by walking through the land, from one end to the other. He was to make a kind of inspection tour, the sort of thing the new owner of a piece of property might want to do. Abram did this, and settled in Hebron, in the southern part of Canaan. Here is where the family of the patriarch lived the longest. Here is where they buried their beloved dead.

The chapter closes on the same note on which it had opened. Abram built an altar to express his personal faith, and to give public testimony to the one true God.

14 At this time Amraphel king of Shinar, Arioch king of Ellasar, Kedorlaomer king of Elam and Tidal king of

Goiim [2] went to war against Bera king of Sodom, Birsha king of Gomorrah, Shinab king of Admah, Shemeber king of Zeboiim, and the king of Bela (that is, Zoar). [3]All these latter kings joined forces in the Valley of Siddim (the Salt Sea). [4]For twelve years they had been subject to Kedorlaomer, but in the thirteenth year they rebelled.

Power politics are nothing new in history. War and bloodshed and conquest are the stuff history has been made of ever since the fall. This chapter tells the story of a military episode that took place about 2100 B.C., the first war recorded on the pages of Scripture. Although Abram was not directly involved, he chose to become involved, and right there is the reason this narrative is included in the Bible.

The story begins in ancient Mesopotamia, present-day Iraq. Four kings from the east joined forces in a military adventure that took them a thousand miles away, to the region around the Dead Sea. What is described here is a major military undertaking, in comparison with which the capture of Abram's nephew is actually only a minor detail. But in the "Account of Terah" this minor detail takes on major significance.

When the four eastern kings invaded, the promised land became a battlefield. God was training Abram to believe his promise of the land even when he saw it trampled and plundered by invading armies. In the region around the Dead Sea the invaders attacked a coalition of five city-states, defeated them on the field of battle, announced a heavy tribute to be paid annually, and returned home. The conquered city-states had no choice but to submit. Year after year they paid the tribute. They did so grudgingly, because it was costly, and it was humiliating. (During the period of Israel's monarchy, for example, King Ahab conquered the neighboring nation of Moab and forced them to pay him an *annual tribute* of 100,000 lambs and the wool of 100,000 rams, 2 Kings 3:4.)

⁵**In the fourteenth year, Kedorlaomer and the kings allied with him went out and defeated the Rephaites in Ashteroth Karnaim, the Zuzites in Ham, the Emites in Shaveh Kiriathaim ⁶ and the Horites in the hill country of Seir, as far as El Paran near the desert. ⁷Then they turned back and went to En Mishpat (that is, Kadesh), and they conquered the whole territory of the Amalekites, as well as the Amorites who were living in Hazazon Tamar. ⁸Then the king of Sodom, the king of Gomorrah, the king of Admah, the king of Zeboiim and the king of Bela (that is, Zoar) marched out and drew up their battle lines in the Valley of Siddim ⁹ against Kedorlaomer king of Elam, Tidal king of Goiim, Amraphel king of Shinar and Arioch king of Ellasar — four kings against five. ¹⁰Now the Valley of Siddim was full of tar pits, and when the kings of Sodom and Gomorrah fled, some of the men fell into them and the rest fled to the hills. ¹¹The four kings seized all the goods of Sodom and Gomorrah and all their food; then they went away. ¹²They also carried off Abram's nephew Lot and his possessions, since he was living in Sodom.**

After a dozen years the five Canaanite kings had had enough. They decided to stop paying the tribute, and the results were predictable. The very next year the armies of the four eastern kings again headed west, with blood in their eye. They swept down on Canaan along an ancient and well-known trade route called "The King's Highway," east of the Jordan, conquering and plundering cities and nations that happened to be in their way. After penetrating far enough into the desert south and west of the Dead Sea to eliminate any danger of attack from the rear, they swung to the north to confront their rebellious vassals.

Moses' report of the decisive battle is brief. The armies of the five kings were easily and soundly defeated. All's fair in war; to the victor belong the spoils. The invaders stole whatever was worth stealing and took some of the population along as slaves (or perhaps as hostages, to guarantee future payment of tribute). In the previous chapter we were told only that Lot had pitched his tents *near Sodom*. Here we learn that he had chosen to live *among the wicked people of Sodom*. As Lot was led away captive he must have regretted his earlier decision. Prisoners of war in ancient times did not have a promising future.

¹³One who had escaped came and reported this to Abram the Hebrew. Now Abram was living near the great trees of Mamre the Amorite, a brother of Eshcol and Aner, all of whom were allied with Abram. ¹⁴When Abram heard that his relative had been taken captive, he called out the 318 trained men born in his household and went in pursuit as far as Dan. ¹⁵During the night Abram divided his men to attack them and he routed them, pursuing them as far as Hobah, north of Damascus. ¹⁶He recovered all the goods and brought back his relative Lot and his possessions, together with the women and the other people. ¹⁷After Abram returned from defeating Kedorlaomer and the kings allied with him, the king of Sodom came out to meet him in the Valley of Shaveh (that is, the King's Valley). ¹⁸Then Melchizedek king of Salem brought out bread and wine. He was priest of God Most High, ¹⁹ and he blessed Abram, saying,

> **"Blessed be Abram by God Most High,**
> **Creator of heaven and earth.**
> **²⁰And blessed be God Most High,**
> **who delivered your enemies into your hand."**

Then Abram gave him a tenth of everything. ²¹The king of Sodom said to Abram, "Give me the people and keep the goods for yourself." ²²But Abram said to the king of Sodom, "I have raised my hand to the LORD, God Most High, Creator of heaven

and earth, and have taken an oath ²³ that I will accept nothing belonging to you, not even a thread or the thong of a sandal, so that you will never be able to say, 'I made Abram rich.' ²⁴I will accept nothing but what my men have eaten and the share that belongs to the men who went with me — to Aner, Eshcol and Mamre. Let them have their share."

At this point Abram became involved. Here for the first time he is referred to as "Abram the Hebrew," a name thought to refer to the fact that his ancestors had come from beyond the Euphrates River — hence, a "foreigner," in contrast to "native-born." When Abram learned the outcome of the battle from one who had escaped, his instinctive reaction might very well have been: "My nephew made his bed; now he can lie in it!"

The previous chapter recorded how Abram's faith in God's promise had made him *unselfish*. This chapter records how Abram's faith made him *bold*. He put weapons into the hands of 318 of his servants, and together with help from friendly neighbors who were allied with him, overtook the enemy armies. Although he was outnumbered, Abram used his advantage of a surprise attack and the protection afforded by darkness. To further confuse the enemy he divided his forces and attacked from several directions. The soldiers from the east panicked and fled, leaving behind all their spoils of war. Abram continued to pursue until he was north of Damascus in Syria — far enough to make sure the enemy would not return.

Two kings came out to meet Abram when he returned to Canaan, and the two could not have been more different. The first was *Melchizedek*, an important person on the pages of the Scripture. He was a worshiper of the true religion of Jehovah handed down from the time of the flood. This passage brings us the only information the Old

Testament gives us about him. He is described as *"king of Salem"* (Jerusalem)...*"and priest of God Most High."* This priest-king brought out food supplies for Abram's hungry and battle-weary servants, and publicly credited God with having granted victory to Abram. Abram identified himself with Melchizedek's testimony by offering this representative of God a tenth part of the spoils of battle. By so doing Abram also showed that he recognized Melchizedek as his spiritual superior.

This would be no more than a fascinating incident from the life of Abram if it were not for some significant light the New Testament sheds on it. For one thing, we learn there that *Melchizedek is an Old Testament picture or type of Jesus*, who also holds the double office of priest and king.

The Epistle to the Hebrews emphasizes a second truth about Melchizedek which is basic to Christianity. Throughout the centuries of the Old Testament God instructed his Israelite people to approach him through mediators known as priests, from the tribe of Levi, Abraham's great-grandson. These Levitical priests daily brought blood sacrifices which symbolized the seriousness of sin and which pointed to God's only remedy for sin. But here, at his return from battle with the eastern kings, Levi's great-grandfather paid a tithe to a priest who had descended from another line. Here is our assurance that all of the religious ceremonies and regulations of the Old Testament — including centuries of blood sacrifices — could not really reconcile a guilty sinner to God. *A better priest* than a sinful Levite, and *a better sacrifice* than an animal victim *were needed*. Jesus is therefore called a "priest in the order of Melchizedek" (Psalm 110:4; Hebrews 5:6; 7:11-17), the one and only priest who can make sinners right with God.

There was another king present the day Abram returned from battle, and that was the *king of Sodom*. He too

136

addressed Abram, but in terms totally different from Melchizedek. "Give me the people, and you can keep the spoils for yourself." Abram was not opposed to accepting gifts. He had accepted bread and wine from the king of Salem, and very generous gifts from the pharaoh of Egypt years earlier. But he knew he couldn't accept *these* gifts to the glory of God. Abram knew he would have been entitled to keep some of the spoils of war; he showed that by making it clear that his allies could take their share. But Abram was not about to give a heathen king credit for making him rich. He hadn't joined battle with the eastern kings in the hope of gain. He owed everything he had to God's blessing, and he even took an oath here to make that very clear.

God Trains Abram to Believe the Promise of the Offspring

15 After this, the word of the LORD came to Abram in a vision:

> **"Do not be afraid, Abram.**
> **I am your shield,**
> **your very great reward."**

²**But Abram said, "O Sovereign LORD what can you give me since I remain childless and the one who will inherit my estate is Eliezer of Damascus?" ³And Abram said, "You have given me no children; so a servant in my household will be my heir." ⁴Then the word of the LORD came to him: "This man will not be your heir, but a son coming from your own body will be your heir." ⁵He took him outside and said, "Look up at the heavens and count the stars — if indeed you can count them." Then he said to him, "So shall your offspring be." ⁶Abram believed the LORD, and he credited it to him as righteousness.**

God had trained Abram to believe the promise o*f the land*. Now a new phase in Abram's development began, as

God trained him to believe the promise *of his offspring*, his descendants.

Once again the Savior-God appeared to Abram, this time *in a vision.* Here God enabled Abram to see things with the eyes of his mind which he could never have seen with his physical eyes. A merciful God knew that fear was tugging away at the corners of Abram's heart, so he assured him: "Do not be afraid; I am your *shield.* In your battle against the eastern kings I protected you. I am your very great *reward.* When the king of Sodom offered you the spoils of battle, you turned down his offer because you recognized that my friendship, my smile is a reward greater than anything he could have offered you."

Abram recognized that God had blessed him abundantly and obviously. But what he wanted most he did not have. God had promised him *a descendant.* But that promised link between Abram and the Savior was still missing, and he and his beloved Sarai were both past child-bearing years. As a result Abram had to make alternate plans. In order to have an heir Abram would have to resort to the customs of the society of that day and legally adopt his servant Eliezer.

Abram was not happy with this arrangement. He couldn't be happy without a descendant, because that was his link to the Savior. For him to go childless was to lose the inheritance God had promised. This is what Abram was afraid of.

God spoke directly to that fear when he said: "Get rid of the idea that Eliezer is to be your heir. The heir I'm speaking about will be *your own flesh and blood.*" If Eliezer were to have succeeded Abram, Abram's blood line would have come to an end; Eliezer's own son would have succeeded him. To strengthen Abram's faith in the promise that he would be the ancestor of many descendants, God — still in the vision — had Abram step outside and look up at a skyful of stars. "Abram, he who can fill a sky with stars can keep his promise to raise up countless descendants from your body." What a promise for an old man, married to a woman past menopause!

"Abram *believed God.*" In the Hebrew language the word for "believe" is a form of the word with which Christians commonly end their prayers. In other words, Abram *said "Amen" to God's promise.* St. Paul describes Abram's attitude this way: "Without weakening in his faith, he faced the fact that his body was as good as dead...and that Sarah's womb was also dead. Yet he did not waver through unbelief regarding the promise of God, but...gave glory to God, being fully persuaded that God had power to do what he had promised" (Romans 4:19-21).

"...and (God) credited it to him as righteousness." In the Bible "righteousness" means "being right with God." The Bible teaches that Abram gained this right standing with God not by what he had done, but by what his great Descendant would do. To believe God, then, is more than to trust his power. *To believe God is to trust his promise*, to take him at his word, to throw oneself on his mercy. This trust God considers as having met his demands for perfection.

It is interesting to note that the Apostle Paul quotes Genesis 15:6 in the two New Testament epistles in which he deals most extensively with the teaching of the sinner's justification (Romans 4:3; Galatians 3:6). God saves sinners not by transforming them into holy people but by declaring them holy. God credits their faith as righteousness. Sinners are saved by faith.

Abram's faith rested *on God's word of promise*, and so must our faith. That's the only safe foundation for faith. My feelings are not a reliable foundation for my faith. *Feelings can mislead.* There may actually be times in my life, for example, when I may not feel forgiven. But *God's promise cannot mislead*, because God cannot lie.

God Seals His Promise With a Solemn Covenant

⁷He also said to him, "I am the LORD, who brought you out of Ur of the Chaldeans to give you this land to take possession of it." ⁸But Abram said, "O Sovereign LORD, how can I know that I will gain possession of it?" ⁹So the LORD said to him, "Bring me a heifer, a goat and a ram, each three years old, along with a dove and a young pigeon."

¹⁰Abram brought all these to him, cut them in two and arranged the halves opposite each other; the birds, however, he did not cut in half. ¹¹Then the birds of prey came down on the carcasses, but Abram drove them away. ¹²As the sun was setting, Abram fell into a deep sleep, and a thick and dreadful darkness came over him.

¹³Then the LORD said to him, "Know for certain that your descendants will be strangers in a country not their own, and they will be enslaved and mistreated four hundred years. ¹⁴But I will punish the nation they serve as slaves, and afterward they will come out with great possessions. ¹⁵You, however, will go to your fathers in peace and be buried at a good old age. ¹⁶In the fourth generation your descendants will come back here, for the sin of the Amorites has not yet reached its full measure."

¹⁷When the sun had set and darkness had fallen, a smoking firepot with a blazing torch appeared and passed between the pieces. ¹⁸On that day the LORD made a covenant with Abram and said, "To your descendants I give this land, from the river of Egypt to the great river, the Euphrates — ¹⁹ the land of the Kenites, Kenizzites, Kadmonites, ²⁰ Hittites, Perizzites, Rephaites, ²¹ Amorites, Canaanites, Girgashites and Jebusites."

As a loving parent, God has never been in the habit of dealing with his children in terms of minimums. In Genesis 15 we are given a glimpse of God's big heart searching for additional ways to reassure his son Abram. Here was a childless old man who had asked for help in believing the promise that his descendants would inherit the land of Canaan. Abram's request was made not in a spirit of doubt or unbelief. He believed God's promise, but he wanted to be more firmly established. God's love found a way to assure his child.

He directed Abram to prepare the materials used in an ancient *Babylonian blood covenant*, the strongest guarantee known to Abram. Incidentally, some Bible scholars separate verses 7-21 from the opening six verses of Genesis 15. In their view, the vision God gave Abram ended at verse 6. But there is no indication of this in the Bible text. The entire chapter is of one piece. It seems more likely, therefore, that the fascinating action described in the second half of the chapter took place in the vision God gave Abram.

If we are to understand the unusual transaction here involving three animals and two birds, we'll need to remember that Abram spent the first 75 years of his life in a Babylonian culture. In that society, when two people wanted to guarantee an important agreement, they did more than affix their signatures to a document; they enacted a blood covenant. One or more sacrificial animals were killed and the half carcasses laid on the ground facing each other, forming a sort of corridor. To seal the contract, the two parties would solemnly walk together between the slain animals.

The symbolism was clear. First of all, the two participants approached the covenant ceremony *as equals*. Each had to contribute something to put the covenant into effect. And, secondly, if either of the persons *violated the terms* of the contract, the gory remains of the animal victims were a silent reminder that he would *forfeit his life*.

As the details of God's vision to him unfolded, Abram saw himself slaughtering the animals and arranging the half-carcasses in rows. The significance of the birds is not stated.

Now all the preparations had been made. All that remained of the covenant ratification ceremony was for the two participants to walk together between the carcasses. Abram waited. In his vision he saw birds of prey swoop down on the bloody carcasses, and he drove them away. As the sun went down, Abram felt a strange feeling of terror. God explained that the birds of prey and Abram's anxiety indicated what would happen to his descendants. Before they would one day inherit their promised land they would spend four centuries as strangers and servants in a foreign land. For part of that time they would even be oppressed. But in his good time God would judge the oppressor and free his people and lead them to a new homeland. To dispossess the previous Canaanite occupants God would send judgment upon them for their wickedness. The father of the Israelite nation must have been relieved to learn of this happy outcome to four turbulent centuries of history.

But now twilight had set in; what about the covenant ratification? Just then Abram saw *a flaming torch* (the form in which nomads usually saw fire) *passing alone between the carcasses.* And Abram heard God's voice reassuring him: "To your descendants I give this land." God even described the rough boundaries ("from Egypt to the Euphrates") and named ten Canaanite tribes who with their sin had forfeited their right to live in the land and who would be dispossessed by Abram's descendants.

During the centuries of the Old Testament God often appeared to his people in *fire* or in *smoke* or in a *cloud* to assure his people of his burning determination to carry out his great plan for them. Think of how Jehovah appeared to Moses in the flame of a burning bush (Exodus 3:1-10) or to the Israelites in a pillar of cloud or of fire (Exodus 13:21). This special appearance (often referred to by its technical name "*the glory of the LORD*") usually came at a time of crisis, when it seemed that either God had forgotten about his promise or that an enemy was about to block its fulfillment.

What was the purpose of its appearance here? Abram had asked God for a sign, and God gave him a *spectacular sign which clarified his plan of salvation*. The flaming torch, symbolizing the very presence of God, appeared all alone as it moved between the pieces of the sacrifice. God's covenant is indeed an agreement between two parties, but the two are by no means equal partners. One party assumes all the obligations, and the other party receives all the benefits. Abram promised nothing, did nothing, said nothing. He merely observed what the LORD was doing, he heard what the LORD was saying, and he believed. St. Paul later put into words what God was teaching Abram here: "It is by grace you have been saved through faith — and this not from yourselves, it is the gift of God — not by works, so that no one can boast" (Ephesians 2:8, 9).

Genesis 15 describes a significant part of God's training program for Abram, who had asked God to guarantee the promise to him. God responded by making a covenant with him, permitting him, first of all, *to hear the promise restated and amplified*. Abram learned that his descendants would grow into a nation which, despite distress and enslavement at the hands of a foreign power, would occupy the land of Canaan. To guarantee his promise to Abram, God also gave him something *to see — a visible symbol of the Savior-God affirming his promise*.

We New Testament believers have received a similar blessing from God — in the sacraments. In Baptism and the Lord's Supper God not only lets us *hear* the message of his mercy in Christ, he given us something to *see*. He connects

earthly elements to his promise, to make it all the more sure
for us. By this visible sign God binds himself to his
promise. Now isn't that evidence of his grace!

Abram Accepts God's Promise, Though in Weakness of Faith

16 Now Sarai, Abram's wife, had borne him no chidren.
But she had an Egyptian maidservant named Hagar; ²so
she said to Abram, "The LORD has kept me from having children. Go, sleep with my maidservant; perhaps I can build a
family through her." Abram agreed to what Sarai said. ³So
after Abram had been living in Canaan ten years, Sarai his
wife took her Egyptian maidservant Hagar and gave her to her
husband to be his wife. He slept with Hagar, and she conceived.
When she knew she was pregnant, she began to despise her
mistress. ⁵Then Sarai said to Abram, "You are responsible for
the wrong I am suffering. I put my servant in your arms, and
now that she knows she is pregnant, she despises me. May the
LORD judge between you and me." ⁶"Your servant is in your
hands," Abram said. "Do with her whatever you think is best."
Then Sarai mistreated Hagar; so she fled from her.

Ten years had elapsed since God had called Abram to
leave homeland and family and had promised him a son.
Genesis 16 records another of the instances where *Abram
and Sarai stumbled* on the path of faith. What we read here
is not pleasant to read, and it's not flattering to either
Abram or Sarai, but the Scripture makes no attempt to hide
the weaknesses of God's saints.

It appears that Sarai took the initiative here. Ten years is
a long time to wait for a baby, especially when you're 75
and your husband is 85. Perhaps Sarai told Abram: "The
LORD promised you a son to come from *your* body, but he
never said that the son would come from *my* body. Really,

he seems to have made it quite clear that I'm not to have any children."

Sarai felt it was *her* fault that God's promise of a son was not being fulfilled. She therefore decided to follow the custom of the day, which allowed a barren wife to give her servant girl to her husband as a secondary wife, with the understanding that any children born of that union would belong to the mistress of the household. (The custom of the day not only *allowed* a childless wife to give her maid to her husband, but may actually have *demanded* it. The spade of the archeologist has uncovered marriage contracts from ancient Nuzi, in what is now Iraq, in which a bride promised to give her husband a maid if she herself was unable to have children.)

Sarai's action of giving her maid to her husband amounts to *using human devices to achieve God's purpose.* Her suggestion to her husband strikes at the very heart of marriage as God gave it to the human race — a lifelong union of one man and one woman.. Perhaps even worse is that their scheme *interfered with God's plan.* Abram went along with Sarai's suggestion. Like Sarai, he was in a hurry to see God's promise fulfilled. Once again sinful human frailty forms the backdrop on which God displays his marvelous mercy.

For reasons known only to him, God often tolerated multiple marriages during the centuries of the Old Testament. He did so here. He even blessed Abram's union with Hagar, and she became pregnant.

One of the evils of polygamy is that it unleashes a person's baser elements. Instead of the *fulfillment* of their hopes, Abram and Sarai got *problems.* Childlessness was looked upon as a disgrace for a married woman, and Hagar seems to have flaunted her pregnancy before her mistress. This wasn't at all how Sarai had hoped things would turn

Sarai mistreats Hagar

out. But this is the sort of thing that inevitably happens when we permit calculation to take precedence over simple trust in God's promise and obedience to his will. Every sidestepping of God's design for marriage, even when done from good motives, invites grief and disruption into one's heart and home.

Sarai reacted predictably. We're told she "mistreated" Hagar. The translation is perhaps too strong. Sarai dealt harshly with Hagar; she humbled her. Hagar may have been Sarai's personal maid; now, as Luther suggests, Hagar may have been asked to live with the servants or to perform more menial tasks. According to ancient law, a slave mother could not be banished from the household. But slaves could run away, and that's what Hagar did. Headstrong and hurt, she headed out on the desert road to Shur. According to 25:18, Shur was near the border of Egypt. It's pretty clear, then, that she was heading for her childhood home. Hagar may have thought that was the best solution to the problem, but God had other plans.

⁷The angel of the LORD found Hagar near a spring in the desert; it was the spring that is beside the road to Shur. ⁸And he said, "Hagar, servant of Sarai, where have you come from, and where are you going?" "I'm running away from my mistress Sarai," she answered. ⁹Then the angel of the LORD told her, "Go back to your mistress and submit to her." ¹⁰The angel added, "I will so increase your descendants that they will be too numerous to count." ¹¹The angel of the LORD also said to her:

"You are now with child
and you will have a son.
You shall name him Ishmael,
for the LORD has heard of your misery.
¹²He will be a wild donkey of a man;
his hand will be against everyone
and everyone's hand against him,

and he will live in hostility
toward all his brothers."
She gave this name to the LORD who spoke to her: "You are
the God who sees me," for she said, "I have now seen the One
who sees me."
¹⁴That is why the well was called Beer Lahai Roi; it is still
there, between Kadesh and Bered. ¹⁵So Hagar bore Abram a
son, and Abram gave the name Ishmael to the son she had
borne. ¹⁶Abram was eighty-six years old when Hagar bore him
Ishmael.

Hagar apparently hadn't gone far on that desert road
when she met a heavenly visitor, "*the angel of the LORD*."
Moses supplies us with a number of clues which make it
clear this was not one of God's *created* angels. For one
thing, he identified himself *as God.* "Go back to your mistress ... I will increase your descendants...." The LORD
spoke through many messengers in the Old Testament, but
none of them ever called himself God. Hagar recognized
that this Angel of the LORD was God himself. She said "You
are the God who sees me." This is the first of many Old
Testament appearances of the Angel of the LORD, the *second person of the Holy Trinity.*

Twenty centuries later this heavenly Messenger assumed
human form permanently when he was born of a Jewish
peasant girl. But the Scripture teaches that the Savior was
active long before Mary gave birth to her child in
Bethlehem — for example, in the work of creation. Here we
learn that during the centuries of the Old Testament he was
also active making sure things developed the way God had
planned them.

The Savior had several reasons for appearing to this lonely, frightened girl. He wanted first to assure her he hadn't
abandoned her. To curb her willfulness he directed her to

return to Sarai; that discipline was part of God's plan for her. And finally the heavenly Messenger gave Hagar a marvelous promise of what the future held for her. For the sake of Abram God would richly bless her. She would give birth to the child she was now carrying, and it would be a son, the ancestor of numerous descendants. His name Ishmael would be a constant reminder that God had heard her in her distress and had answered her plea. The Angel also gave Hagar a thumbnail sketch of the son she was now carrying beneath her heart. He'd be "a wild donkey of a man," an independent sort of fellow who would like to run free, never content to settle down, living in hostility to his relatives and neighbors. This information could warn Hagar to check those traits when she detected them in her son.

Hagar showed her gratitude for the Savior's new revelation of his mercy. She invented a new name for the LORD who had appeared to her. And from the information supplied in verse 15 we conclude that Hagar, now chastened and humbled, returned to Abram's household and submitted to Sarai.

God Emphasizes His Promise by Giving Covenant Seals

17 When Abram was ninety-nine years old, the LORD appeared to him and said: "I am God Almighty; walk before me and be blameless. ²I will confirm my covenant between me and you and will greatly increase your numbers."

³Abram fell facedown, and God said to him, ⁴"As for me, this is my covenant with you: You will be the father of many nations. ⁵No longer will you be called Abram; your name will be Abraham, for I have made you a father of many nations. ⁶I will make you very fruitful; I will make nations of you, and kings will come from you. ⁷I will establish my covenant as an everlasting covenant between me and you and your descendants after you for the generations to come, to be your God and

the God of your descendants after you. ⁸The whole land of Canaan, where you are now an alien, I will give as an everlasting possession to you and your descendants after you; and I will be their God."

Thirteen years had passed since Ishmael's birth, years apparently without any further divine revelation to Abram. It had now been twenty-four years since God had first appeared to Abram with the promise that he would be the ancestor of the Savior. Abram was now ninety-nine, Sarai eighty-nine. Humanly speaking, every shred of hope they had of ever becoming parents had been swept away. Martin Luther once made the statement: "It's God's way to empty a man first before filling him with his blessing." Now God decided that the time had come to make a startling announcement about his covenant.

God once again appeared to Abram. He introduced himself by an unusual name; in Hebrew it's "El Shaddai," apparently from a verb root meaning "to display power," "to deal violently." The God who here appeared with good news for Abram is the God who can compel even nature to do his bidding.

The translation "... and *be blameless*" is misleading (as is also the King James Version's "... *be perfect*"). The word really means "*be complete*." What El Shaddai was asking of Abram was to *live his whole life* before God in the confidence that God's unlimited power could compel even nature to do what is contrary to itself.

God had previously *made* a covenant with Abram, a binding contract in which he had placed himself under obligation to Abram and his future descendants. God had solemnly *ratified* that covenant. Now the time had come to *implement* that covenant, to bring it to fulfillment. For

Abram that had to mean that the birth of the son for whom he had waited a quarter century was near.

At hearing this unbelievably good news, Abram bowed with his face to the ground in humble adoration. Apart from God's grace how could he, a creature of clay, ever have hoped to have numerous descendants, one of whom would be the Savior of the world? This attitude of *humble adoration* is the only proper attitude for the sinner in the presence of God. How tragic that this attitude is often missing when we approach the great God in worship! When we lose sight of our littleness and our unworthiness, when we stop marveling at the sheer magnificence of God's amazing grace, our worship is the poorer.

A Covenant Seal: Abram to Abraham

As a guarantee of the fact that the child of the covenant would soon be born, God *changed Abram's name*. He would no longer be Abram ("exalted father"); he would now be Abraham ("father of many"). This name change was a seal of the covenant, a guarantee that God would keep the promise he had made. If he would fail to keep his covenant promise, the name "Abraham" would constantly testify against him. But with the benefit of hindsight, we can see how appropriate this covenant seal was. Abraham did indeed become the father of multitudes of descendants. Some are *blood* descendants — the Israelites, the Edomites, the Arabs. Some are *spiritual* descendants of Abraham by sharing his faith. The Apostle Paul wrote to the Christians in Rome: "[Abraham] is the father of us all" (Romans 4:16).

As he bowed with his face in the dust, Abraham could hardly believe the good news he was hearing. "Kings will come from you." We think immediately of the royal line of

David, culminating in great David's greater Son, the King of kings.

Abraham was not to think that these blessings were a special favor of God *just for him*. God pledged that this solemn contract with Abraham would remain in force *also for his numerous descendants*, including the ones reading this book right now. The God of the covenant will continue to be a never-ending source of mercy to the fallen children of Adam and Eve.

A quarter century earlier God had promised Abraham that his descendants would *own the land* in which Abraham was a temporary resident. But since then there had been no trace of fulfillment. God now felt it appropriate to renew that promise.

In view of the confusion in the religious world today about ownership of the Holy Land, perhaps it ought to be restated that God's two promises "I will give this land to your descendants" and "I will be their God" are inseparably linked. If in subsequent years Abraham's descendants rejected the second promise, they also forfeited the first. But as long as they remained faithful to their faithful God, they had assurance the land of Canaan would be their home indefinitely.

A Covenant Seal: Circumcision

[9]Then God said to Abraham, "As for you, you must keep my covenant, you and your descendants after you for the generations to come. [10]This is my covenant with you and your descendants after you, the covenant you are to keep: Every male among you shall be circumcised. [11]You are to undergo circumcision, and it will be the sign of the covenant between me and you. [12]For the generations to come every male among you who is eight days old must be circumcised, including those born in your household or bought with money from a foreigner —

those who are not your offspring. [13]Whether born in your household or bought with your money, they must be circumcised. My covenant in your flesh is to be an everlasting covenant. [14]Any uncircumcised male, who has not been circumcised in the flesh, will be cut off from his people; he has broken my covenant."

To serve as an additional guarantee of his covenant, God now gave *circumcision* to his people as another covenant seal. This is not to be understood as saying that circumcision was unknown in the ancient world up to that time. The Prophet Jeremiah (9:25f) makes it clear that circumcision was commonly known among other ancient nations. They practiced it either for hygienic reasons or as a puberty rite, as is still done today. To seal the solemn contract he had made with Abraham's descendants God took this widely-practiced custom and designated it a badge of his covenant.

God's detailed instructions cannot be misunderstood; nothing was left to Abraham's discretion. The male organ was singled out, the instrument of procreation by which sin is transmitted from father to child. Life needs to be purified at its very source.

For Abraham's descendants, then, circumcision was *another seal assuring the certainty of God's covenant*, just as your baptism is a daily reminder that God has elected you to be his very own. Normally ancient covenants were inscribed on clay tablets; this covenant was in the flesh of a man's body.

Furthermore, circumcision *symbolized the removal of defilement*, the putting away of one's inner resistance to God. St. Paul calls it a "seal of the righteousness (Abraham) had by faith" (Romans 4:11). The male Israelite who refused to wear this badge of the covenant in his body was considered to have rejected God's covenant and was to be cut off from God's people (see Exodus 31:14f).

When Christ, the Mediator of the new covenant, came, circumcision lost its purpose. The shadow was replaced by the reality. At the Jerusalem council the early Christian church took a strong stand against those who taught: "Unless you are circumcised according to the custom taught by Moses, you cannot be saved" (Acts 15:1).

A Covenant Seal: Sarai to Sarah

[15]God also said to Abraham, "As for Sarai your wife, you are no longer to call her Sarai; her name will be Sarah. [16]I will bless her and will surely give you a son by her. I will bless her so that she will be the mother of nations; kings of peoples will come from her." [17]Abraham fell facedown; he laughed and said to himself, "Will a son be born to a man a hundred years old? Will Sarah bear a child at the age of ninety?" [18]And Abraham said to God, "If only Ishmael might live under your blessing!" [19]Then God said, "Yes, but your wife Sarah will bear you a son, and you will call him Isaac. I will establish my covenant with him as an everlasting covenant for his descendants after him. [20]And as for Ishmael, I have heard you: I will surely bless him; I will make him fruitful and will greatly increase his numbers. He will be the father of twelve rulers, and I will make him into a great nation. [21]But my covenant I will establish with Isaac, whom Sarah will bear to you by this time next year." [22]When he had finished speaking with Abraham, God went up from him.

Down through the years God had spoken often to Abraham, molding his faith in the promise. Each time God spoke, Abraham understood God's grand plan better; his faith had more to hold on to. In the verses before us God finally spoke the words Abraham had been waiting to hear.

But before doing that God gave an additional covenant seal, another name change. At this late date we're not able

154

to define precisely what the difference is between Sarai and Sarah. We do know that Sarah means "princess." If Abraham's wife was to be the mother of kings, she deserved a royal title, and now she had one.

The heart of God's good news came in the words: "Sarah will bear you a son, and you will call him Isaac. ... Sarah will bear [him] to you by this time next year." These words made it clear why God at the outset introduced himself to Abraham with the name El Shaddai. God's blessing of a son for this aged couple involved a renewal of their reproductive powers.

Now that he had heard the promise he was waiting to hear, Abraham laughed. Does that seem like an appropriate response to a promise so serious and so significant? Abraham's laughter was the unrehearsed expression of the unbelievable joy he felt over what God had just told him. It was as though Abraham was thinking: "Everybody knows ninety-year old women don't have babies, but nobody told that to God!" And his body shook with laughter. His question (verse 17) was asked not in doubt, but in joyful amazement.

Suddenly a disturbing thought creased his brow and stifled his laughter. What God had just said about Sarah's son being the heir of the promises — did that mean Abraham's other son was now to be cut off from God's blessing? Ishmael was, after all, Abraham's firstborn; for thirteen years he had been Abraham's only son. Was he to be forgotten now? Abraham sought a blessing for Ishmael, too.

A Covenant Seal: The Son of Promise Will be Named Isaac

God's response was twofold. He *gave Abraham still another seal* of the covenant. Abraham had laughed for joy when he learned that in a year Sarah would be holding a baby in her arms; now he learned that the baby would be called Isaac ("laughter").

God also *concurred in Abraham's desire* that Ishmael share in God's blessing. For Abraham's sake God promised to multiply Ishmael's descendants, to build him into a great nation with twelve princes (see 25:12-16). But God reaffirmed that Isaac would be the son of the promise, the important link between Abraham and the Savior.

With that, God left Abraham. He had taken Abraham into his confidence. He had shared some of his sacred secrets with him, secrets of his power, of his wisdom, of his grace. With additional information about the promised seed and a number of seals of the covenant, God had bolstered the faith of Abraham.

²³On that very day Abraham took his son Ishmael and all those born in his household or bought with his money, every male in his household, and circumcised them, as God told him. ²⁴Abraham was ninety-nine years old when he was circumcised, ²⁵ and his son Ishmael was thirteen. ²⁶Abraham and his son Ishmael were both circumcised on that same day. ²⁷And every male in Abraham's household, including those born in his household or bought from a foreigner, was circumcised with him.

Abraham's faith now moved into action. God had commanded circumcision without, however, specifying a time deadline. Abraham saw to it that *on that very same day* every male in his household carried the mark of the covenant on his body. With a wealth of detail Moses helps us to see that Abraham's obedience was complete, it was immediate, and it was willing. Most important, it flowed from his trust in God's promise.

God has not called us to follow him blindfolded. Christian faith is not a leap in the dark. Like Abraham, we have

God's word of promise. As we, like Abraham, follow him in trust and obedience, we can say with the Apostle Paul: "I know whom I have believed, and am convinced that he is able to guard what I have entrusted to him" (2 Timothy 1:12).

Martin Luther once made the statement: "There is no more miserable frame of mind than doubt." Doubt questions God's pledged word; it weakens our hold on the blessings God has promised us. In previous appearances to Abraham, God had effectively dealt with Abraham's lingering doubts. But there was another member of Abraham's family whose faith needed God's attention and his help. God therefore made another visit to the home of Abraham in Hebron, in southern Canaan, to *purify Sarah's faith* of its impurities and imperfections.

18 **The LORD appeared to Abraham near the great trees of Mamre while he was sitting at the entrance to his tent in the heat of the day. ²Abraham looked up and saw three men standing nearby. When he saw them, he hurried from the entrance of his tent to meet them and bowed low to the ground.**

³He said, "If I have found favor in your eyes, my lord, do not pass your servant by. ⁴Let a little water be brought, and then you may all wash your feet and rest under this tree. ⁵Let me get you something to eat, so you can be refreshed and then go on your way — now that you have come to your servant." "Very well," they answered, "do as you say." ⁶So Abraham hurried into the tent to Sarah. "Quick," he said, "get three seahs of fine flour and knead it and bake some bread." ⁷Then he ran to the herd and selected a choice, tender calf and gave it to a servant, who hurried to prepare it. ⁸He then brought some curds and milk and the calf that had been prepared, and set these before them. While they ate, he stood near them under a tree.

During the hottest part of the day, the time of siesta, Abraham was sitting in the shade at the door of his tent. Perhaps he had dozed off, or perhaps he was deep in thought about the wondrous promise he had received from God. It was good to think that within a year Sarah would present him with an infant son. At any rate, he was suddenly aware that three travelers had stopped near his tent. Hebron was on the main north-south road that runs along the ridge of the Judean hills, and occasionally there were travelers who needed food and lodging. Hebrews 13:2 informs us that Abraham did not realize who his visitors were until later. Although they appeared in human form, one was the LORD himself (see verse 13), and the other two were angels (see 19:1). The custom of the day required a traveler to stand at some distance from a nomad's tent and wait to be invited in.

Abraham greeted the three travelers humbly and courteously. By our standards his invitation, and especially his hospitality, might seem overdone, but perhaps our standards need adjusting. The Christian who loves his Lord will learn to look upon people not as things to be used, but as creatures designed by God, loved by him and to be loved by us. It is not to our credit if our daily lives touch the lives of others with as little concern as two billiard balls bouncing off each other.

At this lazy hour of the day Abraham's household was suddenly transformed into a beehive of activity. Moses describes meal preparations that must have taken several hours. Abraham instructed Sarah to take three seahs of flour — more than a bushel! — and bake bread. There would surely be no shortage of bread at that meal! He himself ran to the herd, selected a choice bull calf and ordered his men to slaughter it and prepare it. Curds (we'd probably call it cottage cheese) and milk completed the feast he set before his guests.

"They ate." What *condescending love* those two words describe! The three guests ate Sarah's fresh bread and that tender veal. The scene reminds us of what Jesus did when he appeared to his doubting disciples a week after his resurrection. When those frightened men imagined they were seeing a ghost Jesus lovingly asked for something to eat and actually ate a piece of broiled fish. He was showing them there was no barrier blocking their fellowship with God.

What a staggering thought! Abraham and Jesus' disciples were to realize, and you and I are, too, that the almighty God *wants to share our company* as a friend. It is this down-to-earth, seeking, caring love of the Lord which melts down cold and stubborn human hearts and wins them over to himself. We long for fellowship like that which took place under the great tree at Hebron. And God promises that we can look forward to an intimate fellowship with him when we eat and drink at the feast of the Lamb.

⁹"Where is your wife Sarah?" they asked him. "There, in the tent," he said. ¹⁰Then the LORD said, "I will surely return to you about this time next year, and Sarah your wife will have a son." Now Sarah was listening at the entrance to the tent, which was behind him.

¹¹Abraham and Sarah were already old and well advanced in years, and Sarah was past the age of childbearing. ¹²So Sarah laughed to herself as she thought, "After I am worn out and my master is old, will I now have this pleasure?" ¹³Then the LORD said to Abraham, "Why did Sarah laugh and say, 'Will I really have a child, now that I am old?' ¹⁴Is anything too hard for the LORD? I will return to you at the appointed time next year and Sarah will have a son." ¹⁵Sarah was afraid, so she lied and said, "I did not laugh." But he said, "Yes, you did laugh."

It soon became clear that the three visitors had not stopped at Abraham's place just to get a free meal. The purpose of their visit became evident when they asked: "Where is Sarah?"

The question told Abraham several things about his visitors.

> 1. They must be *people of authority*. In that culture a casual visitor would not ask about the lady of the household (who remained in her own tent);
> 2. They knew God had given Sarai *a new name*;
> 3. Their visit concerned Sarah; it was not a chance occurrence.

We can imagine how surprised Sarah must have been to hear these strangers, whom she'd never seen before, mention her name. They were talking about her and had come to bring a message for her.

For reasons that will become clear, Moses explains that Sarah's tent was behind the speaker. The heavenly visitor was sitting in a position where he could not see Sarah. Sarah now heard from God's own lips what he had told Abraham at the time of his previous visit: "At this time next year Sarah will be the mother of a son." For a woman past childbearing age, this was a miracle. Sarah knew very well that miracles don't happen by themselves; only God could bring this to pass.

There's an old proverb something to the effect that "Two things may *seem* the same without *being* the same." It might seem that Sarah's reaction at hearing this birth announcement was the same as Abraham's when God earlier predicted Isaac's birth. Abraham had laughed, and so did Sarah here. But there was a big difference. Abraham had laughed out of sheer joy. Sarah had given up hoping for a child. Her laughter, therefore, was an expression of unbelief; to Sarah

God's promise seemed laughable. Because he is all-knowing, Abraham's heavenly Visitor not only *knew* Sarah's thoughts but was *displeased* by her lack of faith in the promise he had just made. His question "Why did Sarah laugh?" revealed his omniscience and told Sarah who he was. Without seeing Sarah, he knew she was listening at the tent door behind his back.

Imagine how astounded Sarah must have been. Not only had this heavenly Visitor read her secret thoughts, he had considered her doubt unworthy and unbecoming. Surely she should have known that the LORD is not bound by the laws of nature, including the laws of human reproduction.

Sarah, embarrassed, called out from her tent. At first she attempted to defend herself, but then penitently accepted the LORD's rebuke. By faith she received God's promise that she would conceive and bear a child. When the baby was born a year later she spoke differently: "God has brought me laughter, and everybody who hears about this will laugh with me" (21:6).

¹⁶When the men got up to leave, they looked down toward Sodom, and Abraham walked along with them to see them on their way. ¹⁷Then the LORD said, "Shall I hide from Abraham what I am about to do? ¹⁸Abraham will surely become a great and powerful nation, and all nations on earth will be blessed through him. ¹⁹For I have chosen him, so that he will direct his children and his household after him to keep the way of the LORD by doing what is right and just, so that the LORD will bring about for Abraham what he has promised him." ²⁰Then the LORD said, "The outcry against Sodom and Gomorrah is so great and their sin so grievous ²¹ that I will go down and see if what they have done is as bad as the outcry that has reached me. If not, I will know."

There was a second reason why the three heavenly visitors had come to Abraham's home, and God now made that clear to Abraham. As his dinner guests got up to leave, Abraham courteously walked with them to bid them farewell. He noticed that they were heading southeast toward Sodom, forty miles away.

Then the LORD spoke. His words are a sort of soliloquy, spoken softly, yet intended for Abraham's ears. "Shall I hide from Abraham what I am about to do?" There were a number of reasons why God wanted to inform Abraham in advance about his plans to send fiery judgment on Sodom.

Abraham stood in a *special relationship* to God. Abraham was, first of all, God's "friend" (Isaiah 41:8), and here God shared a confidence with his friend. Isn't that an amazing thought? God did not want to proceed with his plans before getting Abraham's reaction.

There was a second reason. God had chosen Abraham not only to continue the Messianic bloodline, but to pass on to his descendants the truth God had revealed to him — in this particular instance, the truth about God's judgment. There are particularly two truths about God's judgments that God wanted Abraham's descendants to know:

1. Whenever God invades human history to pronounce judgment on a person or a group of people, he thereby shows that he hates unbelief and must punish it.
2. God's judgments, however, are always carried out in such a way that they serve the deliverance of his elect. Here God withheld his judgment on Sodom to give Abraham an opportunity to plead for the righteous. In mercy God delayed the onset of the flood (Genesis 6:3). In our day the sins of our country cry to God for judgment, yet

in the interest of gathering all his elect God has graciously delayed his judgment.

Abraham was going to see these truths illustrated in Sodom and Gomorrah. God wanted Abraham to make sure his descendants learned them, too.

God's words "I will go down and see ..." are not to be understood as though God actually had to make a special trip to Sodom for an on-site inspection of the city's corruption before giving the order to destroy it. God here uses a figure of speech in which he ascribes human actions to himself, in order to emphasize an important truth: *God does nothing without possessing all the facts* in the case. He does not act arbitrarily. If he chooses to send punishment on a city or a nation, that judgment is well-deserved.

²²The men turned away and went toward Sodom, but Abraham remained standing before the LORD. ²³Then Abraham approached him and said: "Will you sweep away the righteous with the wicked? ²⁴What if there are fifty righteous people in the city? Will you really sweep it away and not spare the place for the sake of the fifty righteous people in it? ²⁵Far be it from you to do such a thing — to kill the righteous with the wicked, treating the righteous and the wicked alike. Far be it from you! Will not the Judge of all the earth do right?" ²⁶The LORD said, "If I find fifty righteous people in the city of Sodom, I will spare the whole place for their sake." ²⁷Then Abraham spoke up again: "Now that I have been so bold as to speak to the Lord, though I am nothing but dust and ashes, ²⁸what if the number of the righteous is five less than fifty? Will you destroy the whole city because of five people?" "If I find forty-five there," he said, "I will not destroy it." ²⁹Once again he spoke to him, "What if only forty are found there?" He said, "For the sake of forty, I will not do it." ³⁰Then he said, "May the LORD not be angry, but let me speak. What if only thirty can be found there?" He answered, "I will not do it if I find thirty there."

³¹Abraham said, "Now that I have been so bold as to speak to the LORD, what if only twenty can be found there?" He said, "For the sake of twenty, I will not destroy it." ³²Then he said, "May the LORD not be angry, but let me speak just once more. What if only ten can be found there?" He answered, "For the sake of ten, I will not destroy it." ³³When the LORD had finished speaking with Abraham, he left, and Abraham returned home.

When the two angels left for Sodom to carry out their assignment, Abraham detained the LORD. He pleaded with God six times to spare the city for the sake of the believers there. There are some characteristics of Abraham's prayer that are worth noting.

> 1. It was *based on mercy*, not merit. Abraham knew that the same sinful heart that beat in the inhabitants of Sodom and Gomorrah beat within his own breast, and that it was only the grace of God that kept him safe from God's righteous anger.
> 2. It was an *unselfish* prayer. Abraham wanted others to experience the same mercy he had.
> 3. It was *bold*. There's a holy shamelessness to Abraham's prayer. Six times he dared to plead the cause of God's love against God's righteousness. "God, you surely wouldn't want to give the impression that you destroy cities and villages, the innocent and the guilty indiscriminately."

The next chapter of Genesis will help us to see that God *did answer* Abraham's prayer. As a matter of fact, God did *more* than he had promised. Although there were not ten believers in Sodom, God did rescue Lot and his family.

While Abraham was pleading for Sodom and Gomorrah, the inhabitants of those cities were going about their everyday business, blithely unconcerned about the danger that threatened them (Luke 17:18-29), totally unaware that within twenty-four hours a firestorm of divine judgment would consume them.

Abraham knew that God's sovereignty is not blind necessity. God lets himself be "overcome" by the prayers of his children (see Genesis 32:26-28). God actually condescends to take our prayers into consideration as he rules the world. He did so here.

19 The two angels arrived at Sodom in the evening, and Lot was sitting in the gateway of the city. When he saw them, he got up to meet them and bowed down with his face to the ground. ²"My lords," he said, "please turn aside to your servant's house. You can wash your feet and spend the night and then go on your way early in the morning." "No," they answered, "we will spend the night in the square." ³But he insisted so strongly that they did go with him and entered his house. He prepared a meal for them, baking bread without yeast, and they ate. ⁴Before they had gone to bed, all the men from every part of the city of Sodom — both young and old — surrounded the house. ⁵They called to Lot, "Where are the men who came to you tonight? Bring them out to us so that we can have sex with them." ⁶Lot went outside to meet them and shut the door behind him ⁷ and said, "No, my friends. Don't do this wicked thing. ⁸Look, I have two daughters who have never slept with a man. Let me bring them out to you, and you can do what you like with them. But don't do anything to these men, for they have come under the protection of my roof." ⁹"Get out of our way," they replied. And they said, "This fellow came here as an alien, and now he wants to play the judge! We'll treat you worse than them." They kept bringing pressure on Lot and moved forward to break down the door. ¹⁰But the men inside reached out and pulled Lot back into the house and shut the door. ¹¹Then they struck the men who were at the door of the house, young and old, with blindness so that they could not find the door.

The subject matter of this chapter might at first seem to be out of place in a history of Abraham's descendants. And yet we can see a couple good reasons why God saw fit to include it.

1. It's clearly the sequel to the preceding chapters;
2. Genesis 12-25 give us the "Account of Terah," and Lot was Terah's grandson;
3. The site of God's judgment bordered on Israel's promised land and would forever stand as a warning to Israel;
4. The New Testament several times uses Sodom as a type of the final overthrow of the unbeliever.

The two angels whom we last met at Abraham's dinner table now approached the gate of Sodom. In ancient times the city gate was the focal point for much of the activity of the population. The rooms adjoining the gate would, in time of war, be occupied by armed defenders. In times of peace, these rooms would be used as courtrooms and meeting and classrooms for the city fathers and businessmen and teachers and students. Since Lot is described as "sitting in the gateway of the city," we conclude that he was active in the business life of Sodom.

The Bible's description of Lot presents a somewhat mixed picture of the man. On the one hand, St. Peter describes him as "a *righteous* man," who was tormented by the wickedness he saw and heard in Sodom (2 Peter 2:7, 8). When God's angels approached the city gate, Lot generously opened his home to them. When they at first declined his invitation and chose instead to spend the night in the city square he insisted that they be his guests, and with good reason. Lot knew all too well the homosexual tendencies of the men of his city. He knew also that he hadn't been the only one to notice the two male visitors who had just arrived. And when later that evening the men of Sodom paraded their lust and wanted dirty sex with his house guests Lot refused, even at considerable personal risk.

Lot was a righteous man, but living in the immoral climate of Sodom had *blunted his faith* and *dulled his moral sensitivity*. He addressed the rampaging homosexuals threatening to beat down his door as "my brothers." He owed them the full rebuke of God's holy law, but he did not give it. Instead he tried to prevent sin by what he thought was a lesser sin. "My brothers, satisfy your sexual appetite naturally, not unnaturally. I have two virgin daughters. Take them, but spare my guests!" In contrast to his uncle Abraham, Lot gave no evidence of his faith. His disgusting offer could very well have resulted in the death of his daughters (Judges 19:23-28). He demonstrated no love either for his daughters or for the men of Sodom. In Christ's words, Lot was salt that had lost its saltiness.

This page of Scripture has a warning for Christians who must live in a society which wipes its feet on God's Sixth Commandment. We need to speak out for the holy purposes the Creator had in mind when he planted the sex appetite in people. We need also to ask: "Am I, like Lot, becoming insensitive to the obvious abuse of God's gift of sexuality? Is it possible that I appear to approve of conduct I should be reproving?" When in our day homosexual behavior is defended as an "alternate lifestyle," God's people need to let God's voice be heard.

Lot's decision to live in Sodom was far more costly to him than he could ever have imagined. The scriptural record of his life is an unhappy one. When the men of Sodom threatened physical violence, the angels of God intervened. They dragged Lot to safety inside the house and then struck the men outside with miraculous blindness. It was clear that the wickedness of the city was every bit as great as the cry that had reached the ears of God. It was also clear to the angels what their assignment was.

¹²The two men said to Lot, "Do you have anyone else here — sons-in-law, sons or daughters, or anyone else in the city who belongs to you? Get them out of here, ¹³because we are going to destroy this place. The outcry to the LORD against its people is so great that he has sent us to destroy it." ¹⁴So Lot went out and spoke to his sons-in-law, who were pledged to marry his daughters. He said, "Hurry and get out of this place, because the LORD is about to destroy the city!" But his sons-in-law thought he was joking. ¹⁵With the coming of dawn, the angels urged Lot, saying, "Hurry! Take your wife and your two daughters who are here, or you will be swept away when the city is punished." ¹⁶When he hesitated, the men grasped his hand and the hands of his wife and of his two daughters and led them safely out of the city, for the LORD was merciful to them. ¹⁷As soon as they had brought them out, one of them said, "Flee for your lives! Don't look back, and don't stop anywhere in the plain! Flee to the mountains or you will be swept away!" ¹⁸But Lot said to them, "No, my lords, please! ¹⁹Your servant has found favor in your eyes and you have shown great kindness to me in sparing my life. But I can't flee to the mountains; this disaster will overtake me, and I'll die. ²⁰Look, here is a town near enough to run to, and it is small. Let me flee to it — it is very small, isn't it? Then my life will be spared." ²¹He said to him, "Very well, I will grant this request too; I will not overthrow the town you speak of. ²²But flee there quickly, because I cannot do anything until you reach it." (That is why the town was called Zoar.)

There weren't ten believers in the city of Sodom, and God would have lived up to his agreement with Abraham if he had burned the city and inhabitants right down to the ground. But the Savior-God graciously went beyond what he had promised Abraham. He sent the two angels to deliver Lot's family from the nightmare of judgment that was about to strike Sodom. The conversation Lot had with the angels demonstrates how much Sodom had infected him.

When he urged his prospective sons-in-law to leave the city they didn't take him seriously. For Lot suddenly to be concerned about escaping the wicked city seemed out of character for him, and they passed his warning off as a joke. Lot's house guests now revealed their true identity as angels sent by God to rescue him and his family. And yet — unbelievably!— Lot hesitated, unable to take decisive action. He had become so attached to what Sodom had to offer that he was reluctant to make a clean break. The angels had to take him and his wife and daughters as one takes little children by the hand and lead them outside the doomed city. They actually had to force rescue on Lot and his family.

As they passed through the city gate, the angel said: "Leave this area and flee to the mountains! Don't even look back, or you will be swept away!" Here again we see how presumptuous a weak faith can be. Instead of recognizing that it was pure grace that had spared his life Lot asked for further concessions. "Since the disaster will surely overtake us before we reach the mountains, couldn't we escape to Zoar, one of the smaller cities of the plain?" (The name Zoar means "Small.") Even though Lot's request seems unreasonable to us, the angels mercifully granted it.

²³By the time Lot reached Zoar, the sun had risen over the land. ²⁴Then the LORD rained down burning sulfur on Sodom and Gomorrah — from the LORD out of the heavens. ²⁵Thus he overthrew those cities and the entire plain, including all those living in the cities — and also the vegetation in the land. ²⁶But Lot's wife looked back, and she became a pillar of salt. ²⁷Early the next morning Abraham got up and returned to the place where he had stood before the LORD. ²⁸He looked down toward Sodom and Gomorrah, toward all the land of the plain, and he

saw dense smoke rising from the land, like smoke from a furnace. ²⁹So when God destroyed the cities of the plain, he remembered Abraham, and he brought Lot out of the catastrophe that overthrew the cities where Lot had lived.

The precise time of the destruction is pinpointed. Lot and his family were just entering Zoar when suddenly burning sulfur rained down from heaven on the city that had been their home.

We don't know what means God used to produce the firestorm that destroyed the four cities of the plain. Some have theorized that earthquakes and/or volcanic action may have released flammable materials under the earth's surface, which in turn were ignited, perhaps by lightning. Whatever means God used, the fact remains that this was a miracle of divine judgment. When the first two atomic bombs fell on Hiroshima and Nagasaki, there were survivors. When Sodom and Gomorrah were destroyed there were no survivors, except for the four members of Lot's family. Moses tells us that the LORD "overthrew" the cities of the plain; the destruction was so thorough that what was left looked as though the cities had been turned upside down. When on the following morning Abraham stepped out of his tent and looked to the southeast the entire landscape resembled a huge smoking furnace. Many scholars feel that the site of the destruction is today covered by the waters of the Dead Sea.

It is interesting to note the particular divine name Moses used for the One who sent the destruction., "The LORD rained down burning sulfur on Sodom and Gomorrah. ..." It was *the God of grace* who intervened in judgment when his offer of grace was refused. It is *the Savior* who still says: "Do not be deceived; I am not mocked. A man reaps what he sows." Lot's wife found that out from bitter experience when she despised God's warning and turned back to look at the city which had been her home and where her heart's loyalty was. She was struck dead instantly. Her body, embalmed in salt, stood as a grim reminder of the terrible price all will pay who cannot tear their hearts loose from the joys and toys this earthly life offers. It is hardly surprising that, twenty centuries later, when Jesus was warning his disciples against earthly-mindedness, he added: "Remember Lot's wife" (Luke 17:32)!

[30]Lot and his two daughters left Zoar and settled in the mountains, for he was afraid to stay in Zoar. He and his two daughters lived in a cave. [31]One day the older daughter said to the younger, "Our father is old, and there is no man around here to lie with us, as is the custom all over the earth. [32]Let's get our father to drink wine and then lie with him and preserve our family line through our father." [33]That night they got their father to drink wine, and the older daughter went in and lay with him. He was not aware of it when she lay down or when she got up. [34]The next day the older daughter said to the younger, "Last night I lay with my father. Let's get him to drink wine again tonight, and you go in and lie with him so we can preserve our family line through our father." [35]So they got their father to drink wine that night also, and the younger daughter went and lay with him. Again he was not aware of it when she lay down or when she got up. [36]So both of Lot's daughters became pregnant by their father.

[37]The older daughter had a son, and she named him Moab; he is the father of the Moabites of today. [38]The younger daughter also had a son, and she named him Ben-Ammi; he is the father of the Ammonites of today.

There's an ugly postscript to the story of Lot's deliverance from the punishment that overtook Sodom and Gomorrah. The godless and immoral culture that had surrounded Lot's family in Sodom took its toll not only on Lot and his wife, but on their daughters as well. Even though God's angels had led Lot to safety in Zoar he didn't feel safe there. Was he afraid that a belated judgment from God might strike this fifth city of the plain? At any rate, Lot moved with what was left of his family into the mountains and lived in one of the caves common in the Dead Sea area.

Cut off as they were from the outside world, Lot's two daughters rationalized the sin of incest with their father as the only way they could avoid the disgrace of childlessness. Nor can the father escape blame for this sleazy episode. He permitted himself to be seduced by wine and then by his own daughter — and not just once but twice. Their scheme worked, and nine months later each gave birth to a son, both of whom were named by their mothers with shameless disregard of the sin in which they had been conceived. Moab ("from the father") and Ben-Ammi ("son of my people") became the ancestors of two morally degenerate nations that were bitter enemies of Abraham's descendants.

We hear no more of Lot. He doesn't figure in the history of God's people except indirectly, through the Moabites and the Ammonites, Israel's neighbors to the east, across the Jordan. Not only did Lot's descendants display open hostility to the Israelites (see Judges 3:12-14; 1 Samuel 11:1, 2), they actually seduced them into false worship (Numbers 25: 1, 2).

20 Now Abraham moved on from there into the region of the Negev and lived between Kadesh and Shur. For a while he stayed in Gerar, **²** and there Abraham said of his wife Sarah, "She is my sister." Then Abimelech king of Gerar sent for Sarah and took her.

No reason is given why, after living for twenty years in one place, Abraham should have moved. Abraham was not a landowner, but a nomad. The account that follows is similar to 12:10-20. Although there are some *similarities* between the earlier account of Abraham's deception in Egypt and the account here of his deception in Gerar, the reader will note a number of distinct *dissimilarities*. The argument "It's unreasonable that Abraham would have repeated an earlier sin that got him into trouble" is unconvincing. Each of us may very well have a special spiritual weakness which Satan has successfully exploited more than once. Sin is never reasonable.

This lapse on Abraham's part was especially fateful just at this time, because of God's earlier promise: "Within a year Sarah will give birth to the son I promised you." On the very eve of the fulfillment of God's promise, Abraham imperiled the precious hope. Once again the sovereign mercy of God appeared on the dark background of sinful human frailty.

"Abimelech king of Gerar sent for Sarah and took her," namely into his harem. To take the sister of a rich man into his harem would enhance the king's prestige. Behind the king's action we see the prince of hell, seeking to pollute the womb of Sarah. Once again we see God's arch-enemy working in undying enmity against the Descendant of the woman.

3But God came to Abimelech in a dream one night and said to him, "You are as good as dead because of the woman you have taken; she is a married woman." 4Now Abimelech had not gone near her, so he said, "Lord, will you destroy an innocent nation? 5Did he not say to me, 'She is my sister,' and didn't she also say, 'He is my brother'? I have done this with a clear conscience and clean hands." 6Then God said to him in the dream,

"Yes, I know you did this with a clear conscience, and so I have kept you from sinning against me. That is why I did not let you touch her. ⁷Now return the man's wife, for he is a prophet, and he will pray for you and you will live. But if you do not return her, you may be sure that you and all yours will die."

Although the king had acted in good faith, God threatened so drastically because his plan and his promise were at stake. If he had not intervened here, to this day an element of doubt would cling to the ancestry of our Lord. Moses does assure the reader, however, that Abimelech had not approached Sarah sexually. One is reminded of some similar details in the account of our Lord's birth (Matthew 1:25; Luke 1:34). The Holy Spirit surrounds the story of our redemption with intimate detail.

God spoke to the king in a miraculous dream, a dream which allowed for an interchange of thoughts and questions and answers. Abimelech professed his innocence in the matter of taking another man's wife, and God acknowledged it. It is regrettable that, judging by human standards, there are unbelievers who act more responsibly than some who bear Christ's name. Because of Abraham's dishonesty, God had sent a providential sickness which incapacitated the entire royal household. God's miraculous conversation with Abimelech had one important message: "Return the man's wife, for he is a prophet." Although his behavior hadn't shown it, Abraham was a friend of God, a man to whom God had revealed his will, a man who spoke to people for God and who spoke to God for people.

⁸Early the next morning Abimelech summoned all his officials, and when he told them all that had happened, they were very much afraid. ⁹Then Abimelech called Abraham in and said, "What have you done to us? How have I wronged you that you have brought such great guilt upon me and my king-

dom? You have done things to me that should not be done."
¹⁰And Abimelech asked Abraham, "What was your reason for
doing this?" ¹¹Abraham replied, "I said to myself, 'There is
surely no fear of God in this place, and they will kill me
because of my wife.' ¹²Besides, she really is my sister, the
daughter of my father though not of my mother; and she
became my wife. ¹³And when God had me wander from my
father's household, I said to her, 'This is how you can show
your love to me: Everywhere we go, say of me, "He is
my brother."

There's nothing very pretty about seeing Abraham raked
over the coals by someone who, on the scale of spiritual
blessings, ranked much lower than he. And we learn that
this was not just a case of Abraham's being caught off
guard, either. He and Sarah had *rehearsed this lie in
advance.* He had not learned from the incident in Egypt
(12:10-20), but persisted in thinking that his ingenuity was a
surer guarantee of success than the promise of God.

¹⁴Then Abimelech brought sheep and cattle and male and
female slaves and gave them to Abraham, and he returned
Sarah his wife to him. ¹⁵And Abimelech said, "My land is
before you; live wherever you like." ¹⁶To Sarah he said, "I am
giving your brother a thousand shekels of silver. This is to
cover the offense against you before all who are with you; you
are completely vindicated." ¹⁷Then Abraham prayed to God,
and God healed Abimelech, his wife and his slave girls so they
could have children again, ¹⁸ for the LORD had closed up every
womb in Abimelech's household because of Abraham's
wife Sarah.

Under the circumstances, Abimelech's response was
unbelievably generous. In the first place, he restored Sarah.
In addition he gave Abraham a generous present, to remove
any possible embarrassment to Sarah by showing the high

esteem in which he held Abraham and Sarah. And finally he gave Abraham, a temporary resident, the right to live and work in his country. The faithful God of the covenant had again watched over the mother of the child of the covenant.

21 Now the LORD was gracious to Sarah as he had said, and the LORD did for Sarah what he had promised. **²Sarah became pregnant and bore a son to Abraham in his old age, at the very time God had promised him. ³Abraham gave the name Isaac to the son Sarah bore him. ⁴When his son Isaac was eight days old, Abraham circumcised him, as God commanded him. ⁵Abraham was a hundred years old when his son Isaac was born to him. ⁶Sarah said, "God has brought me laughter, and everyone who hears about this will laugh with me." ⁷And she added, "Who would have said to Abraham that Sarah would nurse children? Yet I have borne him a son in his old age."**

God Fulfills His Promise Through Isaac's Birth, Ishmael's Dismissal

With elaborate detail, Moses sketches God's fulfillment of his promise to Abraham and Sarah. By inverting the Hebrew word order of the first sentence he emphasizes that this was the God of the covenant acting in absolute *independence* but also in absolute *constancy*. The long awaited son was born at just the time God had said he would be, and received the name God had selected. At eight days Isaac received circumcision, the sign of the covenant, the seal of the righteousness his great Descendant would earn and which Isaac received by faith.

As she held her infant son in her arms Sarah not only expressed her joy, but she also showed that her repentance was genuine. Recalling her earlier laughter of unbelief at God's promise, she looked lovingly at her little Isaac (whose name means "laughter") and said: "God has really given me something to laugh about. Everyone who hears what great things God has done will laugh with me."

⁸The child grew and was weaned, and on the day Isaac was weaned Abraham held a great feast. ⁹But Sarah saw that the son whom Hagar the Egyptian had borne to Abraham was mocking, ¹⁰ and she said to Abraham, "Get rid of that slave woman and her son, for that slave woman's son will never share in the inheritance with my son Isaac."

¹¹The matter distressed Abraham greatly because it concerned his son. ¹²But God said to him, "Do not be so distressed about the boy and your maidservant. Listen to whatever Sarah tells you, because it is through Isaac that your offspring will be reckoned. ¹³I will make the son of the maidservant into a nation also, because he is your offspring."

Three or four years later, at the time of Isaac's weaning, Abraham held a celebration. It was to be a happy occasion honoring Isaac as the principal heir. But something happened to spoil the happy day for Sarah. She saw Ishmael, fourteen years older than Isaac, mocking her young son. This was not just an older brother innocently teasing his younger brother. St. Paul's epistle to the Galatians describes Ishmael's actions as *persecuting* the young heir of the promise (Galatians 4:29).

Sarah noticed that and told her husband to send Ishmael and his mother away from the household. When Abraham hesitated, God made it clear that her demand did not flow from petty jealousy. Over the years Sarah had noticed that Ishmael had no appreciation for God's covenant promise, but instead made fun of it. He therefore posed a threat to Isaac's inheritance and didn't belong in the same household with Isaac.

God used this unhappy incident as another element in training Abraham to distinguish between his true spiritual descendants and his descendants only according to the flesh. To make it easier for Abraham to expel his older son, God restated his promise to build Ishmael's descendants into a nation, for Abraham's sake. At the same time God reaffirmed that it was through Isaac, not Ishmael, that Abraham's true descendants would be counted. It was through Isaac, not Ishmael, that all nations on earth would be blessed.

This scene provided St. Paul with the features for his well-known comparison in Galatians 4:21-31. There the apostle contrasts Ishmael, "born in the ordinary way" and as a result of earthly-minded planning, with Isaac, "born as a result of a promise." There are not, there cannot be two ways of being saved, one by human merit and one by faith in God's promise. The true heirs of Abraham are heirs according to the promise.

¹⁴Early the next morning Abraham took some food and a skin of water and gave them to Hagar. He set them on her shoulders and then sent her off with the boy. She went on her way and wandered in the desert of Beersheba. ¹⁵When the water in the skin was gone, she put the boy under one of the bushes. ¹⁶Then she went off and sat down nearby, about a bowshot away, for she thought, "I cannot watch the boy die." And as she sat there nearby, she began to sob. ¹⁷God heard the boy crying, and the angel of God called to Hagar from heaven and said to her, "What is the matter, Hagar? Do not be afraid; God has heard the boy crying as he lies there. ¹⁸Lift the boy up and take him by the hand, for I will make him into a great nation." ¹⁹Then God opened her eyes and she saw a well of water. So she went and filled the skin with water and gave the boy a drink. ²⁰God was with the boy as he grew up. He lived in the desert

and became an archer. ²¹While he was living in the Desert of Paran, his mother got a wife for him from Egypt.

You've got to admire Abraham's prompt obedience. Although he realized that at his age he would very likely never see his firstborn son again, he sent Ishmael and his mother away the very next morning. He gave them what supplies of food and water they could carry and, with an ache in his heart, watched them head out into the hot dry southland of Canaan.

This was clearly a difficult time for Hagar, too. When her limited supply of water was gone, she anticipated having to watch her son die of thirst in the desert. But God heard the boy's crying. We're told "the angel of God called to Hagar from heaven." When this divine messenger promised to make of Ishmael a great nation, we once again recognize the speaker as the second person of the Holy Trinity. He first of all assured the young mother that her son would not die in the desert, and then he directed her to a spring of water to satisfy their immediate need.

After this miraculous deliverance, Hagar and her son headed south toward Egypt. Ishmael grew up to be an out-doorsman and later settled in the Sinai Peninsula. Hagar saw to it that he married an Egyptian wife. Moses supplies additional information about Ishmael's descendants in Genesis 25:12-18. For us the most significant feature of Ishmael's line is that it lost all spiritual kinship with Abraham.

²²At that time Abimelech and Phicol the commander of his forces said to Abraham, "God is with you in everything you do. ²³Now swear to me here before God that you will not deal falsely with me or my children or my descendants. Show to me and the country where you are living as an alien the same kind-

ness I have shown to you." ²⁴Abraham said, "I swear it." ²⁵Then Abraham complained to Abimelech about a well of water that Abimelech's servants had seized. ²⁶But Abimelech said, "I don't know who has done this. You did not tell me, and I heard about it only today." ²⁷So Abraham brought sheep and cattle and gave them to Abimelech, and the two men made a treaty. ²⁸Abraham set apart seven ewe lambs from the flock, ²⁹ and Abimelech asked Abraham, "What is the meaning of these seven ewe lambs you have set apart by themselves?" ³⁰He replied, "Accept these seven lambs from my hand as a witness that I dug this well." ³¹So that place was called Beersheba, because the two men swore an oath there. ³²After the treaty had been made at Beersheba, Abimelech and Phicol the commander of his forces returned to the land of the Philistines. ³³Abraham planted a tamarisk tree in Beersheba, and there he called upon the name of the LORD, the eternal God. ³⁴And Abraham stayed in the land of the Philistines for a long time.

It could hardly have been a secret to Abraham's neighbors that Abraham had enjoyed the very special blessing of God. He had become not only rich, but influential as well. Here we see the unusual spectacle of Abimelech, a neighboring king, together with his army commander, approaching Abraham as an equal and showing they were concerned about keeping his good will.

Although this is highly unusual, it's also understandable. It must have been awesome to know a man whom God was so obviously supporting in everything he did — giving him a smashing victory over invading armies, providing abundant food supply in a land of sparseness, delivering him from the consequences of his own stupidity, and miraculously granting him a son in his old age.

King Abimelech reminded Abraham that in the past he had shown him kindness, faithful love. He had permitted Abraham, an alien, not only to live in his land and to move about freely, but also to plant crops, to graze his cattle, to dig wells. His request strikes us as reasonable: "Swear that you will show the same kindness to me and to my children and to my descendants." The proposed alliance between Abimelech and Abraham would also bind their descendants. Abimelech would enjoy the security of a nonaggression pact, and Abraham would continue to enjoy squatter's rights. Abraham was willing to enter into the alliance and to confirm it with an oath.

Before proceeding with the covenant ratification, Abraham happened to mention that a well of his had been taken over by Abimelech's servants. After securing his sole right to use the well Abraham joined in the covenant ceremony. Two significant actions of Abraham after the king and his commander had left are recorded. He acknowledged his indebtedness to the LORD, first by *planting a memorial tree* and then by *publicly worshiping* "the LORD, the Eternal God." Unlike the little, limited, local deities of the surrounding heathen, Abraham's God had promised blessings for all people for all time.

God Brings Abraham's Training in Faith to a Climax

22 **Some time later God tested Abraham. He said to him, "Abraham!" "Here I am," he replied. ²Then God said, "Take your son, your only son, Isaac, whom you love, and go to the region of Moriah. Sacrifice him there as a burnt offering on one of the mountains I will tell you about."**

Sending Ishmael away had been difficult for Abraham, but a much sterner test of his faith now faced him. This testing was not for *God's* benefit (he knew in advance that Abraham was God-fearing), but for *Abraham's* spiritual benefit. Abraham's love for Isaac, right and good though it was, might in time have crowded out his love for God.

181

Jesus once said: "Anyone who loves his son or daughter more than me is not worthy of me" (Matthew 10:37). In God's view, Abraham needed an *opportunity consciously to put God first*. With this test God brought Abraham's training in faith to a climax. The particular sacrifice God asked Abraham to bring is called a "burnt offering," a blood sacrifice which in the Old Testament symbolized a person's complete dedication to God.

It's important to remember that the reader is the only one who is informed that this was a test. Abraham did not learn of this until later. God did not say: "Abraham, don't you worry about the outcome. This is only a test." God had told Abraham that Isaac was to be the bearer of the Messianic promise, and now he told him to kill Isaac. And it is no solution to the dilemma to say: "Well, God performed a miracle once before to give Abraham and Sarah a son: he could repeat the miracle and give them another son." God's words had been too clear for that: "My covenant I will establish *with Isaac*" (17:21). Luther accurately described Abraham's predicament in these words: "To human reason it must have seemed either that God's promise would fail, or else this command must be of the devil and not of God." To Abraham it must have seemed that God's *command* was destroying God's *promise*.

And what further complicated the situation for Abraham was that God's command seemed not only to *violate a father's love* for his son but to *cut off his hope of ever being saved*. If Isaac was the link between Abraham and the only Savior he would ever have, how could he cut off that link and hope to be right with God? And how could he ever hope to live with God forever?

³**Early the next morning Abraham got up and saddled his donkey. He took with him two of his servants and his son Isaac.**

When he had cut enough wood for the burnt offering, he set out for the place God had told him about. ⁴On the third day Abraham looked up and saw the place in the distance. ⁵He said to his servants, "Stay here with the donkey while I and the boy go over there. We will worship and then we will come back to you."

After what must have been a sleepless night Abraham got up early, perhaps so he wouldn't have to discuss with Sarah the gruesome assignment ahead for him. He cut wood for the sacrifice and, with two servants and Isaac, set out for the land of Moriah. We marvel at his prompt and absolute obedience. God got no backtalk from Abraham, no argument, not even a question — just obedience. If "the land of Moriah" is the same area as the hill on which Solomon later built the temple (2 Chronicles 3:1), Abraham had a fifty-mile trip ahead of him. God didn't want Abraham's obedience to flow from spur-of-the-moment enthusiasm. Three days of traveling gave Abraham plenty of time to think. And we can be sure Satan supplied a dozen logical reasons why he should not take the life of his own son.

When he reached the site Abraham ordered the servants to stay, while he and Isaac went on ahead. The servants were not to witness the sacrifice, since they couldn't have understood. Abraham's instructions to the servants are significant, for two reasons. "I and the boy *will worship.* ..." Abraham rightly described the act that was to follow as worship. His act was a declaration: "LORD, you have my heart."

"...and then *we will come back* to you." The Hebrew word translated "we will come back" is an emphatic verb form expressing the speaker's determination. It hints at the answer Abraham had reached to the awful question that was torturing him: "How can a merciful God cut off the

Messianic line?" Abraham's faith answered: "If God commands me to kill Isaac and I obey him, then God is simply going to have to bring Isaac's ashes back to life, and the *two of us are going to come back down this mountain.*"

⁶Abraham took the wood for the burnt offering and placed it on his son Isaac, and he himself carried the fire and the knife. As the two of them went on together, ⁷ Isaac spoke up and said to his father Abraham, "Father?" "Yes, my son?" Abraham replied. "The fire and wood are here," Isaac said, "but where is the lamb for the burnt offering?" ⁸Abraham answered, "God himself will provide the lamb for the burnt offering, my son." And the two of them went on together.

Abraham was silent as he and his son walked to the place of sacrifice. It was Isaac who broke the silence. "Father, where is the lamb for the sacrifice?" The question must have cut Abraham like a knife. His answer was a combination of *considerate love*, which spared Isaac the brutal details, and of *confident faith*, which left the outcome to God.

⁹When they reached the place God had told him about, Abraham built an altar there and arranged the wood on it. He bound his son Isaac and laid him on the altar, on top of the wood. ¹⁰Then he reached out his hand and took the knife to slay his son. ¹¹But the angel of the LORD called out to him from heaven, "Abraham! Abraham!" "Here I am," he replied. ¹²"Do not lay a hand on the boy," he said. "Do not do anything to him. Now I know that you fear God, because you have not withheld from me your son, your only son." ¹³Abraham looked up and there in a thicket he saw a ram caught by its horns. He went over and took the ram and sacrificed it as a burnt offering instead of his son. ¹⁴So Abraham called that place The LORD Will Provide. And to this day it is said, "On the mountain of the LORD it will be provided."

The climax of the sacrifice is described with abundant detail. To obey God's command Abraham had to disregard everything his heart and his reason told him, and to concentrate totally on God's promise; "My covenant I will establish with Isaac" (17:21). The epistle to the Hebrews helps us to understand Abraham's attitude:

> By faith Abraham, when God tested him, offered Isaac as a sacrifice. He who had received the promises was about to sacrifice his one and only son, even though God had said to him,
> > "It is through Isaac that your offspring will be reckoned."
> Abraham reasoned that God could raise the dead, and figuratively speaking, he did receive Isaac back from death. (Hebrews 11:17-19)

If there was a conflict between God's command and his promise, resolving that conflict was *God's* business. *Abraham's* business was to put God first, and he drew his knife.

God knew that in Abraham's heart the necessary sacrifice had been made. He had surrendered his *will* and his *wisdom* — yes, and his *son* — in obedience to the word of his Lord. God deliberately allowed the situation to develop to this point to demonstrate that Abraham had made the inner spiritual sacrifice, and then with a doubly urgent "Abraham! Abraham!" directed him not to harm his son. God had now brought Abraham's spiritual training to a successful climax, and a messenger from heaven announced that.

The "angel of the LORD" called out to Abraham. Who is the speaker? The fact that he says "You have not withheld your son *from me...*" indicates that the speaker was the Angel of the LORD, the Son of God himself. He here made another appearance prior to assuming our flesh and blood in the womb of the virgin.

"Now I know that you fear God," the Angel told Abraham. The fear of God is everywhere in the Scripture a deep feeling of awe in the presence of the great God. It includes an absolute *fear* of doing anything that would displease him, as well as childlike *respect* for him. In the case of the unbeliever only the former is present. Abraham's behavior at Moriah demonstrated that both were present in his heart.

By providing a ram for the sacrifice in place of Isaac, God illustrated a principle that becomes more and more prominent as the Old Testament unfolds. It's the *principle of substitution.* When God *created* the world, he did so by exercising his almighty power. When God *redeemed* the world, he did so by mercifully providing a substitute, whom he punished in place of the sinner.

As Abraham walked down the mountain with his son, he may have remembered what he had said to Isaac as they had walked up the mountain. "My son, God will provide the lamb for the offering." Now Abraham had experienced that the Savior-God had in fact provided, and in testimony of that fact he gave the mountain a new name, "Jehovah-Jireh" ("the LORD will provide").

[15]The angel of the LORD called to Abraham from heaven a second time [16] and said, "I swear by myself, declares the LORD, that because you have done this and have not withheld your son, your only son, [17] I will surely bless you and make your descendants as numerous as the stars in the sky and as the sand on the seashore. Your descendants will take possession of the cities of their enemies, [18] and through your offspring all nations on earth will be blessed, because you have obeyed me." [19] Then Abraham returned to his servants, and they set off together for Beersheba. And Abraham stayed in Beersheba.

The Angel spoke to Abraham once again. He rewarded Abraham's faith by *repeating and expanding the Messianic promise.* Abraham's descendants, as numerous as sand on the seashore, would take possession of the cities of their enemies — a reference to the Israelite conquest of Canaan. God also *confirmed his promise with an oath.* He swore by himself, since there is no higher authority. When Abraham left Moriah his trust in God's promise was deepened, and his love for his son was purified.

God Lets Abraham End His Life in the Calm Contentment of Faith

²⁰Some time later Abraham was told, "Milcah is also a mother; she has borne sons to your brother Nahor: ²¹Uz the firstborn, Buz his brother, Kemuel (the father of Aram), ²²Kesed, Hazo, Pildash, Jidlaph and Bethuel." ²³Bethuel became the father of Rebekah. Milcah bore these eight sons to Abraham's brother Nahor. ²⁴His concubine, whose name was Reumah, also had sons: Tebah, Gaham, Tahash and Maacah.

God's purposes for Abraham had now been achieved. God had called this man away from his former homeland, from his relatives, from his father's house. God had given him a promise that, humanly speaking, was unbelievable, but had taught him to trust that promise implicitly. And then God let Abraham live to see the fulfillment of that promise. What did life still have to offer Abraham? The closing chapters of the "Account of Terah" show us how *God let Abraham end his life in the calm contentment of faith*, first of all, as he received news from Haran.

Half a century had passed since Abraham had left Haran, 500 miles to the north, in present-day Syria. In that time Abraham had most likely lost contact with his only surviving brother Nahor. Now a report reached Abraham about his brother's family. Nahor had eight sons, one of whom was Bethuel. Of Bethuel's children only a daughter Rebekah is named. And here we can see why God had Moses insert a brief and incomplete genealogy into the sacred record at this point. For several generations God had been at work to provide a wife for Isaac, the son of the promise.

Abraham Shows the Calm Contentment of Faith as He Buries Sarah

23 **Sarah lived to be a hundred and twenty-seven years old. ²She died at Kiriath Arba (that is, Hebron) in the land of Canaan, and Abraham went to mourn for Sarah and to weep over her.**

The preceding chapter of Genesis demonstrated how Abraham expressed his faith *under the most unusual and difficult circumstances*. But faith can be expressed in the ordinary and routine events of life as well as in the extraordinary. In this chapter we see how Abraham gave evidence of his faith *under circumstances that presented no extraordinary crisis.*

Sarah is the only woman whose age at her death is recorded on the pages of the Scripture. If Abraham is called the father of believers, then she is the mother of believers. At God's call she too left a comfortable life in Ur of the Chaldeans to spend the last half of her life as a nomad, living in a tent in Canaan's inhospitable southland. Her marriage, which may have lasted a century, was marked by the special blessing of God. She stood by her husband faithfully as God led him from one step in the divine training program to another.

Sarah, the free woman, is a picture of the church of the New Testament, whose children are children of the promise, reborn by the power of the Spirit (Galatians 4:24-31). After Sarah lived to see her son grow to be a man of thirty-seven, God called her to himself. Abraham not only wept tears of sadness at the death of his beloved, he also gave audible expression to his grief, in the custom of that day.

³Then Abraham rose from beside his dead wife and spoke to the Hittites. He said, "'I am an alien and a stranger among you. Sell me some property for a burial site here so I can bury my dead."

Now Abraham faced a problem. For reasons which will become clear, he wanted Sarah to be buried in the land of Canaan. But he was an alien, a stranger in the land. He therefore went to the city gate in Hebron, where he had moved after leaving Beersheba, and appealed to the city fathers. We're surprised to learn these were Hittites, members of a Canaanite people who had originally come from what is today Turkey and had migrated south. Abraham's request shows he realized he was asking for a favor, the right to own land in a country where he was a stranger.

⁵The Hittites replied to Abraham, ⁶"'Sir, listen to us. You are a mighty prince among us. Bury your dead in the choicest of our tombs. None of us will refuse you his tomb for burying your dead." ⁷Then Abraham rose and bowed down before the people of the land, the Hittites. ⁸He said to them, "If you are willing to let me bury my dead, then listen to me and intercede with Ephron son of Zohar on my behalf ⁹ so he will sell me the cave of Machpelah, which belongs to him and is at the end of his field. Ask him to sell it to me for the full price as a burial site among you."

The officials of Hebron answered Abraham's request more favorably than he may have anticipated. They acknowledged him to be a man of high position, a man who enjoyed the special blessing of God. He shouldn't have to *buy* a burial plot; he could choose whichever tomb he wanted, and the owner would not refuse him.

Abraham, however, was interested not only in finding a place for his beloved dead. Abraham was the father of God's ancient covenant people, who would one day own and occupy this land. Canaan was the land which his children's children would one day possess. He therefore wanted Sarah's remains, as well as his own, to rest in the promised land as *a silent testimony to their faith* in God's promise: "To your offspring I will give this land" (Genesis 12:7). Even before his descendants entered Canaan, during the four centuries when they would be living as strangers in Egypt, their ancestor's calm insistence on being buried in the land of promise would reassure them that Canaan would be their future home.

Abraham humbly acknowledged the Hittites' gracious compliment and their generous offer, and pressed his appeal. "If, as you have indicated, you will permit me to bury my dead here, then please speak to Ephron for me. I wish to purchase a cave at one end of his property, and I will pay him the full price in silver." To insure that his request would be granted, he asked the city officials to act for him, instead of dealing with the owner personally. The parcel of land he chose was a cave, unusable for farming or grazing. And he made it clear he was not asking for a gift.

[10]Ephron the Hittite was sitting among his people and he replied to Abraham in the hearing of all the Hittites who had come to the gate of his city. [11]"No, my lord," he said. "Listen to me; I give you the field, and I give you the cave that is in it. I give it to you in the presence of my people. Bury your dead." [12]Again Abraham bowed down before the people of the land

¹³ **and he said to Ephron in their hearing, "Listen to me, if you will. I will pay the price of the field. Accept it from me so I can bury my dead there." ¹⁴Ephron answered Abraham, ¹⁵"Listen to me, my lord; the land is worth four hundred shekels of silver, but what is that between me and you? Bury your dead."**

Ephron, the landowner, was present in the assembly and answered Abraham. His words give the clear impression that he was not particularly interested in giving away his property without compensation. Although he repeated the offer to allow Abraham simply to bury Sarah on his property, he had just learned that was not what Abraham wanted. His offer appears to have been only a polite formality, perhaps indicating no more than that he was ready to begin negotiating the sale with Abraham.

Something else catches our eye in Ephron's answer. Abraham had asked for permission to buy the *cave* at the edge of his property. Ephron countered by offering him the *entire field* along with the cave — something Abraham hadn't asked for. From what we know of Hittite law, ownership of an entire field may well have brought with it certain obligations — perhaps some service to the king. It has been suggested that Ephron may have wanted to unload these responsibilities on somebody else, and saw in Abraham's request an opportunity to do just that.

As a starting point for the negotiations, Ephron suggested that the land was worth 400 shekels of silver. Compared with land values discovered in ancient Babylonian records, the suggested price seems exorbitant. We're led to think that Ephron expected a counter-offer from Abraham, after which serious bargaining could begin.

¹⁶**Abraham agreed to Ephron's terms and weighed out for him the price he had named in the hearing of the Hittites: four**

hundred shekels of silver, according to the weight current among the merchants.

[17]So Ephron's field in Machpelah near Mamre — both the field and the cave in it, and all the trees within the borders of the field — was deeded [18] to Abraham as his property in the presence of all the Hittites who had come to the gate of the city. [19]Afterward Abraham buried his wife Sarah in the cave in the field of Machpelah near Mamre (which is at Hebron) in the land of Canaan. [20]So the field and the cave in it were deeded to Abraham by the Hittites as a burial site.

Ephron must have been surprised when Abraham, an experienced businessman, accepted his initial offer. With the city officials as witnesses, Abraham paid Ephron the full price he had suggested. Since minting coins did not become common for another ten or twelve centuries, Abraham weighed out the purchase price, perhaps in silver bars. The transaction was duly recorded, and the field at Machpelah, including the cave and all the trees on it, was deeded to Abraham.

Abraham buried Sarah in the cave of Machpelah, and thirty-eight years later his sons laid him to rest with Sarah. Subsequent chapters of Genesis will record that the cave was also the last earthly resting place of Isaac and Rebekah, and of Jacob and Leah. One writer has remarked: "No other spot in the Holy Land has as much precious dust as this."

Abraham, "father of believers," was a man who lived by faith in God's promises. He never lived to see the fulfillment of most of them. He never saw his descendants grow into a mighty nation or take possession of the Promised Land. And of course he never lived to see his greatest Descendant, through whose perfect life and innocent death all families of the earth would be blessed. But this chapter emphasizes that Abraham *believed* God's promises, even though he didn't *witness* their fulfillment. And although Abraham could have returned to his relatives in Haran and found a family burial site for Sarah there, Abraham's actions declared: "Haran is not my home any more. The future of my family lies in Canaan, because God has said so. Here is where God's great plan will reach fulfillment, and here is where I am determined to remain."

In the same way, our trust in the promises God has given us in Jesus Christ will transform ordinary and routine details of everyday life into opportunities for bearing witness to the faith that is in us.

Abraham Shows the Calm Contentment of Faith as He Provides a Wife for Isaac

24 Abraham was now old and well advanced in years, and the LORD had blessed him in every way. ²He said to the chief servant in his household, the one in charge of all that he had, "Put your hand under my thigh. ³I want you to swear by the LORD, the God of heaven and the God of earth, that you will not get a wife for my son from the daughters of the Canaanites, among whom I am living, ⁴ but will go to my country and my own relatives and get a wife for my son Isaac."

⁵The servant asked him, "What if the woman is unwilling to come back with me to this land? Shall I then take your son back to the country you came from?" "'Make sure that you do not take my son back there," Abraham said. ⁷"The LORD, the God of heaven, who brought me out of my father's household and my native land and who spoke to me and promised me on oath, saying, 'To your offspring I will give this land' — he will send his angel before you so that you can get a wife for my son from there. ⁸If the woman is unwilling to come back with you, then you will be released from this oath of mine. Only do not take my son back there." ⁹So the servant put his hand under

the thigh of his master Abraham and swore an oath to him concerning this matter.

Three years had elapsed since Sarah's death. Abraham was now 140 years old, and he realized there was an important matter for him to attend to before his time ran out. Isaac needed to have a wife who would share his faith in God's promise. The account we have in Genesis 24 is long and detailed, without parallel in the Scripture.

Abraham called in his chief servant and entrusted to him the responsibility of finding a suitable wife for Isaac. He instructed him to travel 500 miles north to Mesopotamia, to the city of Haran, Abraham's former home. Abraham couldn't attend to this personally, because God had directed him to leave Haran. And although Isaac at forty was old enough to have picked out his own wife, Abraham didn't want him to leave the land of Canaan, either. We take for granted that in this matter Abraham acted with the full knowledge and consent of Isaac.

Abraham placed his servant under oath to follow his instructions to the letter. To seal the oath, the servant placed his hand under Abraham's thigh, the seat of procreative power. The oath was apparently related to the powers of reproduction and would involve Abraham's descendants in the Messianic line.

The very heart of Abraham's concern is summarized in the solemn command: "I want you to swear that...you will not get a wife for my son from the daughters of the Canaanites." Abraham had good reason to be concerned. Canaanite religion was a filthy combination of idolatry and adultery, and a Canaanite wife would not share a common faith with believing Isaac. She could not nourish and transmit that faith in the coming Savior to future generations. And, furthermore, God had promised that the Canaanites would fall under his condemnation because of their shameful idolatry.

The servant showed that he shared his master's deep reverence for the LORD by clarifying his assignment, "What if the woman I find for Isaac is unwilling to marry a man she's never seen? May I then take Isaac there for a visit?" In faith Abraham anticipated no difficulty, and emphatically refused to act contrary to God's will. He knew that the mission on which he was sending his servant was God's will. He was simply applying to this present situation what God had told him. In the same way you and I know that God is committed to making it possible for us to do what he has called us to do.

¹⁰Then the servant took ten of his master's camels and left, taking with him all kinds of good things from his master. He set out for Aram Naharaim and made his way to the town of Nahor. ¹¹He had the camels kneel down near the well outside the town; it was toward evening, the time the women go out to draw water. ¹²Then he prayed, "O LORD, God of my master Abraham, give me success today, and show kindness to my master Abraham. ¹³See, I am standing beside this spring, and the daughters of the townspeople are coming out to draw water. ¹⁴May it be that when I say to a girl, 'Please let down your jar that I may have a drink,' and she says, 'Drink, and I'll water your camels too' — let her be the one you have chosen for your servant Isaac. By this I will know that you have shown kindness to my master."

Abraham was a wealthy man, so he sent along with his servant gifts for the prospective bride and her family, gifts which would reflect favorably on the social standing of the prospective bridegroom.

The Bible narrative says little about the long journey to Mesopotamia, a trip which may have taken a month. Instead the sacred writer focuses our attention on the servant as he stood at the town well and thought about his assignment. Before him he could see the women of the city coming to draw water for family and flocks. How was he to know which one the LORD had picked out for Isaac?

The servant had learned a lot from his master. He talked to God, whose work he was doing. "Give me success today, and show kindness to my master Abraham." God's great plan for saving sinners was involved in finding the right wife for Isaac. The servant was very conscious of that and asked for God's help.

Next, the servant sketched a scenario which would help him identify the woman of the LORD's choice. Does that sound like dictating to the LORD? The servant knew that God's children surely need not assume God will leave them without guidance. He therefore suggested: "If I ask a girl for a drink and she not only gives *me* a drink but offers to draw water also for my *ten camels*, let this be the sign that she is the one you have chosen for Isaac."

What would this sign say about the young lady? It would certainly show friendliness and hospitality and kindness., It would indicate a willingness to serve. And to make repeated trips down to a well to draw enough water to satisfy ten thirsty camels would require physical stamina.

¹⁵Before he had finished praying, Rebekah came out with her jar on her shoulder. She was the daughter of Bethuel son of Milcah, who was the wife of Abraham's brother Nahor. ¹⁶The girl was very beautiful, a virgin; no man had ever lain with her. She went down to the spring, filled her jar and came up again. ¹⁷The servant hurried to meet her and said, "Please give me a little water from your jar." ¹⁸"Drink, my lord," she said, and quickly lowered the jar to her hands and gave him a drink. ¹⁹After she had given him a drink, she said, "I'll draw water for

your camels too, until they have finished drinking." ²⁰So she quickly emptied her jar into the trough, ran back to the well to draw more water, and drew enough for all his camels. ²¹Without saying a word, the man watched her closely to learn whether or not the LORD had made his journey successful.

Before the servant had even finished his prayer his eyes fell on Rebekah. The *servant* didn't know it, but the *reader* is informed that she was the granddaughter of Nahor, Abraham's brother. She gave the servant the drink of water he requested, and then volunteered to draw water for his camels as well. If one camel can drink twenty gallons, her offer may have cost her an extra hour of work at the well. The servant watched wordlessly. Could it be that the LORD had answered his prayer so promptly?

²²When the camels had finished drinking, the man took out a gold nose ring weighing a beka and two gold bracelets weighing ten shekels.

²³Then he asked, "Whose daughter are you? Please tell me, is there room in your father's house for us to spend the night?" ²⁴She answered him, "I am the daughter of Bethuel, the son that Milcah bore to Nahor." ²⁵And she added, "We have plenty of straw and fodder, as well as room for you to spend the night." ²⁶Then the man bowed down and worshiped the LORD, ²⁷ saying, "Praise be to the LORD, the God of my master Abraham, who has not abandoned his kindness and faithfulness to my master. As for me, the LORD has led me on the journey to the house of my master's relatives."

To express his appreciation for the kindness Rebekah had just shown him the servant took out a gold nose ring and gold bracelets which Abraham had sent along and offered them to her as gifts. The bracelets alone weighed four ounces; these were gifts worthy of a rich man.

The servant couldn't wait to ask her the important question. At the well she had met *his* requirements, but did she meet *Abraham's*? "Whose daughter are you?" She gave him the reply he was hoping for, and in answer to his second question assured him there would be lodging at her father's house.

Now there could be no doubt that the LORD had led him to the young woman of his choice, and the servant fell to his knees in humble gratitude. He praised the LORD for as marvelous a display of divine providence as any human being has ever witnessed.

²⁸The girl ran and told her mother's household about these things.

²⁹Now Rebekah had a brother named Laban, and he hurried out to the man at the spring. ³⁰As soon as he had seen the nose ring, and the bracelets on his sister's arms, and had heard Rebekah tell what the man said to her, he went out to the man and found him standing by the camels near the spring. ³¹"Come, you who are blessed by the LORD," he said. "Why are you standing out here? I have prepared the house and a place for the camels." ³²So the man went to the house, and the camels were unloaded. Straw and fodder were brought for the camels, and water for him and his men to wash their feet. ³³Then food was set before him, but he said, "I will not eat until I have told you what I have to say." "Then tell us," Laban said.

Rebekah must have been surprised, too, if not bewildered, at the unusual things that had happened to her at the well. She ran home to tell her family. When her brother Laban saw the jewelry his sister was wearing he ran out to the well to find the man and to invite him to the house. Later chapters of Genesis will reveal some character traits of Laban that are less than noble, but we have no reason to suspect his motives here. The gifts his sister had received from a total stranger were enough to impress anybody, and the brother was understandably interested. He saw to it that the camels were unsaddled and provided with food and shelter. He offered the strangers warm hospitality and invited them to eat with the family.

The pious servant politely declined to eat, however, until he had explained the purpose of his special mission.

³⁴So he said, "I am Abraham's servant. ³⁵The LORD has blessed my master abundantly, and he has become wealthy. He has given him sheep and cattle, silver and gold, menservants and maidservants, and camels and donkeys. ³⁶My master's wife Sarah has borne him a son in her old age, and he has given him everything he owns. ³⁷And my master made me swear an oath, and said, 'You must not get a wife for my son from the daughters of the Canaanites, in whose land I live, ³⁸ but go to my father's family and to my own clan, and get a wife for my son.'

³⁹"Then I asked my master, 'What if the woman will not come back with me?' ⁴⁰He replied, 'The LORD, before whom I have walked, will send his angel with you and make your journey a success, so that you can get a wife for my son from my own clan and from my father's family. ⁴¹Then, when you go to my clan, you will be released from my oath even if they refuse to give her to you — you will be released from my oath.'

⁴²"When I came to the spring today, I said, 'O LORD, God of my master Abraham, if you will, please grant success to the journey on which I have come. ⁴³See, I am standing beside this spring; if a maiden comes out to draw water and I say to her, "Please let me drink a little water from your jar," ⁴⁴ and if she says to me, "Drink, and I'll draw water for your camels too," let her be the one the LORD has chosen for my master's son.'

⁴⁵Before I finished praying in my heart, Rebekah came out, with her jar on her shoulder. She went down to the spring and drew water, and I said to her, 'Please give me a drink.' ⁴⁶She quickly lowered her jar from her shoulder and said, 'Drink, and I'll water your camels too.' So I drank, and she watered

the camels also. ⁴⁷I asked her, 'Whose daughter are you?' She said, 'The daughter of Bethuel son of Nahor, whom Milcah bore to him.'

"Then I put the ring in her nose and the bracelets on her arms, ⁴⁸ and I bowed down and worshiped the LORD. I praised the LORD, the God of my master Abraham, who had led me on the right road to get the granddaughter of my master's brother for his son. ⁴⁹Now if you will show kindness and faithfulness to my master, tell me; and if not, tell me, so I may know which way to turn."

The servant recounted the important assignment his master had given him, and repeated the details of what had happened at the well. These are details which the reader knows, but which Rebekah and her family needed to know if they were to reach a God-pleasing decision in the important matter that lay before them.

Several matters received special emphasis in the servant's presentation. He introduced the matter of Abraham's wealth, and emphasized that at Abraham's death his estate would pass to Isaac. He explained that Isaac was born when Abraham was an old man. (Rebekah's father Bethuel might otherwise have wondered about a possible generation gap between his cousin Isaac and his daughter Rebekah). Most striking in the servant's speech to Rebekah's family is his use of God's Old Testament covenant name. Father Abraham's interest was not just in getting his son married, but in finding a proper wife for the heir of God's covenant promises.

It's interesting to note that the servant did not come right out and ask for Rebekah to be Isaac's wife. He simply restated the facts and let them speak for themselves. The Savior's guiding hand had to be as obvious to Rebekah's family as it was to him.

⁵⁰Laban and Bethuel answered, "This is from the LORD; we can say nothing to you one way or the other. ⁵¹Here is Rebekah; take her and go, and let her become the wife of your master's son, as the LORD has directed." ⁵²When Abraham's servant heard what they said, he bowed down to the ground before the LORD. ⁵³Then the servant brought out gold and silver jewelry and articles of clothing and gave them to Rebekah; he also gave costly gifts to her brother and to her mother.

⁵⁴Then he and the men who were with him ate and drank and spent the night there. When they got up the next morning, he said, "Send me on my way to my master." ⁵⁵But her brother and her mother replied, "Let the girl remain with us ten days or so; then you may go." ⁵⁶But he said to them, "Do not detain me, now that the LORD has granted success to my journey. Send me on my way so I may go to my master." ⁵⁷Then they said, "Let's call the girl and ask her about it." ⁵⁸So they called Rebekah and asked her, "Will you go with this man?" "I will go," she said.

The servant's recital of the astounding chain of events convinced Rebekah's family. It was obvious to them that this was the LORD's will, which they did not dare to oppose. "This is clearly from the LORD. There's nothing more to be said. Here is Rebekah; take her and go." Their use of God's covenant name shows that they were believing children of God and that they were happy Rebekah would be in the family of the promised Savior. Their words make it all the more clear why Abraham wanted his son's wife to come from this background.

The family's response once again brought the servant to his knees in worship. He then distributed the gifts he had brought. Some were gifts for Rebekah, and some were for her parents and her brother. The social custom of the day required a prospective bridegroom to give his future in-laws a special gift known as *the "bride-price."* This gift served a number of purposes. It provided evidence that the marital agreement was made in good faith, and sealed the covenant between the two families. It established the social standing of the groom. Since the bride would be leaving the father's household, the bride-price reimbursed him for the loss of a worker. And it served as a sort of prepaid alimony in case the husband later deserted or divorced his wife.

Now that all the preliminaries had been attended to, Abraham's servant was ready to enjoy a meal and a bed. The following morning, however, he asked the family's permission to return to his master. The old servant might have been excused if he had stayed in Haran a few days to rest, and to rest the animals after a 500-mile journey. The family members encouraged him to do this, and it's easy to understand why. Up to the previous day they hadn't ever seen the man, and once Rebekah left it was unlikely they would ever see her again. The servant knew, however, that delay would only make the eventual parting harder.

They called Rebekah and let her decide. Her answer "I will go" is not to be understood as her consent to be Isaac's wife. Her parents' consent had already been expressed in verse 51, and her acceptance of the bridal gifts indicated that she had concurred in that. Her answer "I will go" announced that she was ready to leave immediately with Abraham's servant.

⁵⁹So they sent their sister Rebekah on her way, along with her nurse and Abraham's servant and his men. ⁶⁰And they blessed Rebekah and said to her, "Our sister, may you increase to thousands upon thousands; may your offspring possess the gates of their enemies."

⁶¹Then Rebekah and her maids got ready and mounted their camels and went back with the man. So the servant took Rebekah and left.

Rebekah's resolute answer decided that the return trip to Canaan would begin at once. Her nurse Deborah (Genesis 35:8), who had cared for her since infancy, went with her, as did several maids. The parting blessing spoken by the family members is remarkable. These were descendants of Noah who were aware of the blessings God had promised to Shem (Genesis 9:26) and to Abraham (Genesis 12:1-3; 22:17). God saw to it that their prayer was granted. Rebekah did become the ancestress of numerous descendants, who later conquered and occupied the cities of Canaan.

[62]Now Isaac had come from Beer Lahai Roi, for he was living in the Negev. [63]He went out to the field one evening to meditate, and as he looked up, he saw camels approaching. [64]Rebekah also looked up and saw Isaac. She got down from her camel [65]and asked the servant, "Who is that man in the field coming to meet us?" "He is my master," the servant answered. So she took her veil and covered herself. [66]Then the servant told Isaac all he had done. [67]Isaac brought her into the tent of his mother Sarah, and he married Rebekah. So she became his wife, and he loved her; and Isaac was comforted after his mother's death.

As was the case with the long trip north, virtually nothing is said about the month-long return trip. Genesis 25:11 tells us Isaac had set up his own camp at the well where God had once appeared to Hagar (16:13, 14). He saw the camel caravan approaching and learned the details of the long-distance courtship from the faithful servant, who once again recited "all he had done." It was as clear to Isaac as it had been to Rebekah's family that God had marvelously directed events to this happy conclusion. Abraham and Isaac had acted responsibly, in the interests of God's covenant. Those who do that will receive God's guidance and will enjoy God's blessing.

No mention is made here of Abraham. Perhaps this is the writer's way of indicating that Isaac is to become the new patriarch of the clan, as Rebekah is its new matriarch.

Abraham Shows the Calm Contentment of Faith as He Dismisses His Other Sons Before His Death

25 Abraham took another wife, whose name was Keturah. **²She bore him Zimran, Jokshan, Medan, Midian, Ishbak and Shuah. ³Jokshan was the father of Sheba and Dedan; the descendants of Dedan were the Asshurites, the Letushites and the Leummites. ⁴The sons of Midian were Ephah, Epher, Hanoch, Abida and Eldaah. All these were descendants of Keturah.**

With this section the *"Account of Terah"* comes to a close, as well as the scriptural *record of the life of Abraham.* Moses records a second marriage of Abraham, who lived another thirty-eight years after Sarah died. Luther felt that Abraham ("father of many nations") recognized that his two sons Ishmael and Isaac hardly furnished the background for "many nations." According to Luther, "Abraham saw that he was to beget more children in order to fulfill the promise of Genesis 17:4, and so in faith he proceeded to enter upon another marriage." Despite the fact that Abraham's relation to Keturah is described in 25:1 as a marriage, she is called a "concubine" in 25:6, perhaps because the sacred writer hesitated to give Keturah equal rank with Sarah, the mother of the promised seed.

Although the table of Abraham's descendants through Keturah is brief, it does document the fact that a number of nations did descend from Abraham. The descendants listed here are the *fathers of Arab tribes* who left southern

Rebekah meets Isaac

Palestine and migrated east and southeast. Of Keturah's six sons, only Midian is subsequently mentioned on the pages of Old Testament history, and always in the context of hostility to the covenant people of Israel.

Unfortunately, the mere fact that these nations descended from Abraham did not automatically guarantee that they shared the faith of Abraham. John the Baptist told the religious leaders of his day: "Produce fruit in keeping with repentance, and don't say: 'We have Abraham for our father'" (Luke 3:8). Each succeeding generation of God's people needs to make God's word and his promise its own through faith, or those blessings will be lost through unbelief.

⁵Abraham left everything he owned to Isaac. ⁶But while he was still living, he gave gifts to the sons of his concubines and sent them away from his son Isaac to the land of the east. ⁷Altogether, Abraham lived a hundred and seventy-five years. ⁸Then Abraham breathed his last and died at a good old age, an old man and full of years; and he was gathered to his people. ⁹His sons Isaac and Ishmael buried him in the cave of Machpelah near Mamre, in the field of Ephron son of Zohar the Hittite, ¹⁰ the field Abraham had bought from the Hittites. There Abraham was buried with his wife Sarah. ¹¹After Abraham's death, God blessed his son Isaac, who then lived near Beer Lahai Roi.

Earlier in his life Abraham had learned through bitter experience that this son Ishmael despised Isaac's favored position in the family. To make sure that there would be no misunderstanding after his death, Abraham gave gifts to each of the concubines' sons and sent them away. With this action he made two things clear. First, *he was giving them their freedom*, along with enough money for a good start in life. According to several ancient Mesopotamian law codes that have come down to us, sons of concubines were ordinarily considered slaves and received no inheritance. But more important, Abraham was *making it clear that Isaac*, and only Isaac, *was the bearer of the covenant*, the future head of the clan, the link between Abraham and the Savior. The "Account of Terah" comes to a close with an elaborate obituary of Abraham. His life span was thirty years shorter than his father Terah's, but it's described as "a good old age." According to Genesis 25:26, Abraham lived to see his twin grandsons Esau and Jacob grow up to be young men. He lived to see his wants and his expectations satisfied.

It's also noteworthy here that although Abraham had dismissed the sons of the concubines from his household with gifts, yet Ishmael took part with Isaac in burying Abraham. Since God had named Ishmael to a special honor (Genesis 17:20), he was elevated above Keturah's sons. We are also glad to note that although there had been a separation between Isaac and Ishmael, there was no alienation.

In accordance with Abraham's wishes, and as a final affirmation of his faith that God would keep his promise to make Canaan his people's homeland, Abraham was buried in the cave of Machpelah.

THE SEVENTH ACCOUNT:
OF ISHMAEL
GENESIS 25:12-18

The book of Genesis traces the early history of God's saving activity, which Moses describes in ten "accounts." The first five of these describe God's saving activity *in the original world*, from the time of creation to the flood. The second group of five "accounts" describe God's saving activity *among the patriarchs*. The sixth "account," that of Terah, records how God chose Abraham, Terah's son, and trained him to be the bearer of the covenant promise.

The next two "accounts" are named after Abraham's sons and continue the survey of how God carried out his saving activity. In instances like this, where a double development is to be traced, Moses customarily *treats that branch of the family first which was less important* for carrying out God's covenant, and then devotes *more attention to the primary branch* of the family.

The "Account of Ishmael" is very brief. It consists primarily of names unfamiliar to us. Since Ishmael and his descendants stood outside of the Messianic line, they played no major role in the history of God's ancient people. Ishmael was, nonetheless, a son of Abraham to whom God had made a gracious promise.

¹²**This is the account of Abraham's son Ishmael, whom Sarah's maidservant, Hagar the Egyptian, bore to Abraham. ¹³These are the names of the sons of Ishmael, listed in the order of their birth: Nebaioth the firstborn of Ishmael, Kedar,**

Adbeel, Mibsam, [14] Mishma, Dumah, Massa, [15] Hadad, Tema, Jetur, Naphish and Kedemah. [16]These were the sons of Ishmael, and these are the names of the twelve tribal rulers according to their settlements and camps. [17]Altogether, Ishmael lived a hundred and thirty-seven years. He breathed his last and died, and he was gathered to his people. [18]His descendants settled in the area from Havilah to Shur, near the border of Egypt, as you go toward Asshur. And they lived in hostility toward all their brothers.

God had made it very clear that the covenant blessing was promised to Isaac and his descendants. When Abraham expressed the hope that his older son Ishmael would not be cut off from God's blessing and simply forgotten, God promised that Ishmael, too, would receive a blessing. For Abraham's sake God promised to increase the family of Ishmael, so that it would grow to become a nation. "[Ishmael] will be the father of twelve rulers," God had promised (17:20).

The "Account of Ishmael" is brief, but it's long enough to record *how God kept his promise*. The names of *twelve tribal rulers* from Ishmael's line are listed, ancestors of many of the Arab nations. God's promises do not fail, even those promises given to people outside the mainstream of Messianic history.

Ishmael's descendants settled in the general area of the Sinai peninsula. God had given Hagar this warning about her son: "He will live in hostility toward all his brothers" (16:12). The history of Ishmael's Arab descendants has borne out the truth of this prophecy.

THE EIGHTH ACCOUNT:
OF ISAAC
GENESIS 25:19-35:29

Now that Moses has dealt briefly with the side issue of Ishmael's line, he can return to the main issue. The eighth "account" is that of Isaac, and it begins a new chapter in the history of God's saving activity among the patriarchs.

Birth of the Twins Esau and Jacob

¹⁹**This is the account of Abraham's son Isaac. Abraham became the father of Isaac, ²⁰ and Isaac was forty years old when he married Rebekah daughter of Bethuel the Aramean from Paddan Aram and sister of Laban the Aramean. ²¹Isaac prayed to the LORD on behalf of his wife, because she was barren. The LORD answered his prayer, and his wife Rebekah became pregnant. ²²The babies jostled each other within her, and she said, "Why is this happening to me?" So she went to inquire of the LORD. ²³The LORD said to her, "Two nations are in your womb, and two peoples from within you will be separated; one people will be stronger than the other, and the older will serve the younger." ²⁴When the time came for her to give birth, there were twin boys in her womb. ²⁵The first to come out was red, and his whole body was like a hairy garment; so they named him Esau. ²⁶After this, his brother came out, with his hand grasping Esau's heel; so he was named Jacob. Isaac was sixty years old when Rebekah gave birth to them.**

As we listen to the record of Isaac and Rebekah's marriage, we hear one of the same sad overtones that we heard in the marriage of Abraham and Sarah a generation earlier.

For twenty years God withheld his blessing of children. Growing up under the training of a pious father and mother, Isaac had learned that parents are not the manufacturers of human life, but that God is the creator of it. He uses human fathers and mothers to pass on the gift of life to another generation, but the gift is his to give or to withhold. During those twenty childless years Isaac was concerned, not only because of his natural desire for children, but because he knew that in the present generation he and Rebekah were the only link to the promised Messiah. Isaac therefore begged the LORD, the God of the covenant, to remove Rebekah's barrenness. The LORD listened to his prayer, and Rebekah became pregnant.

In the months ahead she was awed by the miracle stirring within her. But at the same time Rebekah was bothered by something going on within her that she was sure was not normal. There seemed to be a pushing and shoving going on (the Hebrew verb means "to crush," "to oppress"). What was happening, and why?

Like her husband, Rebekah knew whom to ask, and the LORD gave her a surprising answer. She learned, first of all, that *she was to become the mother of twins*, each of whom would be the founder of a nation. She learned, furthermore, that *there would be conflict*, an ongoing rivalry, between them, as well as between their descendants, and that one would overcome the other. Finally Rebekah learned that contrary to the normal order, *"the older will serve the younger."* In the society of that day, normally the firstborn had the position of privilege in the family. It was the first-born who after the father's death became the head of the clan and received a double share of the inheritance. Rebekah learned that in the case of her twin sons God was going to reverse that natural order. The younger of the twins was going to be the stronger, the dominant one. In the centuries ahead his descendants would consistently hold the upper hand over those of the older twin. The younger twin would also be the son who would continue the Messianic line.

St. Paul refers to this in his epistle to the Romans, to illustrate the truth that God's election is an election *of grace.* "Before the twins were born or had done anything good or bad — in order that God's purpose in election might stand: not by works but by him who calls — [Rebekah] was told: 'the older will serve the younger'" (Romans 9:10-12). The fact that back in eternity God chose us as his dear children before we had done anything good or bad, before we were ever born or had come to faith, is traceable only to the grace of God.

When the time came for Rebekah's babies to be born, there was something unusual about each of them. The first was *completely covered with reddish-brown hair.* That earned him the name Esau, which may mean "hairy"; he was also called Edom, which means "red." The younger twin entered the world with his arms stretched out and *holding on to this brother's heel.* His name ("heel-grabber") perpetuated that memory. Someone present at the birth might even have thought he looked like he wanted to hold his brother back so that he himself could be the firstborn. The name his parents chose for him may have been given innocently enough, but as Jacob's life story unfolds his name came to suggest "one who trips up another, who defrauds him." We know that on at least one occasion the older twin interpreted the name Jacob that way (27:36).

²⁷The boys grew up, and Esau became a skillful hunter, a man of the open country, while Jacob was a quiet man, staying among the tents. ²⁸Isaac, who had a taste for wild game, loved Esau, but Rebekah loved Jacob.

As the twins grew older, sharp differences in temperament began to appear. Esau felt at home in the great out-of-doors; he loved the excitement of the hunt. Father Isaac felt attracted to Esau; perhaps he saw in this older son traits he felt lacking in his own personality.

Jacob, on the other hand, "was a quiet man." The exciting and sometimes dangerous life of the hunter was not for him. He preferred the unglamorous but more secure life of the shepherd, like his father and grandfather. Mother Rebekah quite naturally felt closer to the quiet boy who spent more time in and around the tent. We assume that she shared with him the promise the LORD had made before the twins were born. It was unfortunate that each of the parents had a favorite child. That fact provided fertile soil for future problems to sprout — problems as serious as trying to interfere with God's stated intention to transmit the Messianic blessing through Jacob.

Esau Sells the Birthright

29Once when Jacob was cooking some stew, Esau came in from the open country, famished. 30He said to Jacob, "Quick, let me have some of that red stew! I'm famished!" (That is why he was also called Edom.) 31Jacob replied, "First sell me your birthright." 32"Look, I am about die," Esau said. "What good is the birthright to me?" 33But Jacob said, "Swear to me first." So he swore an oath to him, selling his birthright to Jacob. 34Then Jacob gave Esau some bread and some lentil stew. He ate and drank, and then got up and left. So Esau despised his birthright.

We learned earlier that Jacob was perfectly content to let his brother roam the fields, while he stayed closer to home. Here we meet him boiling a pot of lentil soup. It may very well be that he and his older twin had discussed the privileges that went with being the firstborn, and that he had sensed Esau did not value those privileges highly. Even though God had promised those privileges to the younger twin, Esau considered them his rightful property, and apparently so did his father Isaac (see 27:29). Jacob considered those privileges rightfully his and looked for an opportunity to make sure he got them.

His opportunity came on a day when Esau returned from the hunt, famished and exhausted. He smelled and saw what Jacob was preparing and asked for some to eat. Translated literally, his question comes out something like this: "Let me swallow some of that red stuff, that red stuff there!"

With the exception of the forbidden fruit, that bowl of lentil soup has got to be the most expensive meal anybody ever bought. To buy the soup Esau sold his birthright. His attitude was: "I'm going to die sooner or later, anyway, since hunting is dangerous business, and then what good will a promise once made to my grandfather do me?" He attached no value to the rich promises God had made to Abraham and Isaac — promises about *a chosen nation* which would one day own the land of Canaan and about a *Messianic lineage* that would produce the Savior of the world.

Unfortunately Esau passed that attitude down to his descendants, known as the Edomites. They later became bitter enemies of the people of Israel, and God had to pronounce judgment on them.

Esau's attitude is a common one in our day, too. Most people devote their best efforts and most of their time to satisfying their short-term needs: putting food on the table and a roof over their heads and getting the TV set fixed in time for tonight's favorite show. The result is that a lot of people are making good livings, but mighty poor lives.

We see something here in Jacob that *we don't admire*. When your brother is hungry and asks you for food, you don't answer: "I'll sell you some." It's also difficult to appreciate Jacob's lack of trust in God's ability to keep the promise he had announced before Jacob was born. Instead of waiting for God in his own good time to reverse the social custom which awarded the birthright to the oldest son, Jacob grew impatient and thought perhaps he could help God keep his promise.

But we see one trait in Jacob that *we do admire*: he had an appreciation for spiritual values. He knew what was worth having, and he made sure he got it. Although Esau agreed to sell him the birthright for a bowl of soup, Jacob realized Esau could easily change his mind after his stomach stopped growling, or after sober second thoughts the following morning. And so he asked Esau to swear, to call upon God as his witness, that he was transferring the privileges of the firstborn from his name to Jacob's.

"Keep these two pictures before your eyes," Martin Luther once wrote, "because each of us is either an Esau or a Jacob." Esau stands on the pages of the Scripture as a richly blessed man who despised God's blessings and lost them. "See to it," the Scripture warns, "that no one is godless like Esau, who for a single meal sold his inheritance rights as the oldest son. Afterward, as you know, when he wanted to inherit this blessing, he was rejected. He could bring about no change of mind, though he sought the blessing with tears" (Hebrews 12:15-17).

Isaac's Life in a Hostile Society

26 Now there was a famine in the land — besides the earlier famine of Abraham's time — and Isaac went to Abimelech king of the Philistines in Gerar. ²The Lord appeared

to Isaac and said, "Do not go down to Egypt; live in the land where I tell you to live. ³Stay in this land for a while, and I will be with you and will bless you. For to you and your descendants I will give all these lands and will confirm the oath I swore to your father Abraham. ⁴I will make your descendants as numerous as the stars in the sky and will give them all these lands, and through your offspring all nations on earth will be blessed, ⁵ because Abraham obeyed me and kept my requirements, my commands, my decrees and my laws." ⁶So Isaac stayed in Gerar.

Moses' eighth "account" bears Isaac's name. It draws us a picture of the second patriarch which is quite different from that of his father Abraham and of his son Jacob. Abraham was a man whose faith led to resolute action. Jacob's character was often marred by deceit and dishonesty and by his efforts to help God carry out his plan. By contrast, Isaac's faith showed itself in humble service and in submission to the trials and difficulties God permitted to enter his life.

Like his father before him, Isaac lived in the Negev, in south Canaan. And like his father when famine struck, Isaac was minded to head for Egypt to seek relief. His route took him through Philistine territory, along the Mediterranean coast. It was here that God appeared to Isaac and changed his plans.

"Stay where you are," he told Isaac, "and I will bless you here." To make obedience easier, God confirmed to Isaac the oath he'd originally made to Abraham. The land in which Isaac was living would one day belong to his descendants. They would be as numerous as the stars, and through them all nations of the earth would be blessed. Instructed by God's command and encouraged by his promises, Isaac changed his travel plans and remained in the land of the Philistines.

⁷When the men of that place asked him about his wife, he said, "She is my sister," because he was afraid to say, "She is my wife." He thought, "The men of this place might kill me on account of Rebekah, because she is beautiful." ⁸When Isaac had been there a long time, Abimelech king of the Philistines looked down from a window and saw Isaac caressing his wife Rebekah. ⁹So Abimelech summoned Isaac and said, "She is really your wife! Why did you say, 'She is my sister'?" Isaac answered him, "Because I thought I might lose my life on account of her." ¹⁰Then Abimelech said, "What is this you have done to us? One of the men might well have slept with your wife, and you would have brought guilt upon us." ¹¹So Abimelech gave orders to all the people: "Anyone who molests this man or his wife shall surely be put to death."

It was in the land of the Philistines that Satan successfully used a temptation on Isaac which he had twice used on Isaac's father a generation earlier. Critical scholars have claimed that Genesis 26:1-11 is a duplicate version of the incident recorded in 12:10-20 and again in 20:1-18. In their view it happened only once that a patriarch introduced his wife as his sister, but several different literary traditions incorporated this narrative into the Genesis text in three different places. There is, however, no textual support for this view. Although there are some similarities between the three accounts of attempted deception, there are more points of difference, and these are significant. Unlike the earlier accounts, for example, the king here did not take the beautiful woman into his harem, and the realization that she was the patriarch's wife came not through divine revelation but through the king's personal observation.

Once again it was a fear of the consequences that proved
to be the stumbling block for Isaac's faith, as it had been for
Abraham's. When the men of Gerar asked about Rebekah,
Isaac claimed she was his sister, hoping thereby to protect
his own life. It was a pathetic attempt to deceive, considering that he and Rebekah had two children. The vessels
through which God transmitted and later implemented his
promise were frail jars of clay, indeed.

Once again the LORD had to intervene to protect Rebekah,
although not as forcefully as he had in the instances involving Sarah. And once again God's man had to suffer the
humiliation of being rebuked by a heathen. Although Isaac
made a mockery of his faith, and although his pitiful
attempt at deception put his wife and his marriage in jeopardy and endangered the work of God, the LORD preserved
his people and his plan.

**¹²Isaac planted crops in that land and the same year reaped a
hundredfold, because the LORD blessed him. ¹³The man became
rich, and his wealth continued to grow until he became very
wealthy. ¹⁴He had so many flocks and herds and servants that
the Philistines envied him. ¹⁵So all the wells that his father's servants had dug in the time of his father Abraham, the Philistines
stopped up, filling them with earth. ¹⁶Then Abimelech said to
Isaac, "Move away from us; you have become too powerful for
us." ¹⁷So Isaac moved away from there and encamped in the
Valley of Gerar and settled there. ¹⁸Isaac reopened the wells
that had been dug in the time of his father Abraham, which the
Philistines had stopped up after Abraham died, and he gave
them the same names his father had given them. ¹⁹Isaac's servants dug in the valley and discovered a well of fresh water
there. ²⁰But the herdsmen of Gerar quarreled with Isaac's
herdsmen and said, "The water is ours!" So he named the well
Esek, because they disputed with him. ²¹Then they dug another
well, but they quarreled over that one also; so he named it**

Sitnah. [22]He moved on from there and dug another well, and no one quarreled over it. He named it Rehoboth, saying, "Now the LORD has given us room and we will flourish in the land."

Although Isaac must have been embarrassed when the news of his dishonesty spread throughout the region of Gerar, he didn't immediately leave the area. Perhaps the famine persisted, and he had a large household and immense numbers of cattle to feed. In this situation we again see how true the statement of the psalmist is: "[The LORD] does not treat us as our sins deserve, or repay us according to our iniquities" (Psalm 103:10). Moses' statement in the opening verse of this passage, "The LORD blessed him..." sets the tone for the entire passage.

Although nomads don't ordinarily plant crops, since their flocks and herds are constantly on the move, Isaac did plant crops in Gerar (perhaps on a piece of land Abimelech, as a good will gesture, permitted him to use). His crop yield was unusually large — a hundred times the seed grain he had sowed — all the more impressive if famine conditions were still prevailing.

It was clear to everyone, including Isaac, that more than natural causes were at work here. By showering his blessings on the man, God was telling Isaac something. We might have expected that God's *Creator-name* would be used to describe the one who blessed Isaac with that unexpectedly large harvest. But instead the name "the LORD" is used. It was the *covenant God* who was keeping his promise to this important man, reminding him that God didn't need his dishonesty, that he was very well able without Isaac's scheming to keep his promise to bless the family of promise.

He blessed Isaac's fields, and he blessed his flocks. The man grew richer and richer (and remember, Isaac had been the principal heir of a rich father). His flocks and herds grew so numerous that his Philistine neighbors grew envious. They were landowners, and here this alien, living on the land only by their permission, was prospering. Understandably much of the trouble centered around water rights. Water has always been a problem in Canaan, and it surely was here.

Isaac's neighbors showed their spite in several ways. They stopped up the wells from which Isaac's cattle drank, and when that failed to check his prosperity they asked him to leave.

As a resident alien, Isaac had no alternative but to respect the wishes of the landowners. Besides, he was a man of peace, and to avoid conflict he moved from place to place. As he moved, he reopened some of the wells his father had dug. Isaac dug a new well and discovered fresh water in Gerar Valley, but the local herdsmen contested his ownership. Perhaps with a touch of whimsy, Isaac named that well "Argument Well." He let them have it, moved to another area and dug another well. There was argument over the ownership of that one, too, and it was called "Opposition Well." A man of peace, Isaac moved still farther away, dug still another well, and about this one there was no argument. "Plenty of Room" was the name Isaac gave that well.

Despite all the pettiness and the provocation he had encountered, Isaac showed no bitterness. He knew that it was highly unusual to find water in an area adjoining the Sinai Desert. The fact that his servants had found water each time they attempted to dig a well was to him evidence that the LORD of the covenant was blessing Abraham's descendants as he had promised. "The LORD has given us room, and we will flourish in the land."

²³From there he went up to Beersheba. ²⁴That night the LORD appeared to him and said, "I am the God of your father Abraham. Do not be afraid, for I am with you; I will bless you and will increase the number of your descendants for the sake of my servant Abraham." ²⁵Isaac built an altar there and called on the name of the LORD. There he pitched his tent, and there his servants dug a well. ²⁶Meanwhile, Abimelech had come to him from Gerar, with Ahuzzath his personal adviser and Phicol the commander of his forces. ²⁷Isaac asked them, "Why have you come to me, since you were hostile to me and sent me away?" ²⁸They answered, "We saw clearly that the LORD was with you; so we said, 'There ought to be a sworn agreement between us' — between us and you. Let us make a treaty with you ²⁹ that you will do us no harm, just as we did not molest you but always treated you well and sent you away in peace. And now you are blessed by the LORD." ³⁰Isaac then made a feast for them, and they ate and drank. ³¹Early the next morning the men swore an oath to each other. Then Isaac sent them on their way, and they left him in peace. ³²That day Isaac's servants came and told him about the well they had dug. They said, "We've found water!" ³³He called it Shibah, and to this day the name of the town has been Beersheba. ³⁴When Esau was forty years old, he married Judith daughter of Beeri the Hittite, and also Basemath daughter of Elon the Hittite. ³⁵They were a source of grief to Isaac and Rebekah.

By now it had to be evident to the landowners in south Canaan that Isaac's astounding prosperity was more than just the result of hard work plus a streak of good luck. Even their king had to admit to Isaac: "We saw clearly that the LORD was with you." Once they realized that, they realized something else: it's not only *difficult* to oppose God; it's *useless*. The king realized that since Isaac was going to continue to prosper, he might as well join him as try to oppose him.

Once again Isaac moved with his large household and all his flocks, this time to Beersheba, on the edge of the desert. We're not told why he moved. Had the old rivalries with the local herdsmen over grazing and water rights flared up again?

At any rate, it was here that the Savior God appeared to Isaac the second time, to *reassure him.* "Do not be afraid," he told Isaac. Isaac realized that the strife with the landowners at Gerar had been unpleasant and could get mean. Now he was reassured that although he would remain a stranger in the land of promise he was not alone. His God had told him: "I am with you."

God had one more thing to say. He *restated the promise* originally given to Abraham, reminding Isaac that despite his unworthiness he was the heir of the Messianic promises. God promised to compensate Abraham's descendants for the obedience Abraham had demonstrated in taking the LORD at his word.

In response to the LORD's assurance, Isaac built an altar at Beersheba and proclaimed the LORD's name in public worship. He had learned from his father to give God the credit not only for individual blessings of body and soul, but also for revealing his sacred truth to chosen people in each generation.

Proverbs 16:7 tells us: "When a man's ways are pleasing to the LORD, he makes even his enemies live at peace with him." One day at Beersheba Isaac experienced the truth of this proverb when he received a surprise visit from the king of Gerar with two of his top officials. "A while back you asked me to leave your country. Why do you now come to me?" he asked them. They answered: "We did not molest you but always treated you well." Even after Isaac had deceived them, they showed him the courtesy of permitting him to live in their land. True, they had stopped up his wells and later asked him to leave, but they had dismissed him in peace. Now they wanted an alliance of friendship, and Isaac was willing to make that.

The chapter ends on an unhappy note involving Isaac's older son Esau. Although he was the object of his father's special love, Esau did not return that love. Without the knowledge of his parents and against their will, he married two Hittite wives. With this action he first of all showed *disrespect for God's wishes* regarding marriage as the lifelong union of two people devoted to each other. But with his action Esau showed *disrespect also for God's promises* to his grandfather and his father. Esau had little interest either in being a part of the covenant nation or in having his descendants share the promised blessings. The Hittite wives he chose were unbelievers who couldn't train their children to love the LORD's word and to cling to his promises. Instead they were members of Canaanite tribes who would fall under the judgment of God.

27 **When Isaac was old and his eyes were so weak that he could no longer see, he called for Esau his older son and said to him, "My son." "Here I am," he answered. ²Isaac said, "I am now an old man and don't know the day of my death. ³Now then, get your weapons — your quiver and bow — and go out to the open country to hunt some wild game for me. ⁴Prepare me the kind of tasty food I like and bring it to me to eat, so that I may give you my blessing before I die."**

As God carries out his great good plan for mankind he must often overrule the stubborn, misguided efforts of his own children. This chapter paints a picture of the family of Isaac which is not flattering — not to any of the four people involved.

Isaac was the head of this important family. As husband and father, he had the primary responsibility of leading his family in the way of the LORD. Isaac was now an old man, in declining health; he seems here to have been on a sickbed (see 27:31). His failing eyesight and his generally weakened condition may have reminded him he didn't have long to live. Before he died, however, Isaac wanted to transmit the right of the firstborn to his favored son. It would be at a special meal that he would announce: "Esau will succeed me as head of the family and will receive a double share of my estate," which must indeed have been sizable. Isaac therefore asked Esau to perform one last act of obedience, after which he would receive the blessing of the firstborn.

It's difficult to appreciate or even to defend Isaac's action. He knew that God had designated Jacob, not Esau, to be the bearer of the promise. Perhaps Isaac had convinced himself that even if he gave the blessing to Esau God's original intent would somehow not be violated. Furthermore, even though Esau was his favorite son, Isaac overlooked the flaws in Esau's character which disqualified him from being the covenant link. At the conclusion of the last chapter we noted that by marrying two heathen women Esau had shown total indifference to the LORD's promise. Isaac's intention here to reverse God's decree was sinful.

Esau shared in the guilt of that sin. Surely his parents had told him about the special revelation God had given them prior to his birth: "The older will serve the younger" (25:23). Furthermore, in agreeing to his father's plan, Esau violated his oath to Jacob at the time he had sold the birthright.

⁵Now Rebekah was listening as Isaac spoke to his son Esau. When Esau left for the open country to hunt game and bring it

back, ⁶ Rebekah said to her son Jacob, "Look, I overheard your father say to your brother Esau, ⁷'Bring me some game and prepare me some tasty food to eat, so that I may give you my blessing in the presence of the Lord before I die.' ⁸Now, my son, listen carefully and do what I tell you: ⁹Go out to the flock and bring me two choice young goats, so I can prepare some tasty food for your father, just the way he likes it. ¹⁰Then take it to your father to eat, so that he may give you his blessing before he dies." ¹¹Jacob said to Rebekah his mother, "But my brother Esau is a hairy man, and I'm a man with smooth skin. ¹²What if my father touches me? I would appear to be tricking him and would bring down a curse on myself rather than a blessing." ¹³His mother said to him, "My son, let the curse fall on me. Just do what I say; go and get them for me."

The other two members of the family don't exactly come off smelling like roses here, either. Rebekah's scheming and Jacob's lying do little to glorify God or to demonstrate that they trusted God to carry out his promises. It has been argued, by Luther among others, that it was not wrong for Jacob to take what God had promised to him. God may indeed overrule the evil plans of sinful people, but surely he does not need them or approve of them. All four members of Jacob's family were involved here in dishonest business, and for that each of them paid an awful price, as we shall see.

When Rebekah overheard Isaac explain his perverse plan to give the blessing to his favorite son, she was desperate. She realized that when the patriarchs pronounced the Messianic blessing they did so *as the LORD's spokesmen*, speaking for him as though he were pronouncing the blessing himself. She was afraid that if she didn't act quickly, before Esau returned from hunting, Jacob would forever have lost the blessing. Rebekah knew, on the one hand, that her husband was evading the express will of God. But in

225

her otherwise laudable attempt to further God's will, she likewise stooped to dishonesty. In Rebekah's reaction to Isaac's plan we can hear her sinful nature speaking. Her motivation was not the glory of God but the welfare of her favorite son. She would use her cooking ability to deceive her husband into thinking that the goat meat he was eating was wild game, and she convinced Jacob to deceive his nearly blind father into giving him the coveted blessing while imagining he was blessing Esau.

Jacob's response was entirely unbecoming to the heir of God's Messianic promise. Instead of, "Mother, are you asking me to lie?" his response was, "What if I get caught? I could end up with my father's curse resting on me instead of his blessing!" Rebekah's quick "I'll take the curse. You do as I say" satisfied Jacob.

¹⁴So he went and got them and brought them to his mother, and she prepared some tasty food, just the way his father liked it. ¹⁵Then Rebekah took the best clothes of Esau her older son, which she had in the house, and put them on her younger son Jacob. ¹⁶She also covered his hands and the smooth part of his neck with the goatskins. ¹⁷Then she handed to her son Jacob the tasty food and the bread she had made. ¹⁸He went to his father and said, "My father." "Yes, my son," he answered. "Who is it?" ¹⁹Jacob said to his father, "I am Esau your firstborn. I have done as you told me. Please sit up and eat some of my game so that you may give me your blessing." ²⁰Isaac asked his son, "How did you find it so quickly, my son?" "The LORD your God gave me success," he replied. ²¹Then Isaac said to Jacob, "Come near so I can touch you, my son, to know whether you really are my son Esau or not." ²²Jacob went close to his father Isaac, who touched him and said, "The voice is the voice of Jacob, but the hands are the hands of Esau." ²³He did not recognize him, for his hands were hairy like those of his brother Esau; so he blessed him. ²⁴"Are you really my son Esau?" he

asked. "I am," he replied. ²⁵Then he said, "My son, bring me some of your game to eat, so that I may give you my blessing." Jacob brought it to him and he ate; and he brought some wine and he drank.

The narrative of Jacob's deception is presented in abundant detail. To make his lie more believable, Jacob even put on some of Esau's clothing, knowing it would have Esau's characteristic scent. He tried to imitate Esau's voice, so that the aged patriarch was confused. When Jacob said: "I am Esau," he was not only lying through his teeth, he was behaving lovelessly to his father, to whom he owed obedience and respect. When his father asked how he could have returned from the hunt so quickly, Jacob even dragged God's name into the deceit. That's blasphemy.

In spite of the elaborately staged deception, Isaac was still not convinced. "Come near so I can touch you, my son." To this Luther comments: "If I had been Jacob I would have dropped the dish and run from the scene as though my head were on fire." But Jacob, wearing Esau's clothing and with the skin of goats covering his neck and arms, drew closer and acted out the lie his mother had concocted.

²⁶Then his father Isaac said to him, "Come here, my son, and kiss me." ²⁷So he went to him and kissed him. When Isaac caught the smell of his clothes, he blessed him and said,

"Ah, the smell of my son
    is like the smell of a field
    that the LORD has blessed.
²⁸May God give you of heaven's dew
    and of earth's richness —
    an abundance of grain and new wine.
²⁹May nations serve you
    and peoples bow down to you.

> Be lord over your brothers,
> and may the sons of your mother bow down to you.
> May those who curse you be cursed
> and those who bless you be blessed."

Isaac, still confused but unwilling to suspect his own flesh and blood of deceiving him, finally pronounced the blessing on Jacob. We'll want to note his words carefully. He said nothing about the Messianic blessing but pronounced only *material prosperity* on the son he imagined to be Esau. "May God give you of heaven's dew." In the Negev, a land of minimal rainfall, the dew is an important source of moisture, especially during the long rainless season. "Be lord over your brothers, and may the sons of your mother bow down to you." This was a statement Isaac had no business making. He was *trying to divert to Esau a blessing God had designated for Jacob.*

The fact that God overruled Isaac's presumptuous self-will and saw to it that Jacob got the promised blessing does not excuse the treachery of either Rebekah or Jacob. Sin remains sin, and both mother and son lived to feel God's displeasure over their sin. The fact that God on another occasion overruled Judas's dastardly act of betraying the Savior and actually used it to rescue a whole world of sinners will not excuse Judas on Judgment Day, either.

30After Isaac finished blessing him and Jacob had scarcely left his father's presence, his brother Esau came in from hunting. 31He too prepared some tasty food and brought it to his father. Then he said to him, "My father, sit up and eat some of my game, so that you may give me your blessing." 32His father Isaac asked him, "Who are you?" "I am your son," he answered, "your firstborn, Esau." 33Isaac trembled violently and said, "Who was it, then, that hunted game and brought it

to me? I ate it just before you came and I blessed him — and
indeed he will be blessed!" ³⁴When Esau heard his father's
words, he burst out with a loud and bitter cry and said to his
father, "Bless me — me too, my father!" ³⁵But he said, "Your
brother came deceitfully and took your blessing." ³⁶Esau said,
"Isn't he rightly named Jacob? He has deceived me these two
times: He took my birthright, and now he's taken my blessing!" Then he asked, "Haven't you reserved any blessing for
me?" ³⁷Isaac answered Esau, "I have made him lord over you
and have made all his relatives his servants, and I have sus-
tained him with grain and new wine. So what can I possibly do
for you, my son?" ³⁸Esau said to his father, "Do you have only
one blessing, my father? Bless me too, my father!" Then Esau
wept aloud.

³⁹His father Isaac answered him,
"Your dwelling will be
away from the earth's richness,
away from the dew of heaven above.
⁴⁰You will live by the sword
and you will serve your brother.
But when you grow restless,
you will throw his yoke
from off your neck."

It's not difficult to understand why Isaac trembled violently when Esau returned from the hunt; it's a shattering
discovery to learn one has been deceived by one's own wife
and son. But is it possible Isaac trembled also because he
realized he had just gone head-to-head with God and come
off second-best? Isaac was keenly aware that *God had
rebuked him*, and properly so. He recognized humbly that
God had intervened and that he was helpless to change
what God had done. Penitently Isaac now acted and spoke
in faith (Hebrews 11:20). When Esau asked for a blessing
he answered: "What can I possibly do for you?"

Isaac was unable to give Esau a *blessing*: God had made that very clear. But what the Spirit of God did direct Isaac to give his older son was a *prediction* of what lay ahead for Esau and his descendants. "Your dwelling will be away from earth's richness, away from the dew." Esau's descendants lived in the land south of the Dead Sea — a barren, rocky land, ill-suited for agriculture. It is perhaps worth noting that Isaac's words to his sons about the dew contain a play on words, a pun. The phrases translated "of heaven's dew" (v.28) and "away from the dew of heaven" (v.39) are identical in Hebrew. The sacred writer used a form of literary artistry to make the contrast between the father's words to Jacob and those to Esau all the more striking.

If the future homeland of Esau's descendants, the Edomites, was not suited for agriculture, what did the future hold? *"You will live by the sword,"* by continued violence, "and *you will serve your brother.*" The truthfulness of this prophecy was demonstrated during the reigns of King Saul (1 Samuel 14.47) and of King David (2 Samuel 8:14). The Edomites would be a second-rate power, although on occasion they would manage temporarily to throw off their yoke (2 Kings 8:20-22; 21:8-10).

[41]Esau held a grudge against Jacob because of the blessing his father had given him. He said to himself, "The days of mourning for my father are near; then I will kill my brother Jacob." [42]When Rebekah was told what her older son Esau had said, she sent for her younger son Jacob and said to him, "Your brother Esau is consoling himself with the thought of killing you. [43]Now then, my son, do what I say: Flee at once to my brother Laban in Haran. [44]Stay with him for a while until your brother's fury subsides. [45]When your brother is no longer angry with you and forgets what you did to him, I'll send word for you to come back from there. Why should I lose both of you in one day?" [46]Then Rebekah said to Isaac, "I'm disgusted with

living because of these Hittite women. If Jacob takes a wife from among the women of this land, from Hittite women like these, my life will not be worth living."

Esau realized at once that the future his father had predicted for him was anything but bright. Blinded by anger, he failed to see God's overruling hand in what had happened. One thought, and only one thought, filled his mind: "My brother has again cheated me out of my blessing, and I'm going to kill him."

The whole unlovely transaction, recorded in minute detail in this chapter, must be regarded as a net loss for Rebekah and Jacob. They actually *gained nothing* God hadn't already promised them. Instead they both *lost much*. When Rebekah learned of Esau's murderous scheme, she arranged to have Jacob go to her brother's house in Haran, 500 miles north, "for a while." The Lord of the calendar stretched that "a while" out to twenty years, and by the time her favorite son returned home Rebekah was dead.

And Jacob? God saw to it that he received more than the blessing. Jacob had to enroll in God's training school. Although the blessings of the birthright entitled him to a double share of the inheritance of a very wealthy father, Jacob left home with only a staff in his hand (Genesis 32:10). As he later looked back over his life he said: "My years have been few and difficult" (Genesis 47:9). For the next twenty years God would be working to purify the faith of this patriarch, to cleanse it of self-trust and dishonesty and falsehood.

When Rebekah spoke to her husband about sending Jacob to her family, we note that she again used a subtle deception. Her real reason for sending him out of the country was to spare his life, as well as Esau's. Rebekah realized that she stood to lose both of her sons. If Esau had fulfilled his threat and murdered his twin, Jacob's relatives and friends would have taken vengeance on the murderer.

But Rebekah didn't reveal her real reason to her husband. Instead she used her unhappiness over Esau's Hittite wives to try to persuade Isaac to find a wife for Jacob among her relatives in Mesopotamia, as Abraham had done a generation earlier. This is the last statement of Rebekah we have in the Scripture. At this point she is dismissed from the biblical narrative.

God's Training Program: From Jacob to Israel

28 So Isaac called for Jacob and blessed him and commanded him: "Do not marry a Canaanite woman. ²Go at once to Paddan Aram, to the house of your mother's father Bethuel. Take a wife for yourself there, from among the daughters of Laban, your mother's brother. ³May God Almighty bless you and make you fruitful and increase your numbers until you become a community of peoples. ⁴May he give you and your descendants the blessing given to Abraham, so that you may take possession of the land where you now live as an alien, the land God gave to Abraham." ⁵Then Isaac sent Jacob on his way, and he went to Paddan Aram, to Laban son of Bethuel the Aramean, the brother of Rebekah, who was the mother of Jacob and Esau.**

The household of Isaac was in turmoil. Mother and son had teamed up to deceive the aged father, and the older son hated his twin brother enough to kill him. At this point God once again intervened. He *overruled the petty plans of people, so that his good purpose was served.* Look at some particulars.

If Isaac had been bitter at having been betrayed by his own son, we could perhaps have understood. But his words show he humbly accepted the way things had turned out and was reconciled to the son who had deceived him. When he spoke to Jacob, there was no bitterness in his words, and no criticism.

Rebekah had wanted Jacob to leave Canaan and to go to her relatives for a short time, until things at home had settled down. God overruled Rebekah's plan in favor of his own. Jacob didn't return home until twenty years later. He left as *Jacob, the "heel-grabber,"* the one who was determined to get ahead of the other person, even if that meant taking unfair advantage of him. He returned twenty years later as *Israel, "the man who struggled with God and overcame."* How did God produce this change?

Jacob's Flight from Esau

Part of God's training program for Jacob was to help him, first of all, *to put down his sinful nature*, his inclination to deceive, to seek his own advantage at the expense of others. God let Jacob experience the results of the treachery he had perpetrated on his father. Jacob had to learn the hard way. He, the homebody, had to leave his home. Being forced to run for your life — and with a guilty conscience, at that — is not an easy way to leave one's childhood home and family. "The way of transgressors is hard," God has told us (Proverbs 13:15, KJV). God had to check those sinful impulses, to help Jacob drown his old sinful nature. If unchecked, they could only hamper his spiritual growth as God's child and heir of the promise.

But another part of God's training program for Jacob was *to teach him he could trust God's promises.* Instead of informing Jacob that his dishonesty disqualified him from being the heir of the Messianic promises, God let him hear those promises again — first from the lips of his aged father, and then directly from the lips of God.

233

When Isaac had previously announced the promises to Jacob, he did so unwillingly, thinking he was addressing Esau. Now of his own volition Isaac blessed Jacob. He knowingly and willingly granted the full Messianic blessing to the son who had not been *his* choice, but *God's*. "By faith Isaac blessed Jacob," the apostle tells us (Hebrews 11:20).

"May God Almighty...give you and your descendants the blessing of Abraham!" Jacob's descendants would grow into a large nation and would take possession of the land in which Jacob now lived as an alien. Through one great Descendant Jacob would actually "become a community of peoples." In Christ all nations would share in the blessings originally promised to Abraham and now transmitted to Jacob. Surely this promise of God to an undeserving sinner strengthened the new life of faith struggling to survive and to grow within the heart of Jacob.

And so Jacob set out on the 500-mile journey to the city of Haran, in the country north of Canaan. Today this land is known as Syria; in Old Testament times it was called Aram, home of the Aramean people and of the Aramaic language. As he left, Jacob could hardly have been proud of the fact that through deception he had managed to get the promise he wanted. He was frightened, haunted by the memory of his guilt, but cheered by the promise his father had just repeated to him.

⁶Now Esau learned that Isaac had blessed Jacob and had sent him to Paddan Aram to take a wife from there, and that when he blessed him he commanded him, "Do not marry a Canaanite woman," ⁷ and that Jacob had obeyed his father and mother and had gone to Paddan Aram. ⁸Esau then realized how displeasing the Canaanite women were to his father Isaac; ⁹ so he went to Ishmael and married Mahalath, the sister of

**Nebaioth and daughter of Ishmael son of Abraham, in addition
to the wives he already had.**

Before continuing the narrative of Jacob's journey to his
relatives in Aram, Moses inserts a note about Esau which
once again illustrates his spiritual dullness. Apparently he
hadn't realized how unacceptable his two Canaanite wives
were to his parents. Now he learned that Jacob had been
sent to his mother's relatives to find a proper wife. In a
belated attempt to win his father's good will, Esau took a
third wife, a daughter of Ishmael, from a branch of Abraham's family which was not only outside the promise but
actually hostile to it. Esau's action helps us to understand
better why God did not use Esau in his plan.

¹⁰**Jacob left Beersheba and set out for Haran. ¹¹When he
reached a certain place, he stopped for the night because the
sun had set. Taking one of the stones there, he put it under his
head and lay down to sleep. ¹²He had a dream in which he saw a
stairway resting on the earth, with its top reaching to heaven,
and the angels of God were ascending and descending on it.
¹³There above it stood the LORD, and he said: "I am the LORD,
the God of your father Abraham and the God of Isaac. I will
give you and your descendants the land on which you are lying.
¹⁴Your descendants will be like the dust of the earth, and you
will spread out to the west and to the east, to the north and to
the south. All peoples on earth will be blessed through you and
your offspring. ¹⁵I am with you and will watch over you wherever you go, and I will bring you back to this land. I will not
leave you until I have done what I have promised you."**

Jacob had now been on the road for several days. He had
traveled about 70 miles, and as the sun set he was bone-
weary and lonely. God had a special treat in store for that
young man that night, and the Hebrew text calls attention to

it in a striking way. Moses three times uses a word which calls attention to *something totally unexpected.* (It's the word sometimes translated "behold!"). We might paraphrase Moses' words: "Jacob was dreaming and — a stairway! . . . and angels! . . . and, look, there's the LORD himself!"

To make sure this lonely traveler did not lose heart, the Savior-God surprised him with a vision of God himself. After putting a stone at his head, Jacob had dropped off to sleep under the open sky. He had a dream, in which he saw a stairway reaching from where he was into heaven. On the stairway angels were *ascending,* carrying Jacob's needs and requests to God, as well as *descending,* returning with God's help and assurance. It is interesting to note that the Lord Jesus once referred to Jacob's dream, comparing himself to the stairway Jacob saw (John 1:51). In Jesus Christ God built a bridge on which he comes to us and on which we can return to him.

The climax of Jacob's dream came when the LORD himself stood at the head of the heavenly stairway and repeated to Jacob the promises originally given to his grandfather Abraham. The very promises which Jacob had tricked his father into giving him he now heard from the lips of God. Here was no deception. Jacob was to know where he stood with God. God considered him a child — weak and sinful, but reconciled to God! God promised Jacob that his descendants would be numerous, that they would inherit the land, and that through their one great Descendant all nations on earth would be blessed. And to the lonely, frightened traveler God added one more promise: "I will not leave you but will bring you back to this land."

¹⁶When Jacob awoke from his sleep, he thought, "Surely the LORD is in this place, and I was not aware of it." ¹⁷He was afraid and said, "How awesome is this place! This is none other than

the house of God; this is the gate of heaven." ¹⁸Early the next morning Jacob took the stone he had placed under his head and set it up as a pillar and poured oil on top of it. ¹⁹He called that place Bethel, though the city used to be called Luz. ²⁰Then Jacob made a vow, saying, "If God will be with me and will watch over me on this journey I am taking and will give me food to eat and clothes to wear ²¹ so that I return safely to my father's house, then the LORD will be my God ²² and this stone that I have set up as a pillar will be God's house, and of all that you give me I will give you a tenth."

Jacob woke up the next morning with some mixed emotions. He was grateful for what God had told him, but the dominant emotion was a feeling of awe. Although he was a stranger surrounded by heathen, he had been in the presence of God. In this strange place God had established contact with him, had talked to him, had blessed him. He called the name of the place Bethel (Hebrew for "the house of God").

To commemorate the miraculous vision he'd had, Jacob took the stone which had been at his head and *set it on end* as sort of a monument. He *anointed it* with oil to set it apart, to mark the precious spot where God had appeared to him. Jacob wanted to return to this place later and build an altar (35:7).

God's unexpected goodness to Jacob at Bethel brought forth one more response: *he made a vow*. His statement contained an "if" clause (language teachers call this the "protasis") and a "then" clause (the "apodosis"), and it isn't immediately clear from the text where the division between the two is to be made. It might seem that a translation preferable to that adopted by the NIV and the KJV would be to have the "then" clause begin at verse 22. Jacob's statement would then read: "If God will be with me...and if the LORD will be my God, then this stone that I have set up will be God's house." Regardless of which of the two translations we choose, however, we dare not regard Jacob's words as bargaining with God ("God, if you do such-and-so for me, then you'll be my God, otherwise not"). The Savior God had assured Jacob that he was his God, and that Jacob was a weak but dearly-loved child. How happy we can be that our status before God is a matter determined by God's undeserved love, and is not dependent on our behavior!

Jacob Is Deceived By Laban

29 Then Jacob continued on his journey and came to the land of the eastern peoples. ²There he saw a well in the field, with three flocks of sheep lying near it because the flocks were watered from the well. The stone over the mouth of the well was large. ³When all the flocks were gathered there, the shepherds would roll the stone away from the well's mouth and water the sheep. Then they would return the stone to its place over the mouth of the well. ⁴Jacob asked the shepherds, "My brothers, where are you from?" "We're from Haran," they replied. ⁵He said to them "Do you know Laban, Nahor's grandson?" "Yes, we know him," they answered. ⁶Then Jacob asked them, " Is he well?" "Yes, he is," they said, "and here comes his daughter Rachel with the sheep." ⁷"Look," he said, "the sun is still high; it is not time for the flocks to be gathered. Water the sheep and take them back to pasture." ⁸"We can't," they replied,"until all the flocks are gathered and the stone has been rolled away from the mouth of the well. Then we will water the sheep."

The Bible is silent about the long, lonely miles Jacob traveled to the home of his relatives. If he traveled on foot, the trip probably took him the better part of a month. After his experience at Bethel, though, there was a song in his heart. The Savior God had miraculously appeared to him and promised to protect him and to provide for him.

Now his long journey to Haran was about over. "The land of the eastern peoples" here refers to the territory north and east of Damascus, in present-day Syria. Haran had always been special for Jacob. It was the childhood home of his mother Rebekah. It was the city where his great-grandfather Terah and his grandfather Abraham had lived. And now Haran was to become important to Jacob for another reason. In a way that reminds us of how God had once guided Abraham's servant to find a wife for Isaac (Genesis 24) God now led Jacob to the relatives he was seeking. Even more, he led Jacob to a well where he met the lovely young woman who would be his wife.

Although the sun was still high in the sky, several herdsmen had led their flocks to a well which was capped by a large stone, heavy enough to discourage passers-by from removing it. Apparently by common consent the herdsmen of Haran waited before opening the well until all the herds had been assembled. When Jacob inquired about Laban he was told: "Here comes his daughter Rachel with the sheep."

⁹While he was still talking with them, Rachel came with her father's sheep, for she was a shepherdess. ¹⁰When Jacob saw Rachel daughter of Laban, his mother's brother, and Laban's sheep, he went over and rolled the stone away from the mouth of the well and watered his uncle's sheep. ¹¹Then Jacob kissed Rachel and began to weep aloud. ¹²He had told Rachel that he was a relative of her father and a son of Rebekah. So she ran and told her father. ¹³As soon as Laban heard the news about Jacob, his sister's son, he hurried to meet him. He embraced him and kissed him and brought him to his home, and there Jacob told him all these things. ¹⁴Then Laban said to him, "You are my own flesh and blood."

As he looked at Rachel, Jacob realized that the speedy success he had enjoyed on his mission was no coincidence.

239

He remembered how a generation earlier at a well in Haran God had granted Abraham's servant success on a similar assignment. Singlehandedly he removed the stone covering the well and drew water for Rachel's flocks. After she learned who the kind stranger was, she ran home to tell her parents. Father Laban hurried out to the well to meet his sister's son and to invite him into his home. "There Jacob told him all these things" — the reason for his coming to Haran, and his joy at meeting his lovely cousin.

15After Jacob had stayed with him for a whole month, Laban said to him, "Just because you are a relative of mine, should you work for me for nothing? Tell me what your wages should be." 16Now Laban had two daughters; the name of the older was Leah, and the name of the younger was Rachel. 17Leah had weak eyes, but Rachel was lovely in form, and beautiful. 18Jacob was in love with Rachel and said, "I'll work for you seven years in return for your younger daughter Rachel."

19Laban said, "it's better that I give her to you than to some other man. Stay here with me." 20So Jacob served seven years to get Rachel, but they seemed like only a few days to him because of his love for her. 21Then Jacob said to Laban, "Give me my wife. My time is completed, and I want to lie with her."

Up to now Jacob's mission to Haran had been remarkably trouble-free. God had led him without delay to his destination and had prepared a warm welcome in his uncle's home. Things would soon change, however. *A new session in the Lord's training school was about to begin* for Jacob.

Jacob had been in Haran only a month, but that was long enough for Laban to recognize what an unusually capable herdsman he was, a valuable man to have around. When Laban offered Jacob a job he *seemed to have Jacob's interest at heart*. "Why should you work for me for nothing? Tell me what your wages should be." What could be fairer?

Throughout all his dealings with Jacob, however, Laban showed himself to be not only greedy, but *willing to take advantage of another person.* He had noticed that Jacob's heart was drawn to the beautiful cousin he had met at the well and shrewdly asked himself: "Could I perhaps use Jacob's love for her to my advantage?" When he permitted Jacob to name his wages, Laban *recognized that Jacob was bargaining from a point of weakness.* The very reason he had come to Haran was to find a wife, and he had found one — Laban's daughter. Laban knew, furthermore, that although Jacob was the son of a very wealthy father he had no money to offer a prospective father-in-law as bride-price (see the comment on Genesis 24:53), and so he would have to earn it. Jacob was at a distinct disadvantage in these salary negotiations.

At this point Moses provides information the reader will need to know in order to understand what follows. We're introduced to Leah, Rachel's older and less attractive sister. In a culture where bright, flashing eyes were considered a mark of beauty in a woman, Leah's "weak eyes" were a handicap, especially when she was compared to her sister, a young woman of lovely face and figure.

Jacob's response to Laban's offer, "Name your wages," strikes one as extremely generous. In return for the privilege of marrying Rachel he would offer Laban seven years of his labor as the bride-price. Laban knew Jacob *couldn't afford to set the terms of his employment too low.* That could be interpreted either as "I can't afford any more" or "She isn't worth more to me." Jacob would also want to be sure his offer would be one Laban couldn't refuse. By accepting the bride-price offered Laban got the benefit, for the next seven years, of Jacob's skill in handling cattle.

²²So Laban brought together all the people of the place and gave a feast. ²³But when evening came, he took his daughter Leah and gave her to Jacob, and Jacob lay with her. ²⁴And Laban gave his servant girl Zilpah to his daughter as her maid-servant. ²⁵When morning came, there was Leah! So Jacob said to Laban, "What is this you have done to me? I served you for Rachel, didn't I? Why have you deceived me?" ²⁶Laban replied, "It is not our custom here to give the younger daughter in marriage before the older one. ²⁷Finish this daughter's bridal week: then we will give you the younger one also, in return for another seven years of work." ²⁸And Jacob did so. He finished the week with Leah, and then Laban gave him his daughter Rachel to be his wife. ²⁹Laban gave his servant girl Bilhah to his daughter Rachel as her maidservant. ³⁰Jacob lay with Rachel also, and he loved Rachel more than Leah. And he worked for Laban another seven years.

Laban, greedy man that he was, *wanted another seven years of free labor* from his new son-in-law, and he devised a mean way to get it. Jacob, the "heel-grabber," the one who usually managed to get ahead of the other person by fair means or foul, met his match in Laban.

Laban treacherously arranged it that on the night when Jacob should have received Rachel as his bride he got Leah instead. The question is inevitable: "How could a man as intelligent as Jacob have let this happen to him?" The answer usually given is that Leah was in on the deception, that she was veiled, and in the fragrant darkness of the wedding night spoke softly so her voice would not be recognized. In addition Jacob was caught completely off guard; he had no reason to suspect foul play.

The real answer to the question, however, goes deeper. *God permitted this unhappiness to enter Jacob's life.* God had been displeased with Jacob when, to make sure he would receive the birthright, he had deceived his own father. God recognized as flaws in Jacob's character his *willingness to compromise his principles* for the sake of personal gain, and his *reliance on his own cleverness* to outwit an adversary and get ahead of him. A loving Father also knew that these impurities in Jacob's spiritual makeup could only hinder the great plans he had for this man.

God therefore had to help Jacob learn to *despair of his own cleverness.* For the next seven years Jacob had plenty of time to ask himself: "You're really quite clever, aren't you — clever enough to get yourself married to a woman you didn't want!" Seven years also offered plenty of opportunity to reflect on the irony of his situation. Leah, at her father's direction, had deceived him, just as he, at Rebekah's suggestion, had deceived his father.

As part of Jacob's training program, God was teaching him that dishonesty and self-trust are repugnant to God. This is not to say that God still held Jacob's sin against him. As believers we know that our sin has been forgiven, and that God's forgiveness is complete. Christ's substitutionary work on our behalf has intercepted God's judgment, and we know we are at peace with him. Jacob knew that, too. But the results of the sin we have committed may remain to plague us, to serve as a necessary reminder that yielding to the promptings of our sinful nature can only frustrate the grace of God. God's chastisement also reminds us that we need the help God has promised to put down the evil nature that opposes his good will for us.

The following morning in response to Jacob's anguished cry, "What is this you have done to me?" Laban offered a halfhearted explanation which smacks of further deception. If it was unthinkable in Haran for a father to give his younger daughter in marriage before her older sister, why hadn't Laban mentioned that to Jacob when he first asked to marry Rachel?

We marvel at the patience of Jacob. Was God's chastening already having an effect? Luther remarked: "I wouldn't have put up with this. I'd have taken Laban to court and demanded that he be ordered to give me the bride for whom I served him under contract." Perhaps mindful of how he had taken advantage of his brother and his aged father, Jacob submitted meekly to the dreadful disappointment God had permitted to enter his life. He declined to humiliate Leah by demanding that the marriage be annulled. Instead, as Laban suggested, he spent the bridal week with Leah and then married Rachel. For the rest of his life he had to live in a divided family, the husband of two wives, one of whom he loved more, the other less.

³¹When the LORD saw that Leah was not loved, he opened her womb, but Rachel was barren. ³²Leah became pregnant and gave birth to a son. She named him Reuben, for she said, "It is because the LORD has seen my misery. Surely my husband will love me now." ³³She conceived again, and when she gave birth to a son she said, "Because the LORD heard that I am not loved, he gave me this one too." So she named him Simeon. ³⁴Again she conceived, and when she gave birth to a son she said, "Now at last my husband will become attached to me, because I have borne him three sons." So he was named Levi. ³⁵She conceived again, and when she gave birth to a son she said, "This time I will praise the LORD." So she named him Judah. Then she stopped having children.

The LORD compensated Leah for the difficult role she had to play as the less-loved wife by giving her a son, whom she named *Reuben*. She explained the name as a double word play. The two Hebrew words making up the name mean "Look! a son!" Now her husband's line would be carried on for at least another generation. Leah explained,

Rachel and Leah

however, that the Hebrew components of the name sound very much like "He has seen my misery."

With the LORD's continued blessing Leah bore several more children. The names she chose for them hint at the ongoing heartache Leah felt at having to be satisfied with second place in her husband's heart. She named her second son *Simeon* ("one who hears") because "The LORD heard that I am not loved." The third son's name *Levi* ("attached") expressed her hope that her marriage could be a true union of two hearts, a hope that was never realized. When she bore her fourth son she named him *Judah* ("praise"). This was not just a fond wish: Leah was expressing her determination: "I will praise the LORD!"

Leah's fourth son is noteworthy, for two reasons. It was from his name that the Jewish people got their name. More important, it was through this fourth son that Leah, the less-loved wife, became an ancestress of King David and of Jesus Christ. God used even a shabby case of deception to bring Leah into the Savior's family line.

> Oh, the depth of the riches
> of the wisdom and knowledge of God!
> How unsearchable his judgments,
> and his paths beyond tracing out!

(Romans 11:33)

Jacob's Family

30 When Rachel saw that she was not bearing Jacob any children, she became jealous of her sister. So she said to Jacob, "Give me children, or I'll die!" ²Jacob became angry with her and said, "Am I in the place of God, who has kept you from having children?" ³The she said, "Here is Bilhah, my maidservant. Sleep with her so that she can bear children for me and that through her I too can build a family." ⁴So she gave him her servant Bilhah as a wife. Jacob slept with her, ⁵ and she became pregnant and bore him a son. ⁶Then Rachel said, "God has vindicated me; he has listened to my plea and given me a son." Because of this she named him Dan. ⁷Rachel's servant Bilhah conceived again and bore Jacob a second son. ⁸Then Rachel said, "I have had a great struggle with my sister, and I have won." So she named him Naphtali. ⁹When Leah saw that she had stopped having children, she took her maidservant Zilpah and gave her to Jacob as a wife. ¹⁰Leah's servant Zilpah bore Jacob a son. ¹¹Then Leah said, "What good fortune!" So she named him Gad. ¹²Leah's servant Zilpah bore Jacob a second son. ¹³Then Leah said, "How happy I am! The women will call me happy." So she named him Asher.

Christians today are often bothered by the fact that in Old Testament times some of God's people practiced polygamy without being rebuked by God for violating his creation regulation regarding marriage. How do you answer that?

Several truths of the Scripture need emphasizing here. Truth #1: The *Scripture makes no attempt to hide the sins* of God's ancient people. It is clear that they did things they should not have done. Truth #2: *God does not approve of everything he tolerates.* Genesis 30 points out the awful problems that resulted from the fact that Jacob had more than one wife. The loving relationship between sisters was destroyed. Closest friends became bitter rivals. Truth #3: *God can overrule* the evil intent of people and bend their wicked deeds *to serve his good purposes.* God actually used Jacob's polygamous marriage relationship to produce the twelve sons who fathered the twelve tribes of Israel.

This page of the Bible makes it clear that polygamy brings out the worst in marriage partners. Unable to handle the truth that she was childless while her sister had given birth to four sons, Rachel took out her frustrations on her husband. "Give me children, or I'll die," of a broken heart.

Rachel showed the same impatience Sarah had showed earlier when she gave Abraham her maid Hagar to bear a child for her. When Bilhah bore Jacob a son, Rachel named him *Dan* explaining "God has *vindicated* me: he has stood up for my rights." There's a certain irony in the fact that Rachel sidestepped God's will in ordering her husband into an illicit sexual union and then praised God for blessing her disobedience with a child. When Bilhah bore a second son, Rachel named him *Naphtali* ("my struggle"), explaining: "In my struggle with my sister I have won. My sister's fruitfulness seems to be at an end, and mine is just beginning!" What had been designed by God to be a loving relationship between two sisters had degenerated into a fleshly struggle between rivals. The Scripture surely is not silent about the evils of polygamy.

Rachel's boastful words seem to have fired the competitive spirit in Leah. Not willing to be outdone, she gave her maid Zilpah to Jacob, and the man who had traveled to Haran to find a God-fearing wife now found himself instead with a fourth bed-partner. That relationship led to the birth of two more sons. Leah named the first one *Gad* ("good fortune"), explaining: "What good fortune! Now my sister won't get ahead of me after all!" Zilpah's second son was named *Asher* ("happy"). Leah explained: "How happy I am! Because of my fruitfulness the women will call me happy!"

Reading the crude details of the unholy competition between the sisters is not pleasant. It is good to remind ourselves that the petty jealousies and the family bickering Jacob had to put up with in his marriage were part of the mechanism the LORD was using to train Jacob, to make him more alert to sinful tendencies in his own personality, to assist him in putting down his sinful nature, and to shape him into God's kind of man.

[14]During wheat harvest, Reuben went out into the fields and found some mandrake plants, which he brought to his mother Leah. Rachel said to Leah, "Please give me some of your son's mandrakes." [15]But she said to her, "Wasn't it enough that you took away my husband? Will you take my son's mandrakes too?" "Very well," Rachel said, "he can sleep with you tonight in return for your son's mandrakes." [16]So when Jacob came in from the fields that evening, Leah went out to meet him. "You must sleep with me," she said. "I have hired you with my son's mandrakes." So he slept with her that night. [17]God listened to Leah, and she became pregnant and bore Jacob a fifth son. [18]Then Leah said, "God has rewarded me for giving my maidservant to my husband." So she named him Issachar. [19]Leah conceived again and bore Jacob a sixth son. [20]Then Leah said, "God has presented me with a precious gift. This time my husband will treat me with honor, because I have borne him six sons." So she named him Zebulun. [21]Some time later she gave birth to a daughter and named her Dinah.

By this time Reuben, Leah's firstborn, was old enough to accompany the reapers out into the field at the time of harvest. We're told he found some yellow berries and brought them to his mother. She recognized them as mandrakes, also known as "love apples," thought to be a cure for barrenness and to promote human fertility.

When Rachel learned of this she asked her sister for some of the mandrakes. Since her maid Bilhah had apparently stopped bearing children, Rachel was interested in any means that offered to help her have a child. Her request brought an angry reply from her older sister. "You've already taken my husband from me (although I had him first). Now you want to take everything I have!"

Jacob became aware of this unlovely exchange when he returned from the harvest field and was informed that his evening schedule had been planned for him by his two wives. God again blessed that sexual union, and Leah bore a fifth son named *Issachar* ("reward"). Leah, who knew that Jacob was destined to be the ancestor of a great nation, explained her baby's name. "God is rewarding me for giving my maid to my husband," to guarantee the fulfillment of God's promise. The fact that she said this does not mean that the opinion she expressed about God was true.

When Leah bore her sixth son, she named him *Zebulun* ("honor"). The name expressed her hope that now her husband might treat her with the honor which he had so far reserved for his beloved Rachel. Dinah is the only one of Jacob's daughters named here, although we know from Genesis 37:35 that there were more. Moses' reasons for mentioning Dinah here may be to prepare the reader for the events recorded in Genesis 34.

²²Then God remembered Rachel; he listened to her and opened her womb. ²³She became pregnant and gave birth to a son and said, "God has taken away my disgrace." ²⁴She named him Joseph, and said, "May the LORD add to me another son."

Enough time had elapsed for Rachel to realize the mandrakes hadn't worked. The words "God *listened to her* and opened her womb" indicate that she had prayed to the One who doesn't need love potions to grant the blessings of pregnancy and birth.

We have met the expression "*God remembered*" earlier in the book of Genesis. In 8:1 Moses reported that God "remembered Noah" and caused the floodwaters to recede. By using the term Moses was not suggesting that God had temporarily forgotten about Noah, or in this case about Rachel. His love had continually surrounded them. But now he *made his loving care evident*. Rachel became pregnant and bore a son. Although previously she had been impatient and even haughty, she now gave credit to God for having taken away the disgrace of her childlessness. She named her son *Joseph* ("may he add") with the prayer: "May the LORD add to me another son!" Several years later Rachel's prayer was answered (35:16-20), but at the cost of her life.

²⁵After Rachel gave birth to Joseph, Jacob said to Laban, "Send me on my way so I can go back to my own homeland. ²⁶Give me my wives and children, for whom I have served you, and I will be on my way. You know how much work I've done for you." ²⁷But Laban said to him, "If I have found favor in your eyes, please stay. I have learned by divination that the LORD has blessed me because of you." ²⁸He added, "Name your wages, and I will pay them." ²⁹Jacob said to him, "You know how I have worked for you and how your livestock has fared under my care. ³⁰The little you had before I came has increased greatly, and the LORD has blessed you wherever I have been. But now, when may I do something for my own household?" ³¹"What shall I give you?" he asked. "Don't give me anything," Jacob replied. "But if you will do this one thing for me, I will go on tending your flocks and watching over them: ³²Let me go through all your flocks today and remove from them every speckled or spotted sheep, every dark-colored lamb and every spotted or speckled goat. They will be my wages. ³³And my honesty will testify for me in the future, whenever you check on the wages you have paid me. Any goat in my possession that is not speckled or spotted, or any lamb that is not dark-colored, will be considered stolen." ³⁴"Agreed," said Laban. "Let it be as you have said."

³⁵That same day he removed all the male goats that were streaked or spotted, and all the speckled or spotted female goats (all that had white on them) and all the dark-colored lambs, and he placed them in the care of his sons. ³⁶Then he put a three-day journey between himself and Jacob, while Jacob continued to tend the rest of Laban's flocks.

Jacob had now served out the seven years he owed Laban in return for Rachel; now he was eager to return to Canaan, his home. Not only was he looking forward to leaving Haran, where he had tasted the bitterness of dishonesty and heartache, he was eager to return to his parents and to the land of promise. He therefore asked his father-in-law for permission to leave.

Laban was aware of how he had been enriched during the years Jacob took care of his flocks and responded: "Please stay." This was a *selfish request*, as can be seen from Jacob's answer: "When may I do something for my household?" Although Laban had benefited from Jacob's expertise in raising cattle, his greed had been evident in his unwillingness to share the profits with Jacob. And now he stood to lose this valuable man. It's not surprising that he offered Jacob a blank check. "What shall I give you, to induce you to stay?"

Jacob's answer seems to have caught Laban completely off-guard. To appreciate that, we'll need to know that in the ancient Near East sheep were normally solid white in color, goats dark brown or black.

Speckled or spotted animals were unusual, as were black lambs. Laban could hardly believe his ears when he learned that all Jacob was asking for were *the uncommon animals, the "irregulars."* And if Laban were to find any normally colored animals in with Jacob's flock, he could consider them to have been stolen from his. One would like to think that by making this offer Jacob was leaving his economic future totally in God's hands.

Laban must have thought his son-in-law's offer was foolish, but he agreed to it instantly, since he certainly stood to come out ahead. We might have hoped Laban would decline and instead offer a counter-proposal more favorable to Jacob. But again his greed surfaced here, as did his suspicious nature. Jacob had suggested: "Let *me* go through your flocks today and remove the unusually colored animals." Instead Laban *took it upon himself* to remove the uncommon animals from his flocks, insinuating that he couldn't trust Jacob to do it. And then, to add insult to injury, he placed *his own sons* in charge of *Jacob's* flocks. As still a further expression of his suspicions, he put a three-day journey between the major flock (under Jacob's care) and Jacob's irregulars. That would guarantee, first, that there could be no crossbreeding between the two flocks and, secondly, that Jacob's share of the flock would remain small.

³⁷Jacob, however, took fresh-cut branches from poplar, almond and plane trees and made white stripes on them by peeling the bark and exposing the white inner wood of the branches. ³⁸Then he placed the peeled branches in all the watering troughs, so that they would be directly in front of the flocks when they came to drink. When the flocks were in heat and came to drink, ³⁹ they mated in front of the branches. And they bore young that were streaked or speckled or spotted. ⁴⁰Jacob set apart the young of the flock by themselves, but made the rest face the streaked and dark-colored animals that belonged to Laban. Thus he made separate flocks for himself and did not put them with Laban's animals. ⁴¹Whenever the stronger females were in heat, Jacob would place the branches in the troughs in front of the animals so they would mate near the branches, ⁴² but if the animals were weak, he would not place them there. So the weak animals went to Laban and the strong ones to Jacob. ⁴³In this way the man grew exceedingly prosperous and came to own large flocks, and maidservants and menservants, and camels and donkeys.

Jacob resented the unloving and unwarranted suspicion his father-in-law showed toward him. Under Laban's persistent provocation, Jacob's old tendency to practice deception showed itself here. He yielded to the temptation to take matters into his own hands. Since his father-in-law was once again taking advantage of him, Jacob decided to give him a taste of his own medicine.

To induce solid-colored animals to bear spotted young, Jacob cut branches and peeled off the bark to expose spots or stripes of white wood underneath. At breeding time he would put these branches into the animals' drinking troughs. Whether this trick actually had prenatal influence on the female sheep and goats and actually resulted in the birth of larger numbers of "irregulars" is really beside the point. Whether this technique is scientifically accurate or just country superstition doesn't matter here. The point is that Jacob, the "heel-grabber," listened to the whispering of his evil nature, which urged him: "Don't get angry; get even!" This was not Jacob's new nature speaking; the shenanigans at breeding time was not evidence of a new life of faith. Jacob was not yet ready to graduate from the Lord's training school.

Believing that his strategy had worked, Jacob added several refinements. When speckled or spotted young were born he separated them from their mothers as soon as possible and let them mingle with the rest of the flock, to encourage interbreeding. And he began to limit the use of his peeled branch technique, using it only when the strong animals were breeding. By this selective breeding he built a flock of strong animals for himself, leaving the weaker animals for Laban's flock.

In the vision God had granted Jacob at Bethel years earlier (28:15) he had promised to bless Jacob, but he surely did not need Jacob's scheming to help him keep his promise. God later made it clear to Jacob that he blessed him *not because of* his scheming *but in spite of* it (31:10-12).

Jacob Leaves Laban

31 Jacob heard that Laban's sons were saying, "Jacob has taken everything our father owned and has gained all this wealth from what belonged to our father." **²And Jacob noticed that Laban's attitude toward him was not what it had been. ³Then the LORD said to Jacob, "Go back to the land of your fathers and to your relatives, and I will be with you."**

For six more years — that makes twenty in all — the tug-of-war between Laban and Jacob went on. Jacob did everything he knew to guarantee that there would be larger numbers of newborn cattle that were irregular in color. Laban, on the other hand, changed Jacob's wages repeatedly. In spite of such dishonesty, however, the LORD continued to bless Jacob, and his growing prosperity irritated Laban and his sons. They looked upon him not as a member of their family, not as a man whom God had blessed. They saw him only as an outsider who through dishonesty had managed to get his hands on what was rightfully their inheritance.

News of this bad blood reached Jacob's ears. He became more and more convinced: "The time has come for me to leave."

The LORD, the God of the covenant, settled the matter for Jacob in a dream one night. As the bearer of the Messianic promise, Jacob did not belong in Haran, but in Canaan, the future homeland of his descendants. Jacob realized, of course, that for him to return home meant facing Esau. Was Esau still seeking to kill him? God's promise to Jacob made it easier for him to obey.

⁴So Jacob sent word to Rachel and Leah to come out to the fields where his flocks were. ⁵He said to them, "I see that your father's attitude toward me is not what it was before, but the

God of my father has been with me. ⁶You know that I've worked for your father with all my strength, ⁷ yet your father has cheated me by changing my wages ten times. However, God has not allowed him to harm me. ⁸If he said, 'The speckled ones will be your wages,' then all the flocks gave birth to speckled young; and if he said, 'The streaked ones will be your wages,' then all the flocks bore streaked young. ⁹So God has taken away your father's livestock and has given them to me. ¹⁰In breeding season I once had a dream in which I looked up and saw that the male goats mating with the flock were streaked, speckled or spotted. ¹¹The angel of God said to me in the dream, 'Jacob.' I answered, 'Here I am.' ¹²And he said, 'Look up and see that all the male goats mating with the flock are streaked, speckled or spotted, for I have seen all that Laban has been doing to you. ¹³I am the God of Bethel, where you anointed a pillar and where you made a vow to me. Now leave this land at once and go back to your native land.' "

Jacob's first job was to convince his wives that the time had come to return to Canaan. He called them out to the fields, so they could speak privately. He recounted the sacrificial, faithful service he had given their father for twenty years, only to be rewarded with suspicion and dishonesty and ill will. To keep peace Jacob had repeatedly allowed Laban to change the terms of their wage agreement and to tilt in in his own favor. But no matter how often Laban revised the agreement, the LORD saw to it that Jacob came out ahead. "And," Jacob added, "if the rapid increase in the size of my flocks and herds alone were not a clear indication that the LORD has blessed me, God told me that in a strange dream."

Jacob identified the one who had sent the dream as "the angel of God," a reference to God himself (verse 13). We have met this speaker several times before in Genesis — when he appeared to Hagar (16:7-11), and to Abraham

(22:11.14-16). The Son of God himself appeared to Jacob at this critical time. Jacob may have thought that his work of peeling branches with his pocket knife had contributed to his success as a herdsman, but the dream showed him that God was controlling even the details of his cattle breeding. In his dream Jacob saw Laban's flocks during the breeding season. Although Laban's cattle were the solid-colored ones the only male goats that were mating were the irregulars, which meant that all of their offspring would belong to Jacob. The dream served as a gentle reminder to Jacob that if God wanted to grant him material blessing he didn't need Jacob's help.

Jacob's dream ended with God's clear directive: "Now *leave* this land at once and *go back* to your native land." To make obedience easier for Jacob, God identified himself as "the God of Bethel." Twenty years earlier it had been *at Bethel* that God had appeared to Jacob with some precious promises.

"I'll give you and your descendants this land."

"Your descendants will be as numerous as the dust of the earth."

"All people on earth will be blessed through you."

"I will watch over you and bring you back to this place."

In the face of a direct command from God, and in view of the promises of God, *Jacob* knew that his assignment was clear. But what did *his wives* think about leaving Haran and moving to Canaan?

14Then Rachel and Leah replied, "Do we still have any share in the inheritance of our father's estate? 15Does he not regard us as foreigners? Not only has he sold us, but he has used up what was paid for us. 16Surely all the wealth that God took away from our father belongs to us and our children. So do whatever God has told you."

¹⁷Then Jacob put his children and his wives on camels, ¹⁸ and he drove all his livestock ahead of him, along with all the goods he had accumulated in Paddan Aram, to go to his father Isaac in the land of Canaan. ¹⁹When Laban had gone to shear his sheep, Rachel stole her father's household gods. ²⁰Moreover, Jacob deceived Laban the Aramean by not telling him he was running away. ²¹So he fled with all he had, and crossing the River, he headed for the hill country of Gilead.

Jacob may have been surprised at this wives' immediate willingness to leave their childhood home. They, too, had been aware of a change in their father's attitude — not only toward Jacob, but toward them. "He no longer looks upon us as daughters," they said, "but as foreigners," as slaves whom one uses only for his own advantage.

Another action of their father's that embittered them was that "he has *used up* what was paid for us." According to Mesopotamian law a father was supposed to *retain* a portion of the price paid for his daughter at the time of her marriage. He could invest it, but he was supposed to return it to her if at some in her life she needed it, since the bride-price was the daughter's insurance policy. Because Laban had selfishly appropriated what Jacob had paid for Leah and Rachel with fourteen years of labor, they felt that whatever Jacob had gotten from their father was rightfully theirs.

One of the little ironies of Jacob's checkered career is that twenty years earlier he'd had to flee Canaan to go to Haran. Now he had to flee Haran to return to Canaan. He was able to leave without being detected because Laban had put considerable distance between his flocks and Jacob's (30:36). Jacob also timed his leave to coincide with Laban's sheep-shearing, a time of special activity.

A detail in this episode that puzzles Bible students is Rachel's theft of her father's household gods. Various reasons have been advanced to explain her thievery. Some have thought she was *secretly an idolatress* and actually looked to these little gods for protection. Some scholars feel there was *economic significance* in possessing the father's gods, that after the father's death the child who inherited the father's gods succeeded him as head of the clan. If this is so, we can understand why Laban was so upset at the thought that Jacob had his household gods.

At any rate, Jacob's large caravan — including wives and children, manservants and maidservants, cows and sheep and goats, camels and donkeys — headed out south from Haran. We get some idea of the size of Jacob's flocks and herds when, in advance of his meeting with Esau (recorded in the next chapter of Genesis), he sent Esau a gift of *580 animals*. The large caravan crossed the Euphrates river and slowly made its way toward Canaan. After a week they had reached the land of Gilead, east of the Sea of Galilee, leaving a trail that could not have been difficult for Laban to follow.

²²On the third day Laban was told that Jacob had fled. ²³Taking his relatives with him, he pursued Jacob for seven days and caught up with him in the hill country of Gilead. ²⁴Then God came to Laban the Aramean in a dream at night and said to him, "Be careful not to say anything to Jacob, either good or bad." ²⁵Jacob had pitched his tent in the hill country of Gilead when Laban overtook him, and Laban and his relatives camped there too. ²⁶Then Laban said to Jacob, "What have you done? You've deceived me, and you've carried off my daughters like captives in war. ²⁷Why did you run off secretly and deceive me? Why didn't you tell me, so I could send you away with joy and singing to the music of tambourines and harps? ²⁸You didn't even let me kiss my grandchildren and my daughters good-by. You have done a foolish thing. ²⁹I have the power to harm you; but last night the God of

your father said to me, 'Be careful not to say anything to Jacob, either good or bad.' ³⁰Now you have gone off because you longed to return to your father's house. But why did you steal my gods?"

Laban picked up the trail three days later when he learned that Jacob had left. Just before he caught up with Jacob, Laban had a dream in which God warned him not to try to harm his son-in-law. It's conceivable that a bitter and vengeful man, with a small force of armed men, could simply have taken the livestock and forced Jacob and his household back to Haran, this time as slaves.

Laban's greeting to his son-in-law was: "What have you done?" Answering his own question, he accused Jacob of dealing deceitfully with him, of treating his daughters like prisoners of war, and of stealing his household gods. There's hypocrisy in his words, as he described himself as a hurt father who had enjoyed a tender and loving relationship with his daughters. He pretended that he had nothing but respect and goodwill for Jacob, whereas both of them knew better. Laban probably came closest to the truth when he admitted that only the fear of God's vengeance had restrained him from resorting to violence.

³¹Jacob answered Laban, "I was afraid, because I thought you would take your daughters away from me by force. ³²But if you find anyone who has your gods, he shall not live. In the presence of our relatives, see for yourself whether there is anything of yours here with me; and if so, take it." Now Jacob did not know that Rachel had stolen the gods. ³³So Laban went into Jacob's tent and into Leah's tent and into the tent of the two maidservants, but he found nothing. After he came out of Leah's tent, he entered Rachel's tent. ³⁴Now Rachel had taken the household gods and put them inside her camel's saddle and was sitting on them. Laban searched through everything in the

tent but found nothing. ³⁵Rachel said to her father, "Don't be angry, my lord, that I cannot stand up in your presence; I'm having my period. So he searched but could not find the household gods.

³⁶Jacob was angry and took Laban to task. "What is my crime?" he asked Laban. "What sin have I committed that you hunt me down? ³⁷Now that you have searched through all my goods, what have you found that belongs to your household? Put it here in front of your relatives and mine, and let them judge between the two of us. ³⁸I have been with you for twenty years now. Your sheep and goats have not miscarried, nor have I eaten rams from your flocks. ³⁹I did not bring you animals torn by wild beasts; I bore the loss myself. And you demanded payment from me for whatever was stolen by day or night. ⁴⁰This was my situation: The heat consumed me in the daytime and the cold at night, and sleep fled from my eyes. ⁴¹It was like this for the twenty years I was in your household. I worked for you fourteen years for your two daughters and six years for your flocks, and you changed my wages ten times. ⁴²If the God of my father, the God of Abraham and the Fear of Isaac, had not been with me, you would surely have sent me away empty-handed. But God has seen my hardship and the toil of my hands, and last night he rebuked you."

It must have been difficult for Jacob to keep a straight face as he listened to Laban's self-righteous tirade. Everybody present knew that Laban's charges against Jacob were simply not true, and Jacob saw no need to respond to each of them. Unaware that Rachel had stolen her father's household gods, he invited Laban to see for himself that his charge of thievery was untrue. And if he should happen to find his gods with some member of Jacob's household, that person would die.

Rachel appears to have inherited her father's cunning. As Laban proceeded to search through all of Jacob's tents and baggage, Rachel hid the gods in her camel's saddle and managed to keep her father from looking for them there.

It was then that Jacob exploded in anger. "What is my crime? What sin have I committed that you hunt me down like a common thief? I served you faithfully for twenty years, and you know your livestock received the best of care. While I was out on the range away from home, I never killed any of your animals for food." (Clay tablets discovered at the site of ancient Nuzi record lawsuits brought by cattle owners against herdsmen, for slaughtering animals without permission.) "If one of your animals was torn by wild beasts or was stolen, you demanded compensation from me. I *entered your employ* a pauper, and if the God of my fathers hadn't been looking out for my welfare, I would *still* be a pauper. That is the God who spoke to you last night!"

⁴³Laban answered Jacob, "The women are my daughters, the children are my children, and the flocks are my flocks. All you see is mine. Yet what can I do today about these daughters of mine, or about the children they have borne? ⁴⁴Come now, let's make a covenant, you and I, and let it serve as a witness between us." ⁴⁵So Jacob took a stone and set it up as a pillar. ⁴⁶He said to his relatives, "Gather some stones." So they took stones and piled them in a heap, and they ate there by the heap. ⁴⁷Laban called it Jegar Sahadutha, and Jacob called it Galeed. ⁴⁸Laban said, "This heap is a witness between you and me today." That is why it was called Galeed. ⁴⁹It was also called Mizpah, because he said, "May the LORD keep watch between you and me when we are away from each other. ⁵⁰If you mistreat my daughters or if you take any wives besides my daughters, even though no one is with us, remember that God is a witness between you and me." ⁵¹Laban also said to Jacob, "Here is this heap, and here is this pillar I have set up between you and me. ⁵²This heap is a witness, and this pillar is a witness,

262

that I will not go past this heap to your side to harm you and that you will not go past this heap and pillar to my side to harm me. [53]May the God of Abraham and the God of Nahor, the God of their father, judge between us." So Jacob took an oath in the name of the Fear of his father Isaac. [54]He offered a sacrifice there in the hill country and invited his relatives to a meal. After they had eaten, they spent the night there. [55]Early the next morning Laban kissed his grandchildren and his daughters and blessed them. Then he left and returned home.

Jacob's emotional outburst must have cut Laban like a knife to the heart. There was no way he could refute Jacob's charges. Wanting to save face before his relatives he claimed that his love for his daughters and his grandchildren prevented him from forcibly reclaiming what rightfully belonged to him. His suspicious nature showed itself again when he asked Jacob to make a covenant, a solemn contract, never to return to take revenge. Jacob was perfectly willing to agree to this, and sealed the agreement with an oath.

As visible testimony to the agreement, a large stone was set on end as a pillar, and additional stones were gathered into a heap. Laban gave it its name in Aramaic, Jacob in Hebrew. The two names mean the same thing: "a heap of witness." The stone monument was also called Mizpah ("watchtower").

For Jacob the stones represented a monument to a *peaceful separation*. Laban gave the monument an ugly significance. "May the LORD keep watch between you and me." In other words, may the LORD keep an eye on Jacob and prevent him from harming me. And, Jacob, if you mistreat my daughters, I may not be around to see it, but this monument will be a constant reminder that *God* sees what you're doing." It was an *unkind word, full of suspicion*. To emphasize the solemnity of the contract, Laban invoked the God of Nahor (his grandfather) and the God of Abraham (Jacob's grandfather). This is usually interpreted as evidence that Laban was a polytheist.

Since he was thankful that an unpleasant chapter in his life had been brought to a peaceful conclusion, Jacob offered a sacrifice to God. His long absence from his home, his painful twenty-year exile in the household of Laban, were at last coming to an end.

Laban, too, returned home. For two successive generations, Abraham's relatives in Haran had provided wives for men who were bearers of the covenant promise. But since the rest of Laban's family was *outside the Messianic line*, Laban is at this point dismissed from the pages of Genesis. From this point on, the reader's attention will be directed away from the land of Aram to the land of promise, where Jacob's descendants were to grow into a great nation.

Jacob's Spiritual Crisis

32 **Jacob also went on his way, and the angels of God met him. ²When Jacob saw them, he said, "This is the camp of God!" So he named that place Mahanaim.**

Jacob had now been enrolled in the LORD's training school for twenty years. The master Teacher had worked persistently and purposefully with his problem student. He patiently sought to purify Jacob's faith of the impurities that weakened it, impurities like deceitfulness and self-reliance. Although throughout those years of God's training Jacob was constantly tempted to revert to his old ways of thinking, the chapter before us offers convincing evidence that God's training program had been successful.

After Laban headed back to his home north of Canaan, Jacob and his large caravan continued their journey south.

Now Jacob's thoughts turned to his reunion with his brother Esau, a confrontation that promised to be far more dangerous than the one with Laban had been. Would Esau meet him with love in his heart, or with blood in his eye and a dagger in his hand?

Twenty years earlier, when Jacob had first left home, *God had permitted him to see angels* in a dream at Bethel. There Jacob had seen angels carrying his prayers to God and returning with God's help. Now Jacob was returning home, and God again let him see angels, except this time not in a dream. Jacob was wide awake when "the angels of God met him." Angels are normally invisible; they don't have flesh and bone and blood. But at this critical juncture in Jacob's life God wanted to reassure him that he was not heading into an uncertain future all alone. He therefore *let Jacob see two encampments of angels* (to his left and his right, or ahead of him and behind him). Though unseen, "the angel of the LORD encamps around those who fear him and he delivers them" (Psalm 34:8).

³Jacob sent messengers ahead of him to his brother Esau in the land of Seir, the country of Edom. ⁴He instructed them; "This is what you are to say to my master Esau: 'Your servant Jacob says, I have been staying with Laban and have remained there till now. ⁵I have cattle and donkeys, sheep and goats, menservants and maidservants. Now I am sending this message to my lord, that I may find favor in your eyes.' " ⁶When the messengers returned to Jacob, they said, "We went to your brother Esau, and now he is coming to meet you, and four hundred men are with him."

While still in Haran, Jacob must have learned that Esau had moved away from his father's household and settled in the land of Edom. That was south of the Dead Sea, perhaps a hundred miles from where Jacob was now encamped.

Esau had apparently gathered a group of family and friends and followers who later conquered the inhabitants of Edom and took possession of their land.

Jacob sent messengers to bring this double message to his twin brother:

"I, your brother, am coming to meet you"; and

"I, your servant, humbly request your good will."

Jacob's reference to his livestock holdings would assure Esau that Jacob's purpose in returning home was not to file his claim for a double share of his father's possessions. He didn't need that, and he didn't want that.

The messengers brought back no reply from Esau. They did, however, bring Jacob the ominous report that Esau was on his way to meet him with 400 men. Apparently, then, Esau still bore a grudge.

⁷In great fear and distress Jacob divided the people who were with him into two groups, and the flocks and herds and camels as well. ⁸He thought, "If Esau comes and attacks one group, the group that is left may escape." ⁹Then Jacob prayed, "O God of my father Abraham, God of my father Isaac, O LORD, who said to me, 'Go back to your country and your relatives, and I will make you prosper,' ¹⁰I am unworthy of all the kindness and faithfulness you have shown your servant. I had only my staff when I crossed this Jordan, but now I have become two groups. ¹¹Save me, I pray, from the hand of my brother Esau, for I am afraid he will come and attack me, and also the mothers with their children. ¹²But you have said, 'I will surely make you prosper and will make your descendants like the sand of the sea, which cannot be counted.' "

When Jacob heard the news his messengers had brought back, he anticipated a hostile confrontation with Esau. He immediately *took steps to minimize his losses* if the meeting with his brother turned ugly and led to bloodshed. He divid-

266

ed the people who were with him, as well as his livestock, into two groups. If Esau's men attacked one group, perhaps the other could escape.

And then he *had a talk with God.* Throughout the last few chapters of Genesis we have repeatedly observed attitudes and actions of Jacob that we would not want to imitate. Not so here. Jacob's prayer to God before meeting Esau is a *model prayer* which can teach us much that will improve our prayer life.

He first of all *confessed his unworthiness* to have God answer his prayer. "I am unworthy of all the kindness and faithfulness you have shown your servant." The word translated "kindness" stresses God's covenant mercy, the kindness he shows people not because they deserve it, but because in his covenant God has placed himself under obligation to them. What a far cry this humility is from the attitude Jacob had displayed earlier in life, when his motto seemed to be: "I'm entitled to this, and I'm going to make sure I get it!" When in his prayer Jacob referred to God's "faithfulness," he couldn't help contrasting it with the fickleness he had given God in return. Jacob realized very well that he had no right to come barging into God's throne room and expect God to hear him out.

Another characteristic of effective prayer which we can learn from Jacob is to *admit our inability* by ourselves to handle the problems that face us, and to *declare our total dependence on God.* Twenty years earlier Jacob wouldn't have been ready to say that. At that time in his life he might instead have said; "Let's see: I've got to think of a way to outsmart Esau. That shouldn't be too difficult. I did it once; I ought to be able to do it again." Not now. Now his prayer was: "Save me, I pray, from the hand of my brother...."

A third aspect of God-pleasing prayer which we can learn from Jacob is to *remind God of his promise*. Listen to Jacob's prayer: "LORD, you promised me:

'I will surely make you prosper.

I will make your descendants like the sand of the sea.'

If Esau comes here tomorrow and puts my household to the sword, your promise would fail. LORD of the covenant, keep your promise!"

What a marvelous prayer! Jacob was not bitter. ("Lord, Esau is an unspiritual fellow, and a mean one at that. Put him in his place.") There was no feeble attempt to excuse his own sin. ("Lord, I know I probably shouldn't have lied to my father, but under the circumstances can't you understand why I did?") Simply: "Lord, you promised!" Martin Luther said it well: "The only ground on which godly men can stand in times of trouble is God's word."

¹³He spent the night there, and from what he had with him he selected a gift for his brother Esau: ¹⁴ two hundred female goats and twenty male goats, two hundred ewes and twenty rams, ¹⁵ thirty female camels with their young, forty cows and ten bulls, and twenty female donkeys and ten male donkeys. ¹⁶He put them in the care of his servants, each herd by itself, and said to his servants, "Go ahead of me, and keep some space between the herds." ¹⁷He instructed the one in the lead: "When my brother Esau meets you and asks, 'To whom do you belong, and where are you going, and who owns all these animals in front of you?' ¹⁸Then you are to say, 'They belong to your servant Jacob. They are a gift sent to my lord Esau, and he is coming behind us.' " ¹⁹He also instructed the second, the third and all the others who followed the herds: "You are to say the same thing to Esau when you meet him. ²⁰And be sure to say, 'Your servant Jacob is coming behind us.' " For he thought, "I will pacify him with these gifts I am sending on ahead; later, when I

see him, perhaps he will receive me." ²¹So Jacob's gifts went on
ahead of him, but he himself spent the night in the camp.

Jacob was not a fatalist ("What will be will be"). He
knew *God often uses human means to carry out his good
will.* Jacob therefore took one more significant action which
he hoped God might use to produce a change in Esau's attitude.

He assembled whatever livestock he could quickly lay his
hands on into five herds, one each of goats, sheep, camels
("the Cadillac of the desert"), cows, and donkeys — a total
of 580 animals. He appointed drivers for each of the herds,
and directed them to *offer the herds, one at a time, to Esau
as a gift.* The first group of animals to meet Esau would be
a herd of 220 goats — a very generous gift in itself. Some
time later another herd would appear on the scene, and
another, and another. Each time, when Esau would ask
about the herd, he was to be told: "They're a gift from your
servant Jacob, and he is coming behind us." If each of the
five herds came separately, the size of Jacob's gift would be
more likely to impress Esau. Jacob also hoped that this pro-
cedure would delay Esau's arrival and would allow more
time for his anger to cool down.

²²That night Jacob got up and took his two wives, his two
maidservants and his eleven sons and crossed the ford of the
Jabbok. ²³After he had sent them across the stream, he sent over
all his possessions. ²⁴So Jacob was left alone, and a man wrestled with him till daybreak. ²⁵When the man saw that he could
not overpower him, he touched the socket of Jacob's hip so that
his hip was wrenched as he wrestled with the man. ²⁶Then the
man said, "Let me go, for it is daybreak." But Jacob replied, "I
will not let you go unless you bless me." ²⁷The man asked him,
"What is your name?" "Jacob," he answered. ²⁸Then the man
said, "Your name will no longer be Jacob, but Israel, because

you have struggled with God and with men and have overcome." ²⁹Jacob said, "Please tell me your name." But he replied,
"Why do you ask my name?" Then he blessed him there. ³⁰So
Jacob called the place Peniel, saying, "It is because I saw God
face to face, and yet my life was spared." ³¹The sun rose above
him as he passed Peniel, and he was limping because of his hip.
³²Therefore to this day the Israelites do not eat the tendon
attached to the socket of the hip, because the socket of Jacob's
hip was touched near the tendon.

Jacob and his caravan had reached the Jabbok, a stream
that flows into the Jordan from the east just about midway
between the Sea of Galilee and the Dead Sea. After leading
family and flocks south across the Jabbok under cover of
darkness, Jacob himself went back across the stream, apparently to spend some time alone with the Lord in prayer. As
he began once again to pour out his heart to God, he suddenly became aware that out of the darkness some one had
grabbed hold of him and was wrestling him to the ground.
The mysterious struggle continued — for hours — until the
first streaks of dawn appeared in the eastern sky.

In commenting on this passage, Martin Luther said: "This
text is one of the most obscure in the Old Testament."
Although there are elements of this wrestling match that are
difficult to understand and to explain, there are some basic
truths that are immediately clear.

Jacob was struggling with God in earnest prayer. This
struggle involved a *spiritual striving with God* for his blessing, but it involved a *physical struggle* as well. Jacob's
opponent, referred to as "the man," later identified himself
as God.

But why should God appear to one of his children as an
opponent, as an enemy fighting against him? Surely not to
crush the life out of him. If God had been minded to crush

270

Jacob, the wrestling match would have been over in half a second. In the heat of the struggle Jacob may have been tempted to think of God as his enemy; in that case he would not have *wanted* to bless Jacob. But God had *promised* to bless, and Jacob knew that God cannot lie.

The struggle continued until Jacob's divine opponent, by merely touching Jacob's hip, threw the entire hip socket out of joint. Now Jacob couldn't continue the painful struggle any longer, so he threw his arms around his opponent and held on to him. His opponent said: "Let me go, for it is daybreak." He was delighted to hear Jacob answer: "I will not let you go unless you bless me." God didn't want Jacob (and he doesn't want us) to be timid with him. He *delights to let us win victories over him on the basis of humble, believing prayer.* Jacob clung in faith to God and to God's promise, and he received the blessing he desired.

"What is your name?" the LORD asked him, not because he had forgotten, but to remind Jacob that he had been a "heel-grabber," one who took unfair advantage of a rival. That old name no longer fit this man, and so God gave him a new one. "Your name will no longer be *Jacob*, but *Israel*, because you have struggled with God and with men and have overcome." Bible names often serve as more than convenient labels for people. Here Jacob's new name describes the new nature and character the Spirit of God had patiently and painstakingly created in him. No longer would he rely on his own cleverness to overcome anyone who opposed him. *The heel-grabber had become the persistent fighter who clung to God's promise and won God's blessing legitimately.* He had learned to lean on God.

God apparently felt that Jacob needed a memento of his victory, as a warning against relapsing into his old "Jacob" nature. And so, as Jacob left the scene of the wrestling match, he was limping. All of God's children need to learn that in and of ourselves we have no strength, no power with God or man. Our only strength, like Jacob's, lies in holding firmly to what God has promised.

For Jacob another blessed fruit of the mysterious struggle was that he was free from the terror that had gripped his heart when he learned Esau was coming for him with 400 men. But now, with the Savior's promise ringing in his ears, he was ready to meet Esau, ready for whatever surprises that new day might bring.

God still appears to his people on occasion as though he were an opponent. Each of us has known dark hours when we were unable to see God's mercy, but saw only a face that looked angry. Jacob held on to God even when he appeared as his opponent, and he won a blessing. We will have that same experience when in faith we learn to say: "My Savior, I will not let you go unless you bless me."

Reunion With Esau and Return to Canaan

33 Jacob looked up and there was Esau, coming with his four hundred men; so he divided the children among Leah, Rachel and the two maidservants. ²He put the maidservants and their children in front, Leah and her children next, and Rachel and Joseph in the rear.

³He himself went on ahead and bowed down to the ground seven times as he approached his brother. ⁴But Esau ran to meet Jacob and embraced him; he threw his arms around his neck and kissed him. And they wept.

During the eventful night Jacob had spent at the Jabbok he had been separated from his family and flocks: he had sent them on ahead. Now he rejoined them, and the caravan resumed its southward march. Suddenly a cloud of dust on the horizon signaled the approach of a band of riders. Nobody had to tell Jacob who they were.

Esau and Jacob reunited

He lined up his children, with the four sons of the maid-servants in front, then Leah with her seven, and finally Rachel and her son Joseph — perhaps the order in which he planned to introduce them to Esau. Then came the moment of truth. Jacob stepped forward to meet his brother, not knowing what kind of reception he would receive.

It doesn't take much imagination to picture the drama of the scene. A comparison of several passages in Genesis (47:9; 41:46; 45:11; 29:27; 31:38) reveals that Jacob and Esau were *in their nineties* when they met here. Here were two grey-haired men, twins who had not seen each other for twenty years.

As Jacob stepped toward Esau, he fell to his knees with his forehead to the ground, got up, walked a step or two, and bowed again. He did this *seven times*. Although he knew God had announced that the older twin was to serve the younger, Jacob repeatedly referred to himself as "servant," and to his brother as his "lord," treating him with the utmost respect. If in years gone by Esau had detected arrogance in his twin brother, he saw none now. At the sight of his brother humbly bowing before him, Esau's bitterness melted.

And suddenly any unanswered question that Jacob might have had about how Esau would receive him was answered. Moved by Jacob's evident humility, Esau dismounted from his camel, ran to his brother, threw his arms around him, kissed him and wept. Amazing! We have noted that God's powerful grace had produced changes *in Jacob*: we see here that that same powerful grace had brought about changes *in Esau*. Although Jacob had done everything humanly possible to assist in the reconciliation, finally *it's only God who can change hearts*. He used Jacob's prayers and his generous gifts and his deferential attitude, but only he can soften a hard heart.

⁵Then Esau looked up and saw the women and children. "Who are these with you?" he asked. Jacob answered, "They are the children God has graciously given your servant." ⁶Then the maidservants and their children approached and bowed down. ⁷Next, Leah and her children came and bowed down. ⁸Esau asked, "What do you mean by all these droves I met?" "To find favor in your eyes, my lord," he said. ⁹But Esau said, "I already have plenty, my brother. Keep what you have for yourself." ¹⁰"No, please!" said Jacob. "If I have found favor in your eyes, accept this gift from me. For to see your face is like seeing the face of God, now that you have received me favorably. ¹¹Please accept the present that was brought to you, for God has been gracious to me and I have all I need." And because Jacob insisted, Esau accepted it.

Esau saw more than a dozen children with their mothers and wondered out loud: "Who are all these people?" He pointed to the hundreds of cattle Jacob had sent ahead as a gift and asked: "What's this army of animals supposed to mean?" The answer he received was: "Please accept them as a token of my gratitude that in your face I can see God's love reflected." What a change God had brought about in Jacob over a twenty-year period! Instead of wanting to *deprive* Esau of a blessing, Jacob almost had to force Esau to *accept* this tangible evidence of the LORD's blessing.

¹²Then Esau said, "Let us be on our way; I'll accompany you." ¹³But Jacob said to him, "My lord knows that the children are tender and that I must care for the ewes and cows that are nursing their young. If they are driven hard just one day, all the animals will die. ¹⁴So let my lord go on ahead of his servant, while I move along slowly at the pace of the droves before me and that of the children, until I come to my lord in Seir." ¹⁵Esau said, "Then let me leave some of my men with you." "But why do that?" Jacob asked. "Just let me find favor in the eyes of my lord."

Esau had undergone a change of heart, and he showed
that not only with words but with actions. He realized that
marauding bands hiding out near the desert edge threatened
a caravan as large and vulnerable as Jacob's. He therefore
offered to be their bodyguard, to escort them wherever they
were going.

Jacob declined his brother's offer, for several reasons,
only one of which is stated. *"My group*, with its young children and young cattle, *can't travel as fast as yours* can. If
we were to drive them hard for just a single day, we could
lose them." Jacob had other reasons for declining Esau's
offer of protection. A few days earlier God had opened his
eyes to let him see the angel host surrounding him (32:1).
Even though that *angel escort* was invisible to him now, it
was the only escort he needed.

Perhaps to avoid hurting Esau's feelings Jacob was silent
about still another reason for not inviting Esau to accompany him back to Canaan. Esau had shown little appreciation
for the Messianic covenant. Two of his wives were heathen
Canaanites; the third was an Ishmaelite — all three outside
of the family of promise. Jacob wanted his descendants to
remain separate from those who despised their heritage.

And so the brothers parted, but they remained united in
heart. Moses informs us later that when Isaac died, *Esau
and Jacob* buried their father (35:29). We conclude from
this that the brothers' reconciliation was not only genuine, it
was permanent.

[16]So that day Esau started on his way back to Seir. [17]Jacob,
however, went to Succoth, where he built a place for himself
and made shelters for his livestock. That is why the place is
called Succoth. [18]After Jacob came from Paddan Aram, he
arrived safely at the city of Shechem in Canaan and camped
within sight of the city. [19]For a hundred pieces of silver, he

bought from the sons of Hamor, the father of Shechem, the plot of ground where he pitched his tent. ²⁰There he set up an altar and called it El Elohe Israel.

Esau said good-bye to his brother and returned to his home in the land of Edom, south of the Dead Sea. Jacob settled temporarily near the east bank of the Jordan river, in the valley of the Jordan known as the Arabah. Here he and his household enjoyed relief from the exertion and the tension of the long march from Haran. Jacob built a dwelling for himself and shelters for his cattle near the site where the city of Succoth ("shelters") later stood.

It is interesting that Jacob did not immediately head west across the Jordan and south to Hebron, where his father was living (35:27). After staying in Succoth for several years, he crossed the Jordan and settled in Shechem, in central Canaan. He made it clear, furthermore, that he wanted to live *not as an alien*, but permanently *as a landowner*. He therefore purchased a piece of property, establishing legal residence in the land. He was the ancestor of a nation that would bear his name, the people of Israel, who would one day possess this land as their homeland. Just as Abraham had insisted on purchasing a burial plot for Sarah in the land of promise, so Jacob wanted to pitch his tent *on land he owned*. His descendants were to know *he believed God's promise* that the Israelites would one day own this land. And by establishing a household independent of his father Isaac's, Jacob demonstrated that *he was a patriarch* in his own right.

The statement "He arrived safely in the city of Shechem *in Canaan...*" offers an example of what has been called *internal evidence that Moses is the author of Genesis.* If, as some Bible critics today claim, Genesis was not written until long after Israel entered its promised land, this phrase "in Canaan" is superfluous. After the Israelite conquest, what Israelite would need to be informed that one of the most prominent of Israelite cities, the nation's first capital, was located in the land of Canaan?

There are several interesting sidelights in later Israelite history to the real estate transaction recorded here. Several centuries later, after the Israelites had occupied the land of Canaan, they buried Joseph's mummified remains in Shechem, as he had requested (50:25; Joshua 24:32). And one of the most interesting conversations the Lord Jesus had was with a Samaritan woman whom he met at a well in Sychar (Shechem), on the piece of property Jacob had bought (John 4:5).

A very eventful and highly significant chapter of Jacob's life had come to an end. Jacob felt this called for special recognition. He therefore established an altar at Shechem, a place of public worship. There he proclaimed the name of the mighty God, the God of Israel, using the new name God had given him. Through the might and the mercy of the covenant God a tumultuous twenty-year period of Jacob's life had now reached a victorious conclusion.

Tragedy At Shechem

34 Now Dinah, the daughter Leah had borne to Jacob, went out to visit the women of the land. ²When Shechem son of Hamor the Hivite, the ruler of that area, saw her, he took her and violated her. ³His heart was drawn to Dinah daughter of Jacob, and he loved the girl and spoke tenderly to her. ⁴And Shechem said to his father Hamor, "Get me this girl as my wife."

We like to think of the autumn years of a believer's life as golden ones — basking in the love of a devoted family, seeing the blessed fruits of Christ-centered child training.

The record of Jacob's later years, however, is stained by a *series of family tragedies*, the first of which is recorded in Genesis 34. In the hand of a gracious Father these tragedies were again a discipline for Jacob, reminding him of his former character as "heel-grabber," leading him to pray God to keep him from surrendering to his sinful nature and lapsing into his old ways.

If an estimated ten years had elapsed since Jacob had returned from Haran, his daughter Dinah may have been at least 16. Perhaps she was invited by one of her Canaanite friends to meet some Canaanite girls her age or to attend some Canaanite festival. During her visit she was raped by the son of the chief of the Hivites, a Canaanite tribe. The father, incidentally, was the man from whom Jacob had earlier purchased the piece of property on which he was living.

His son Shechem, who had grown up in a culture of sexual permissiveness and perversion, wasn't able to distinguish love from lust. The Hebrew verb describes his act as an act of violence, of humiliating another person. Shechem viewed the sexual act as a conquest, which is understandable when we remember he was a heathen. It's only God who can teach us that love is an unselfish emotion which seeks primarily *the welfare of the beloved*. "God so loved the world that he *gave...*" not "*...grabbed.*"

⁵When Jacob heard that his daughter Dinah had been defiled, his sons were in the fields with his livestock; so he kept quiet about it until they came home. ⁶Then Shechem's father Hamor went out to talk with Jacob. ⁷Now Jacob's sons had come in from the fields as soon as they heard what had happened. They were filled with grief and fury, because Shechem had done a disgraceful thing in Israel by lying with Jacob's daughter — a thing that should not be done.

Perhaps Jacob first became aware that something had happened to Dinah when she didn't return home that evening. It seems that since young Shechem had secured his father's permission to marry Dinah he took her to his home. Jacob remained silent about the matter until his sons returned from the range with the cattle. Was it because of his age (probably well over a hundred by this time) that he decided to discuss the matter with Dinah's brothers first, before taking decisive action? He would know, of course, that Leah's other children would feel a special responsibility to stand up for the rights of their sister. Or was Jacob gradually relinquishing the leadership of the family to his sons? Would he have acted more decisively if it had been Rachel's daughter instead of Leah's who had been attacked? Jacob's behavior leaves us with some unanswered questions.

The brothers' initial reaction upon hearing what had happened to their sister strikes us as commendable. They were *sad* over what had happened, and they were *angry*. It is to their credit that they recognized Jacob as a patriarch and his family as very special to God. (By contrast, Esau had not shown that awareness when he entered a marital alliance with two Canaanite women.) "We are the convenant people," the brothers seemed to be saying. "God has set us apart as the people of the promise. For Shechem to have violated a woman of the covenant family shows no respect for God's great promise." And they were right. God equated contempt for his special people with contempt for him.

⁸But Hamor said to them, "My son Shechem has his heart set on your daughter. Please give her to him as his wife. ⁹Intermarry with us; give us your daughters and take our daughters for yourselves. ¹⁰You can settle among us; the land is open to you. Live in it, trade in it, and acquire property in it." ¹¹Then Shechem said to Dinah's father and brothers, "Let me

find favor in your eyes, and I will give you whatever you ask. [12]Make the price for the bride and the gift I am to bring as great as you like, and I'll pay whatever you ask me. Only give me the girl as my wife."

When Hamor, the tribal chief, came with his son to visit Jacob to try to arrange for the marriage, he could sense the brothers' anger, and made a very generous offer to try to pacify them. He knew, of course, that he was speaking to men who were aliens and who did not enjoy the same rights Canaanite citizens enjoyed. If Hamor's offer was made sincerely (and in the light of verse 23 one must question that), he offered Jacob's family privileges that resident aliens did not normally enjoy: the right *to settle* in the land, the right *to intermarry* with the Canaanites, the right *to acquire property*, and the right *to transact business*. These were major concessions the father was offering.

The would-be bridegroom entered the conversation at this point: "About *the bride-price*. Make it as high as you like, and I'll pay it." Shechem's willingness to pay whatever price they would name for their sister had precisely the opposite effect on the brothers from what he had hoped. His offer to pay her price signaled to the brothers that he was treating their sister like a prostitute (verse 31).

[13]**Because their sister Dinah had been defiled, Jacob's sons replied deceitfully as they spoke to Shechem and his father Hamor. [14]They said to them, "We can't do such a thing; we can't give our sister to a man who is not circumcised. That would be a disgrace to us. [15]We will give our consent to you on one condition only: that you become like us by circumcising all your males. [16]Then we will give you our daughters and take your daughters for ourselves. We'll settle among you and become one people with you. [17]But if you will not agree to be circumcised, we'll take our sister and go."**

"Jacob's sons replied deceitfully." They owed the truth to the people in whose land they were guests. Instead they pretended to be considering the marriage proposal when in fact they had already decided in favor of revenge. The message they gave Shechem was: "We'd be willing to give our sister to you in marriage except that it's against our religion to give her to an uncircumcised man."

By dragging the matter of circumcision into the conversation, the brothers were treating flippantly the special covenant sign God had given his people several generations earlier. Like applying water in baptism, and like eating and drinking bread and wine in the Lord's Supper, the act of circumcision had no special value in and of itself. God had given circumcision to his people *as a seal of the righteousness that comes through faith*. For the Shechemites to receive the badge of the covenant in their bodies without faith in Israel's God would make a mockery of God's *covenant* as well as of the *convenant sign*, and Jacob's sons knew that. "But if you will not agree to be circumcised, we'll come to your home, take our sister (by force, if necessary), and leave this area of the country, where we've been so humiliated."

[18]Their proposal seemed good to Hamor and his son Shechem. [19]The young man, who was the most honored of all his father's household, lost no time in doing what they said, because he was delighted with Jacob's daughter. [20]So Hamor and his son Shechem went to the gate of their city to speak to their fellow townsmen. [21]"These men are friendly toward us," they said. "Let them live in our land and trade in it: the land has plenty of room for them. We can marry their daughters and they can marry ours. [22]But the men will consent to live with us as one people only on the condition that our males be circumcised, as they themselves are. [23]Won't their livestock, their property and all their other animals become ours? So let us

**give our consent to them, and they will settle among us." ²⁴All
the men who went out of the city gate agreed with Hamor and
his son Shechem, and every male in the city was circumcised.**

To agree to respect the religious scruples of Dinah's family was really no big deal for these religiously indifferent
Canaanites. Shechem had the operation performed on himself without delay.

Father and son next appeared in the gate of the city, the
official meeting place where the city's business was trans-
acted, to try to persuade their fellow townsmen to agree to
the demands of Dinah's brothers. They offered these arguments:

1. "The members of Jacob's family are peaceably
   inclined toward us."
2. "The land is big enough. There's room for their
   family."
3. "They are very well-to do, and if we let them
   transact business, we stand to benefit. Their
   wealth — large herds and flocks — will become
   ours. Submitting to their religious scruples is
   really a small price to pay for what we stand to
   gain."

It becomes clear that *Jacob's sons* were not the only ones
who were dealing deceitfully here. *Hamor and Shechem*
were actually not offering the unusual privileges to Jacob's
family they claimed to be offering. Instead they intended to
swallow up this family, to incorporate them into their
Canaanite society and ultimately gain possession of their
flocks.

But their arguments persuaded the men of the town. Since
Hamor was a tribal official and since his son was held in
high respect, the townsmen consented to have themselves
circumcised.

²⁵**Three days later, while all of them were still in pain, two of Jacob's sons, Simeon and Levi, Dinah's brothers, took their swords and attacked the unsuspecting city, killing every male. ²⁶They put Hamor and his son Shechem to the sword and took Dinah from Shechem's house and left. ²⁷The sons of Jacob came upon the dead bodies and looted the city where their sister had been defiled. ²⁸They seized their flocks and herds and donkeys and everything else of theirs in the city and out in the fields. ²⁹They carried off all their wealth and all their women and children, taking as plunder everything in the houses. ³⁰Then Jacob said to Simeon and Levi, "You have brought trouble on me by making me a stench to the Canaanites and Perizzites, the people living in this land. We are few in number, and if they join forces against me and attack me, I and my household will be destroyed." ³¹But they replied, "Should he have treated our sister like a prostitute?"**

Three days later the treachery of the brothers became apparent to all. While the Shechemites were incapacitated, unable to defend themselves, Simeon and Levi, two of Leah's other children, full brothers of Dinah, took swords and killed the men of Shechem.

What started out as righteous anger over a sexual attack on their sister had degenerated into a bloodbath. And after the grim and bloody business was over, it seems the other sons of Jacob also indulged their sinful natures by plundering the dead bodies and taking the women and children as slaves.

What a dreadful example for God's people to set before the Canaanites! The brothers' vengeance brought little honor to God and to his covenant, and may indeed have hardened the Canaanites in their unbelief.

In view of that, it's difficult to appreciate Jacob's reaction. As he here delivered a rebuke (a very mild one) to his sons, he spoke only of the *consequences* the family could now expect to receive from other Canaanite tribes. What Jacob owed his sons was the *full rebuke of God's law* on their bloodthirst, their cruelty and their greed, but that he withheld.

In fairness two things should be added. When later on his deathbed Jacob spoke his parting words to his twelve sons, he expressed his horror to Simeon and Levi over the moral depravity of their deed and let them know what the consequences would be for them (49:5-7). And let it not be forgotten that Moses, the man through whom the Holy Spirit recorded this narrative, was himself a descendant of Levi. He surely did not hesitate to describe the sin of his ancestor in all of its ugliness and depravity.

In this chapter and in ones to follow the reader will note a lack of spirituality among the sons of Jacob, a spiritual insensitivity which does not bode well for the future. When people who call themselves God's people fail to act like God's salt, God's yeast, what can be expected of the society in which they live?

Genesis 34 sounds remarkably contemporary. Like Jacob, you and I live not in a nice, neat world but in a disorderly world, a world in rebellion against God. We see evidence of this rebellion all about us. What is most distressing, however, is to see evidences of this rebellion among those who claim to be members of the family of God. In a world like this, a world with an easy conscience about sin, the church of God must *rebuke sin* and reaffirm that to abuse God's grace is to invite God's condemnation.

But that isn't the whole story. This world is not only Satan's playpen, but the workshop of our God. In his Son Jesus Christ he met the problem of sin head-on. Still more. Through the *message of his law* God is ceaselessly at work restraining the evil power within us that strives to dominate our hearts and lives. And through the *message of his love* he assures us that even when we fall — through stubbornness or through weakness — he is able to overrule evil and force it to serve his good purpose. God will be glorified — whether in judgment or in mercy.

Covenant Renewal At Bethel

35 Then God said to Jacob, "Go up to Bethel and settle there, and build an altar there to God, who appeared to you when you were fleeing from your brother Esau." ²So Jacob said to his household and to all who were with him, "Get rid of the foreign gods you have with you, and purify yourselves and change your clothes. ³Then come, let us go up to Bethel, where I will build an altar to God, who answered me in the day of my distress and who has been with me wherever I have gone." ⁴So they gave Jacob all the foreign gods they had and the rings in their ears, and Jacob buried them under the oak at Shechem. ⁵Then they set out, and the terror of God fell upon the towns all around them so that no one pursued them.

One would think that after the tension and trauma of his twenty-year stay in Haran Jacob would have *headed straight for Bethel* after meeting Esau. Bethel was that special place where the LORD had *appeared* to Jacob when he was fleeing from Esau, and where God had *assured* him: "I will protect you, and I will bless you." At that time Jacob had been so impressed by God's goodness that he vowed: "LORD, if you bring me back to this land, I'll establish a sanctuary here at Bethel."

But what had happened since then? It's difficult to escape the impression that *Jacob had been dragging his feet.* After saying good-bye to Esau Jacob spent time at *Succoth*, east of the Jordan, enough time to build a house there. Then after a while he moved across the Jordan to *Shechem*, purchased some land and lived there. It was at Shechem that

286

the tragedy described in the previous chapter occurred. If we may judge from the age of Jacob's children, it seems he spent something like ten years in Succoth and Shechem.

Why did he stay in the area around Shechem? Surely Jacob knew that his testimony to the true God had been blunted by the activities of his children. In that neighborhood Jacob's usefulness to God must have been severely limited. Why hadn't he returned *to Bethel* earlier to fulfill his vow?

We don't know. It's not likely he had forgotten his vow. It's difficult to review the facts as the Bible reports them without seeing *evidence of spiritual decline* in Jacob.

Perhaps he realized that fulfilling his vow at Bethel would call for a pretty thorough religious reformation in his household. Perhaps Jacob's delay stemmed from a misguided deference to his wives, who seem to have brought elements of pagan worship along with them from Haran (31:19). The Shechemite women who had joined Jacob's household (34:29) may also have brought their paraphernalia of idolatry along.

Whatever Jacob's reason was, God finally had to appear to him to remind him of the vow he had made. "Go up to Bethel...and build an altar there to God." It wasn't just that God was insisting on receiving payment of an overdue vow. Thirty years earlier, when Jacob was running for his life and the LORD appeared to reassure him, Jacob had been very conscious of the LORD's great mercy and vowed to remember that. Since his return to Canaan, however, his memory of God's grace had begun to dim. He was taking it for granted. God did not want the record of his love and his promise to Abraham's descendants to be lost to succeeding generations. He expected better things from the patriarch after whom the promised nation would be named.

In God's call to him Jacob heard a *call to repentance*. There was no way he could return to Bethel and establish a sanctuary to the true God while at the same time tolerating the worship of false gods in his own household. Jacob therefore gave the order: "Get rid of the foreign gods!"

Those who had them brought them to him, along with earrings which may have been charms for practicing superstition. Jacob disposed of them permanently. There are many things God will put up with in the human heart, but second place is not one of them. He has made it clear:

I am the LORD; that is my name!
I will not give my glory to another
or my praise to idols. (Isaiah 42:8)

The distance from Shechem to Bethel is only twenty miles, but the journey led through Canaanite territory. Since the news of the slaughter at Shechem (34:25) had spread, and since the Canaanites vastly outnumbered Jacob's household, they would gladly have taken revenge for the slaughter of their Shechemite friends. God, therefore, miraculously protected Jacob. "The terror of God fell on all the towns around them so that no one pursued them."

⁶Jacob and all the people with him came to Luz (that is, Bethel) in the land of Canaan. ⁷There he built an altar, and he called the place El Bethel, because it was there that God revealed himself to him when he was fleeing from his brother. ⁸Now Deborah, Rebekah's nurse, died and was buried under the oak below Bethel. So it was named Allon Bacuth. ⁹After Jacob returned from Paddan Aram, God appeared to him again and blessed him. ¹⁰God said to him, "Your name is Jacob, but you will no longer be called Jacob; your name will be Israel." So he named him Israel. ¹¹And God said to him, "I am God Almighty; be fruitful and increase in number. A nation and a community of nations will come from you, and kings will come from your body. ¹²The land I gave to Abraham and Isaac

I also give to you, and I will give this land to your descendants after you." [13]Then God went up from him at the place where he had talked with him. [14]Jacob set up a stone pillar at the place where God had talked with him, and he poured out a drink offering on it; he also poured oil on it. [15]Jacob called the place where God had talked with him Bethel.

Upon arriving at Bethel Jacob fulfilled his vow. He found the stone which had been at his head during the solemn night when the LORD appeared to him and which he had upended the following morning to form a monument. Now that stone became the central stone in an altar Jacob built to God, to give public recognition to the great things God had done for him and his family, and would continue to do.

The note is inserted here that Deborah, Rebekah's nurse, died and was buried at Bethel. We take from this that her mistress Rebekah must have died earlier, perhaps while Jacob was still in Haran; after that Deborah apparently made her home with Jacob's family. Martin Luther had this interesting comment about Deborah: "I imagine her to have been a wise and pious woman, whom the children in the family considered a sort of grandmother. She would have been of great service to Jacob, even giving him advice in time of danger or distress."

As he had done thirty years earlier, God again appeared to Jacob at Bethel, for two important reasons. God felt it necessary, first of all, to *confirm the name change* from Jacob ("the heel-grabber") to Israel ("the man who fought with God and overcame"). Jacob's new name had, as it were, been dirtied during the gory goings-on in Shechem. By failing to rebuke his sons, and by ignoring the idolatry practiced in his own household, the patriarch had lapsed back into his old Jacob nature. "But you will no longer be called Jacob," he now heard God say. That wasn't his real nature. By restating and ratifying his new name, God was reaffirming the convenant relationship the patriarch had with him. By so doing he was announcing: "I have forgiven you."

God had one more announcement to make at Bethel, and this one was intended not only for Jacob's ears. He *restated the promise* he had made thirty years earlier to a lonely, frightened fugitive. Perhaps while the household of Jacob — including the twelve men who would head the tribes of Israel — were joining the patriarch at worship at the brand new altar, they heard the voice of the covenant God announcing: "A nation and a community of nations will come from you. ...and I will give this land to your descendants after you." God has always dealt with his people not primarily in terms *of command and demand*, but in terms *of promise*.

In addition to building the altar at Bethel, Jacob erected a stone monument to mark the place where God had twice invaded his life and spoken to him. He poured out a thankoffering of wine on that monument, and by anointing it with oil he consecrated the place as a permanent sanctuary, formally dedicated to the God who had appeared to him there. Just as the LORD had seen fit to ratify Jacob's name change and to restate his great promise, so Jacob now felt constrained to reaffirm: "This is indeed Bethel ("the house of God"), where God has appeared in all his saving grace!" (The term El Bethel in verse 7 means "God of Bethel.")

¹⁶Then they moved on from Bethel. While they were still some distance from Ephrath, Rachel began to give birth and had great difficulty. ¹⁷And as she was having great difficulty in childbirth, the midwife said to her, "Don't be afraid, for you have another son." ¹⁸As she breathed her last — for she was dying — she named her son Ben-Oni. But his father named

him Benjamin. [19]So Rachel died and was buried on the way to Ephrath (that is, Bethlehem). [20]Over her tomb Jacob set up a pillar, and to this day that pillar marks Rachel's tomb. [21]Israel moved on again and pitched his tent beyond Migdal Eder. [22]While Israel was living in that region, Reuben went in and slept with his father's concubine Bilhah, and Israel heard of it.

Jacob's business at Bethel was finished. Now that God had straightened out his thinking and adjusted his priorities, there was one thing on Jacob's mind — to head south to Hebron to see his father Isaac. And so he and his household set out on the road that runs along the crest of Canaan's central ridge.

As they headed south out of Jerusalem toward Bethlehem, Rachel went into labor — difficult and painful labor. To encourage the mother-to-be, the midwife comforted her: "Don't be afraid; you have another son." Rachel knew, however, that she would not live to enjoy her new son, and named him Ben-Oni ("the son of my trouble," "the son who will cost me my life"). After Rachel's death Jacob, unwilling to have his youngest son's name forever remind him of the sorrow that accompanied his birth, renamed him Benjamin ("son of my right hand"). Jacob buried Rachel along the road that they were traveling. The pillar he erected to mark her grave was still standing in Moses' day. Today travelers on the road from Jerusalem to Bethlehem can still see the traditional site of Kever Rahel ("Rachel's Tomb").

There was heartache awaiting Jacob, however, that was even more painful than that caused by Rachel's death. Reuben, his firstborn, slept with Bilhah, his father's concubine and the maid of Rachel, who had just died. The death of loved ones is something that, ever since the fall, we know we can expect. But Reuben's behavior was totally unexpected. Besides indicating that he had turned his back on the godly training he had received from his father, besides being a calculated insult to his father (actually a form of incest), with his action Reuben presumed to serve notice that he, the oldest son, was expecting to take over the headship of the family after his father's death.

At the time this news reached Jacob's ears he said nothing to Reuben. He would have something to say about it later, and what he would say would be shattering news for a man who expected to succeed his father as patriarch. When on his deathbed Jacob prophesied the future of his sons, he informed Reuben that with his crude and shameless act of disrespect he had forfeited his right to the privileges of the firstborn (49:4). The *Messianic line* would instead pass to Judah, the fourth son (49:10). The *double share* normally received by the firstborn would be received by Joseph (1 Chronicles 5:1).

Jacob had twelve sons: ²³The sons of Leah: Reuben the firstborn of Jacob, Simeon, Levi, Judah, Issachar and Zebulun. ²⁴The sons of Rachel: Joseph and Benjamin. ²⁵The sons of Rachel's maidservant Bilhah: Dan and Naphtali. ²⁶The sons of Leah's maidservant Zilpah: Gad and Asher. These were the sons of Jacob, who were born to him in Paddan Aram. ²⁷Jacob came home to his father Isaac in Mamre, near Kiriath Arba (that is, Hebron), where Abraham and Isaac had stayed. ²⁸Isaac lived a hundred and eighty years. ²⁹Then he breathed his last and died and was gathered to his people, old and full of years. And his sons Esau and Jacob buried him.

When Jacob had left home to flee to Haran, he had been alone; his worldly goods consisted of a shepherd's staff. But what a difference thirty years had made! Moses lists what the blessing of God had made of this solitary traveler.

With the birth of Benjamin, the roster of the twelve tribal heads was now complete. The descendants of these dozen men were the tribes that later made up the promised nation of Israel.

Jacob now established his home in Hebron and was able to spend about a dozen years with his father. Isaac died at the age of 180, the oldest of the three patriarchs. We're told that Esau was present for his father's funeral. Jacob had undoubtedly notified his brother in Edom when he noticed that their father's end was drawing near.

The sons buried their father Isaac in the tomb at Machpelah, in Hebron (49:31), which Abraham had originally purchased. There Abraham had buried Sarah; there Isaac and Ishmael had buried Abraham; and there Isaac had buried Rebekah. Now his body would lie there, to give testimony to later generations of Israelites: "I believe God's promise that my descendants will one day inherit this land. I want my last earthly resting place to be the land I know my descendants will occupy."

And so the eighth of Moses ten mini-histories, the "Account of Isaac," comes to a close. Although not as dominant a character in the history of the Old Testament as his father Abraham, Isaac expressed his faith in submitting to many trials. Now the son who succeeded him had returned home after years of wandering. God's intended purpose for Isaac had been carried out.

THE NINTH ACCOUNT:
OF ESAU
GENESIS 36:1-43

A quick look at Genesis 36 is enough to make some Bible readers skip to chapter 37. At first glance it seems to be no more than a list of Esau's descendants, and might seem to make about as interesting reading as a telephone directory.

To appreciate this chapter one must *remember the role Moses assigned to it* in his ten-part outline of the book of Genesis. It is the ninth of ten "accounts" which *trace the early history of God's saving activity.* The tenth and final "account," which brings the book to its conclusion, is the "Account of Jacob." But before picking up the thread of that narrative, the sacred writer disposes of the less important "Account of Esau." He *documents how this son of Isaac,* although not continuing the Messianic line, nevertheless *did develop into a nation, as God had promised* before Esau was born. This was a distinct blessing of God, and Genesis 36 traces how this blessing took shape.

36 This is the account of Esau (that is, Edom). ²Esau took his wives from the women of Canaan: Adah daughter of Elon the Hittite, and Oholibamah daughter of Anah and granddaughter of Zibeon the Hivite — ³ also Basemath daughter of Ishmael and sister of Nebaioth. ⁴Adah bore Eliphaz to Esau, Basemath bore Reuel, ⁵ and Oholibamah bore Jeush, Jalam and Korah. These were the sons of Esau, who were born to him in Canaan. ⁶Esau took his wives and sons and daughters

and all the members of his household, as well as his livestock
and all his other animals and all the goods he had acquired in
Canaan, and moved to a land some distance from his brother
Jacob. ⁷Their possessions were too great for them to remain
together; the land where they were staying could not support
them both because of their livestock. ⁸So Esau (that is, Edom)
settled in the hill country of Seir.

At the funeral of their father, Esau and Jacob came
together, perhaps for the last time. Esau had learned from
his father that Jacob's descendants were to inherit the land
of Canaan. During the time Jacob was in Haran Esau therefore moved his household into the hilly region south of the
Dead Sea. One of the factors that contributed to this decision was that, with God's blessing, Esau had grown enor-
mously wealthy. Finding range land for his cattle was a
major problem, and since the land on which he had been
living was destined for his brother's descendants, Esau
moved.

Before dismissing Esau from the sacred record, however,
Moses lets us see how the prophecy spoken to Isaac and
Rebekah about their twin sons was fulfilled. Before the
twins were born, God had prophesied that Esau's descendants would grow into an independent nation. The first
eight verses of chapter 36 *list the names of Esau's wives
and children* and inform us of his place of settlement. The
second and longer section of the chapter (beginning with
verse 9) *traces the development of this family group into a
nation*, including tribal chiefs and kings.

A problem confronting the reader is that the names
recorded here don't always agree with the corresponding
names listed elsewhere in Genesis (26:34 and 28:9). It's
possible that some of the people listed here had more than

one name (just as Esau is often referred to as Edom). Another possibility is that two people had the same name.

When he married two Hittite wives Esau had introduced a Canaanite strain into the bloodline of Abraham. By taking as his third wife a daughter of Ishmael, Esau introduced still another foreign element into his line. The narrative of chapter 36 suggests that Esau's *descendants continued that practice* when the family moved into the hilly terrain south of the Dead Sea. The end result was that Esau's line came to be the dominant one in that land.

⁹This is the account of Esau the father of the Edomites in the hill country of Seir. ¹⁰These are the names of Esau's sons: Eliphaz, the son of Esau's wife Adah, and Reuel, the son of Esau's wife Basemath. ¹¹The sons of Eliphaz: Teman, Omar, Zepho, Gatam and Kenaz. ¹²Esau's son Eliphaz also had a concubine named Timna, who bore him Amalek. These were grandsons of Esau's wife Adah. ¹³The sons of Reuel: Nahath, Zerah, Shammah and Mizzah. These were grandsons of Esau's wife Basemath. ¹⁴The sons of Esau's wife Oholibamah, daughter of Anah and granddaughter of Zibeon, whom she bore to Esau: Jeush, Jalam and Korah. ¹⁵These were the chiefs among Esau's descendants: The sons of Eliphaz the firstborn of Esau: Chiefs Teman, Omar, Zepho, Kenaz, ¹⁶ Korah, Gatam and Amalek. These were the chiefs descended from Eliphaz in Edom; they were grandsons of Adah. ¹⁷The sons of Esau's son Reuel: Chiefs Nahath, Zerah, Shammah and Mizzah. These were the chiefs descended from Reuel in Edom; they were grandsons of Esau's wife Basemath. ¹⁸The sons of Esau's wife Oholibamah: Chiefs Jeush, Jalam and Korah. These were the chiefs descended from Esau's wife Oholibamah daughter of Anah. ¹⁹These were the sons of Esau (that is, Edom), and these were their chiefs.

We learn here that five of Esau's sons and ten of his grandsons became tribal chiefs. The family of Esau was growing in size and in strength, and was ready for its next move.

²⁰These were the sons of Seir the Horite, who were living in the region: Lotan, Shobal, Zibeon, Anah, ²¹ Dishon, Ezer and Dishan. These sons of Seir in Edom were Horite chiefs. ²² The sons of Lotan: Hori and Homam. Timna was Lotan's sister. ²³The sons of Shobal: Alvan, Manahath, Ebal, Shepho and Onam. ²⁴The Sons of Zibeon: Aiah and Anah. This is the Anah who discovered the hot springs in the desert while he was grazing the donkeys of his father Zibeon. ²⁵The children of Anah: Dishon and Oholibamah daughter of Anah. ²⁶The sons of Dishon: Hemdan, Eshban, Ithran and Keran. ²⁷The sons of Ezer: Bilhan, Zaavan and Akan. ²⁸The sons of Dishan: Uz and Aran. ²⁹These were the Horite chiefs: Lotan, Shobal, Zibeon, Anah, ³⁰ Dishon, Ezer and Dishan. These were the Horite chiefs, according to their divisions, in the land of Seir. ³¹These were the kings who reigned in Edom before any Israelite king reigned: ³²Bela son of Beor became king of Edom. His city was named Dinhabah. ³³When Bela died, Jobab son of Zerah from Bozrah succeeded him as king. ³⁴When Jobab died, Husham from the land of the Temanites succeeded him as king. ³⁵When Husham died, Hadad son of Bedad, who defeated Midian in the country of Moab, succeeded him as king. His city was named Avith. ³⁶When Hadad died, Samlah from Masrekah succeeded him as king. ³⁷When Samlah died, Shaul from Rehoboth on the river succeeded him as king. ³⁸When Shaul died, Baal-Hanan son of Acbor succeeded him as king. ³⁹When Baal-Hanan son of Acbor died, Hadad succeeded him as king. His city was named Pau, and his wife's name was Mehetabel daughter of Matred, the daughter of Me-Zahab. ⁴⁰These were the chiefs descended from Esau, by name, according to their clans and regions: Timna, Alvah, Jetheth, ⁴¹ Oholibamah, Elah, Pinon, ⁴² Kenaz, Teman, Mibzar, ⁴³ Magdiel and Iram. These were the chiefs of Edom,

according to their settlements in the land they occupied. This was Esau the father of the Edomites.

Moses introduces us to the *second major group* which entered into the making of the people known as the Edomites. *Seir the Horite* was an early inhabitant of the territory south of the Dead Sea who had actually given his name to the prominent mountain range of the country. Seir had seven sons, and they were all Horite chiefs.

What happened when the family of Esau moved into the territory occupied by Seir the Horite? Deuteronomy 2:12 tells us: "The Horites used to live in Seir, but the descendants of Esau drove them out. They destroyed the Horites and settled in their place." The *tribal chiefs descended from Esau* took the place of the Horite leaders whom they had defeated and *took control of the country of Edom.* If this process had started already during the lifetime of Esau, it is not surprising Esau could readily assembly 400 men to confront his brother Jacob (32:6).

Moses informs us that Edom had kings "before any Israelite king reigned" (verse 31). Years later, when the Israelites had been freed from Egyptian slavery and were approaching their new homeland from the south, they requested permission of the king of Edom to pass through his country. He refused permission and came out to meet them with a large and powerful army (Numbers 20:14-21). Eight Edomite kings are listed in verses 31-39. Although we don't know their exact relationship to Esau we know they must have descended from him, for the closing verse of the chapter calls Esau "the father of the Edomites."

And with this, Esau is dismissed from Moses' sacred narrative. From this point forward Moses is concerned only with tracing the development of that branch of Abraham's family that *carried the promise*. From this point on the

Edomites are mentioned only when they came into direct contact with the nation of Israel.

"This was Esau, the father of the Edomites," *head of a nation,* just as God has prophesied, but a nation *that despised, as Esau did, the spiritual heritage he had received* from Abraham and Isaac. Throughout its history the nation of Edom remained hostile to God's covenant people.

THE TENTH ACCOUNT:
OF JACOB
GENESIS 37:1—50:26

The last and longest of Moses' ten "accounts" presents the subsequent history of Jacob and his family. Although the preceding chapters have provided much information about Jacob, most of it has dealt with *personal family matters*. In this last of the ten mini-histories, the emphasis shifts in the direction of *Israel's becoming a nation*, as God had promised to Abraham and Isaac and Jacob.

There is a second point of emphasis in this tenth and final "account." God had predicted to Abraham that his descendants would be strangers and slaves in a foreign land. The instrument God used to carry out this particular segment of his promise was Jacob's son Joseph. In God's marvelous management of history, the same country in which *Joseph* grew to manhood, spent time in prison and was later raised to honor, became the place where *the family of Jacob* grew to nationhood, endured bitter slavery, and then was rescued by a miracle of God. The concluding fourteen chapters of Genesis prepare for the exodus by recording how Jacob's twelve sons grew into a family of seventy souls who, under the remarkable guidance of God, journeyed to Egypt. There they awaited the next step in God's fulfillment of his promise to them.

From Favored Son to Foreign Slave

37 Jacob lived in the land where his father had stayed, the land of Canaan. ²This is the account of Jacob. Joseph, a young man of seventeen, was tending the flocks with his brothers, the sons of Bilhah and the sons of Zilpah, his father's wives, and he brought their father a bad report about them. ³Now Israel loved Joseph more than any of his other sons, because he had been born to him in his old age; and he made a richly ornamented robe for him. ⁴When his brothers saw that their father loved him more than any of them, they hated him and could not speak a kind word to him.

Actually 37:1 is the closing verse of the previous "account," the Account of Esau. In contrast to *Esau*, whose descendants lived in Edom and gradually took over the country (Genesis 36), *Jacob* continued to live as a temporary resident in the land of Canaan, as had his fathers before him.

Joseph, son of Jacob's beloved wife Rachel, was the favorite of his father. When Moses picks up the narrative here Joseph was seventeen and worked as a shepherd along with his brothers, especially with those closest to him in age.

The picture we get of Joseph in this and the following chapters is that of a young man of *exceptional ability and talents*. He recognized that his father loved him, and he returned that love. He strikes us also as a man of *high moral principle*. If he saw his brothers conducting themselves in a way that did not reflect favorably on their father, Joseph realized he had to say something, also to his father. Understandably, this trait did not endear him to his brothers.

Complicating Joseph's relationship with his brothers was the fact that as his father's favorite he received preferential treatment. And here father Jacob must share some of the blame for the friction that developed in his family. He should have been aware that, as God's representative in his home, he had no business loving some sons less than others. Jacob should have remembered from his own youth how his father Isaac had loved one of his twin sons more than the other and how that led to envy and hatred that tore the family apart. The richly ornamented robe he gave Joseph singled that son out from his brothers for special distinction. Jacob later was to pay dearly for that favoritism.

⁵Joseph had a dream, and when he told it to his brothers, they hated him all the more. ⁶He said to them, "Listen to this dream I had: ⁷We were binding sheaves of grain out in the field when suddenly my sheaf rose and stood upright, while your sheaves gathered around mine and bowed down to it." ⁸His brothers said to him, "Do you intend to reign over us? Will you actually rule us?" And they hated him all the more because of his dream and what he had said. ⁹Then he had another dream, and he told it to his brothers. "Listen," he said, "I had another dream, and this time the sun and moon and eleven stars were bowing down to me." ¹⁰When he told his father as well as his brothers, his father rebuked him and said, "What is this dream you had? Will your mother and I and your brothers actually come and bow down to the ground before you?" ¹¹His brothers were jealous of him, but his father kept the matter in mind.

God had special plans for Joseph, and he signaled that to him at an early age through special dreams. Although people usually believe that dreams originate in a person's subconscious mind, the Bible teaches that *God often spoke through dreams*, as he did to Joseph. This was not the first time God did this in Bible times, nor would it be the last. Through a dream God alerted the Egyptian pharaoh about years of plenty and years of famine. Centuries later God warned the Magi from the east in a dream not to return to wicked King Herod.

The dreams God gave to young Joseph revealed to him something of what the future held for him. Sometimes the dreams God gave to people included *verbal communication*; here the dream consisted only of *symbols*: the brothers' sheaves gathering around Joseph's sheaf and bowing down to it. Joseph's second dream showed the sun, moon and eleven stars bowing down to him. Without speaking a word, God was letting Joseph know that *God had singled him out for a significant position of leadership*. God's purpose in revealing this to Joseph in advance was not just to give Joseph something to brag about. God knew that difficult days lay ahead for this young man — difficult *years*, actually — and the advance knowledge which Joseph's dreams gave him of how the whole situation was going to turn out would reassure Joseph. He was going to need that.

Joseph's brothers lacked the spiritual maturity and the brotherly love to handle the special divine revelation Joseph shared with them. They hated him, first of all, because of the preferential treatment he received, and after they heard about his dreams they hated him even more.

In view of the brother's reaction, Joseph should probably be faulted for sharing his second dream with them. He must have been overwhelmed that God had now spoken to him the second time, and felt he owed it to them to let them know what God had in store for the family. But Joseph seems to have been insensitive to the fact that his dreams irritated his brothers. He should have realized that hearing again how God planned to elevate him above them could only fan the flames of jealousy and hatred. Father Jacob meanwhile "kept the thing in mind." Although he did not understand the significance of Joseph's dreams, he realized that God was conveying important truth to his beloved son.

¹²Now his brothers had gone to graze their father's flocks near Shechem, ¹³ and Israel said to Joseph, "As you know, your brothers are grazing the flocks near Shechem. Come, I am going to send you to them." "Very well," he replied. ¹⁴So he said to him, "Go and see if all is well with your brothers and with the flocks, and bring word back to me." Then he sent him off from the Valley of Hebron. When Joseph arrived at Shechem, ¹⁵ a man found him wandering around in the fields and asked him, "What are you looking for?" ¹⁶He replied, "I'm looking for my brothers. Can you tell me where they are grazing their flocks?" ¹⁷"They have moved on from here," the man answered. "I heard them say, 'Let's go to Dothan.'" So Joseph went after his brothers and found them near Dothan.

Grazing land was in short supply in ancient Canaan, especially as the hot, rainless summer wore on. Since the brothers could not find adequate pasturage for their flocks in the vicinity of their home in the south, they headed farther and farther north. We're surprised to learn that they actually traveled as far as Shechem, fifty miles north of their home in Hebron. Perhaps the fact that their father also owned some land there led them to Shechem.

Jacob feared for the welfare of his sons and their flocks. He hadn't forgotten that it had been at Shechem that his sons had made him a stench to the Canaanite neighbors (34:30). Jacob also knew he wasn't the only one who remembered that. The memory of how his sons had treated the people of Shechem with treachery and cruelty would still be very much alive throughout that entire area.

We can therefore understand why Jacob instructed Joseph to visit his brothers to see if all was well with them. When Joseph got to Shechem he learned that his brothers had moved their flocks fifteen miles still farther north — to Dothan, a city situated on one of the ancient trade routes from Mesopotamia to Egypt.

[18]But they saw him in the distance, and before he reached them, they plotted to kill him. [19]"Here comes that dreamer!" they said to each other. [20]"Come now, let's kill him and throw him into one of these cisterns and say that a ferocious animal devoured him. Then we'll see what comes of his dreams." [21]When Reuben heard this, he tried to rescue him from their hands. "Let's not take his life," he said. [22]"Don't shed any blood. Throw him into this cistern here in the desert, but don't lay a hand on him." Reuben said this to rescue him from them and take him back to his father.

The Apostle James warns us: "Each one is tempted when, by his own evil desire, he is dragged away and enticed. Then, after desire has conceived, it gives birth to sin" (James 1:14f). There were evil desires in the hearts of the brothers toward Joseph, thoughts of envy, of anger, of hatred. Given time, those evil thoughts gave birth to evil actions. When the brothers saw Joseph coming to them, they plotted to kill him.

It's difficult to understand the intensity of the brothers' hatred of Joseph. He was not only their flesh and blood; he and they shared membership in the family of the promise. They had not grown up like savages, or like heathen; they had heard of the promises God had made to their great-grandfather Abraham. They knew that in the present generation theirs was the family — the only family on earth — from whose descendants the Savior of the world would be born. In the brothers' attitude we can see the awful power of sin; their hatred had blinded them to what they were doing.

[23]So when Joseph came to his brothers, they stripped him of his robe — the richly ornamented robe he was wearing — [24] and they took him and threw him into the cistern. Now the cistern was empty; there was no water in it. [25]As they sat down

to eat their meal, they looked up and saw a caravan of Ishmaelites coming from Gilead. Their camels were loaded with spices, balm and myrrh, and they were on their way to take them down to Egypt. ²⁶Judah said to his brothers, "What will we gain if we kill our brother and cover up his blood? ²⁷Come, let's sell him to the Ishmaelites and not lay our hands on him; after all, he is our brother, our own flesh and blood." His brothers agreed. ²⁸So when the Midianite merchants came by, his brothers pulled Joseph up out of the cistern and sold him for twenty shekels of silver to the Ishmaelites, who took him to Egypt.

"After desire has conceived, it gives birth to sin" (James 1:15). Now, sixty-five miles away from the eye of a doting father, the brothers could once and for all settle accounts with their hated brother. Reuben managed to head off their murderous intent by suggesting they throw Joseph into a cistern. Cisterns were commonly used in ancient Canaan to catch the runoff during the rainy season. To minimize loss of water by evaporation they were frequently bell-shaped, with an opening no larger than a man's shoulders. Cisterns would be gradually emptied by farmers and herdsmen during the rainless months of summer. Reuben may have intended to return later to rescue Joseph, but the brothers seem to have been perfectly willing to let Joseph die there in the cistern. And then what would come of all his wild dreams and his high-flying plans? Meanwhile the brothers casually and calmly sat down to enjoy their lunch, deaf to their brother's pleas for his life (42:21).

Reuben sought to prevent one sin by suggesting a different sin. Now Judah tried the same compromise. A camel caravan was coming down the highway that led south to Egypt. It was a caravan from Gilead, east of the Jordan, bearing spices and resins valued highly by the Egyptians for medicinal purposes, as well as for embalming. Judah didn't want Joseph killed, but he knew his brothers would not let him release Joseph. Perhaps they might compromise and sell him as a slave. Then they wouldn't have to witness any more preferential treatment or listen to any more of his self-centered dreams. Besides, they'd be twenty shekels of silver richer. How deadly it is to compromise with sin! To choose what may seem a lesser sin in preference to what may seem a greater sin is a temptation of the devil.

Bible critics have made much of an alleged error here in the names of the merchants who bought Joseph. In verse 27 they're called Ishmaelites, and in the following verse they're called Midianites. Some have used these different names to argue that the subject matter for this chapter came from different written sources, and that not all of the original sources had the facts straight. On the other hand, others have suggested that perhaps the Ishmaelites were the caravaneers, since the Midianites are here called the merchants. Whoever they were, they could see that some herdsmen were eager to sell a seventeen-year-old young man, so they bought him for twenty shekels of silver — less than the usual price of a slave (Exodus 21:32).

29When Reuben returned to the cistern and saw that Joseph was not there, he tore his clothes. 30He went back to his brothers and said, "The boy isn't there! Where can I turn now?" 31Then they got Joseph's robe, slaughtered a goat and dipped the robe in the blood. 32They took the ornamented robe back to their father and said, "We found this. Examine it to see whether it is your son's robe." 33He recognized it and said, "It is my son's robe! Some ferocious animal has devoured him. Joseph has surely been torn to pieces." 34Then Jacob tore his clothes, put on sackcloth and mourned for his son many days. 35All his sons and daughters came to comfort him, but he refused to be comforted. "No," he said, "in mourning will I go

down to the grave to my son." So his father wept for him.
³⁶Meanwhile, the Midianites sold Joseph in Egypt to Potiphar,
one of Pharaoh's officials, the captain of the guard.

Where Reuben was during this transaction we're not told,
but he was shocked when he discovered Joseph was no
longer in the cistern. Apparently he felt the primary responsibility for the welfare of his brother was his, since he was
the oldest. "Where can I turn now?" he asked.

The brothers had an answer. They slaughtered a goat,
took the hated coat, so richly ornamented, dipped it in the
blood and headed back home, rehearsing the story they
would tell their father. When they got home several days
later their father saw the dried, caked blood on the familiar
garment and drew his own conclusion, without their help.

Perhaps they sought to defend themselves by saying, "We
didn't actually tell our father Joseph was killed. We asked
him only whether this was his son's robe." But a lie doesn't
begin on the lips. It begins in a false heart, a heart which
receives the love God has poured into it but withholds that
love from others.

The brothers had not anticipated their father's reaction.
He tore his clothes and dressed in coarse sackcloth. The
person who did this showed no concern for his outward
appearance or his personal comfort; his only concern was to
express the sadness which overwhelmed his heart. "Don't
try to comfort me," he told his sons. "The ache I feel in my
heart will be with me until I join my son in the grave." This
the brothers had not bargained for.

With consummate literary art, the sacred writer breaks off
the narrative about Joseph's father and his brothers at this
point. He has let us share the hopeless grief of the father
and the futile attempts of the family to comfort him. Now
the writer drops that subject; it won't be mentioned again

for another 20 years. The reader can only imagine the grief that continued to gnaw at the heart of Jacob over the years, and the guilt that continued to lie like lead on the consciences of the brothers. They had imagined they were getting away with something; now their consciences gave them no rest. Those 20 years were a dark period for all concerned — for Jacob, for the brothers and for Joseph. Only God could make light shine out of that darkness, and subsequent chapters will tell us how he did. But for the moment the dark hour of that family's grief was oppressive and overwhelming.

Meanwhile, considering that the lot of a slave in ancient times was not an enviable one, there had to be silent grief in the heart of a certain seventeen-year-old as he was led to far-off Egypt. He wasn't a slave, he told himself, but the son of a rich man. Furthermore, he was a member of the family that had received God's promises. What a strange way for the faithful covenant God to treat those who put their trust in him!

Although the father and the brothers and the seventeen-year-old weren't aware of it, God had just worked out the first step in his magnificent plan to shelter the chosen family in Egypt. He saw to it that Joseph was placed in the household of a high ranking officer of the pharaoh, the man in charge of the royal bodyguard.

Moral Laxity of Judah

38 **At that time, Judah left his brothers and went down to stay with a man of Adullam named Hirah. ²There Judah met the daughter of a Canaanite man named Shua. He married her and lay with her; ³ she became pregnant and gave birth to a son, who was named Er. ⁴She conceived again and gave birth to a son and named him Onan. ⁵She gave birth to still another son**

and named him Shelah. It was at Kezib that she gave birth to him.

Genesis 38 is an interlude which the sacred writer inserted before his narrative returns to Joseph in Egypt. By so doing he supplies some unflattering information about one of Joseph's brothers which, strangely enough, played an important role in God's long-range plan.

This chapter does not make for comfortable reading, because it shows us again *how insensitive Jacob's sons were in spiritual matters*. Reuben had committed incest. Simeon and Levi had masterminded the savage revenge on the Shechemites for dishonoring their sister. And most of the brothers had been involved in selling Joseph into slavery. In the chapter before us we learn that Judah took a *Canaanite* wife, surely against better knowledge. He knew how his ancestors had gone out of their way to find *God-fearing* wives for their sons. The Canaanites did not worship the true God; nor would Judah's Canaanite wife be likely to teach her children to love the God of the covenant and trust his promises. Furthermore, the Canaanites were under God's curse because of their national religion — a vile mixture of idolatry and adultery — and would be driven out of their national homeland.

It's not difficult to imagine that after the brothers sold Joseph into slavery, living conditions around Jacob's household were anything but pleasant. The brothers had to observe the ongoing grief of their father. No doubt they heard "I told you so" from Reuben. They had to watch their words constantly, lest an inadvertent slip give their uncomfortable secret away.

For whatever reasons, Judah decided to make a break with his father's household and to strike out on his own. He moved to Adullam, about ten miles west of Jacob's home in

Hebron. Here he met and married a Canaanite woman, who bore him three sons. If it had been up to Judah, that branch of Jacob's family which would later carry the Messianic promise would have been canaanized.

⁶Judah got a wife for Er, his firstborn, and her name was Tamar. ⁷But Er, Judah's firstborn, was wicked in the LORD's sight; so the LORD put him to death. ⁸Then Judah said to Onan, "Lie with your brother's wife and fulfill your duty to her as a brother-in-law to produce offspring for your brother." ⁹But Onan knew that the offspring would not be his; so whenever he lay with his brother's wife, he spilled his semen on the ground to keep from producing offspring for his brother. ¹⁰What he did was wicked in the LORD's sight; so he put him to death also.

When his oldest son Er reached marriageable age, Judah chose a wife for him named Tamar. Since she came from the same area, it's usually taken for granted that she, like Judah's wife, was Canaanite. Her marriage to Er was cut short, however, when the LORD put him to death because of his wickedness. Life, after all, is a gift from God, which we hold in trust. If we abuse our life, God has every right to withdraw his gift.

> The fear of the LORD adds length to life,
> but the years of the wicked are cut short.

(Proverbs 10:27)

So that Er's line would not die out in Israel, Judah instructed his second son Onan to take the widow as his wife and produce offspring for his brother. This is the first Bible reference to the so-called "levirate marriage," although the custom has been found in a number of ancient cultures. This custom of having the next of kin marry a childless widow was definitely fixed by the LORD at Mt. Sinai, where it became part of the sacred constitution governing life among God's people, thereby perpetuating the

311

family of the dead first husband. The first child born of a levirate marriage would live with his father and mother, but in the genealogical tables he would be listed as the son of the dead husband. Moses' farewell address to Israel makes it clear that this practice must not be considered *an absolute command* from God, but as an *act of love* for the departed brother (Deuteronomy 25:5-10)

Onan did not appreciate the situation in which he found himself. As things stood, he was the oldest surviving heir of Judah and as such was entitled to a double share of his father's inheritance. If, however, he fathered a son for Tamar's first husband, that double share would go to the son, the legal descendant of Er. To Onan it seemed ironic: the son would actually be his flesh and blood but would not bear his name and would one day cause him to lose a sizable share of Judah's estate. Onan therefore refused to complete the sex act with Tamar. He was willing to enjoy the *physical gratification* but wanted none of the *responsibilities* involved. God showed his disapproval of that wicked attitude by putting Onan to death.

¹¹**Judah then said to his daughter-in-law Tamar, "Live as a widow in your father's house until my son Shelah grows up." For he thought, "He may die too, just like his brothers." So Tamar went to live in her father's house. ¹²After a long time Judah's wife, the daughter of Shua, died. When Judah had recovered from his grief, he went up to Timnah, to the men who were shearing his sheep, and his friend Hirah the Adullamite went with him. ¹³When Tamar was told, "Your father-in-law is on his way to Timnah to shear his sheep," ¹⁴ she took off her widow's clothes, covered herself with a veil to disguise herself, and then sat down at the entrance to Enaim, which is on the road to Timnah. For she saw that, though Shelah had now grown up, she had not been given to him as his wife. ¹⁵When Judah saw her, he thought she was a prostitute,**

for she had covered her face. ¹⁶Not realizing that she was his daughter-in-law, he went over to her by the roadside and said, "Come now, let me sleep with you." "And what will you give me to sleep with you?" she asked. ¹⁷"I'll send you a young goat from my flock," he said. "Will you give me something as a pledge until you send it?" she asked. ¹⁸He said, "What pledge should I give you?" "Your seal and its cord, and the staff in your hand," she answered. So he gave them to her and slept with her, and she became pregnant by him. ¹⁹After she left, she took her veil and put on her widow's clothes again.

Father Judah had now lost two of his three sons, and he unfairly considered Tamar responsible. In his view, she was "bad luck," and he was not willing to give her his youngest son Shelah. Instead he told Tamar: "Return to your father's house and live as a widow until Shelah has reached marriageable age." He said this with intent to deceive; he never intended to keep his promise and risk losing his only surviving son.

When Shelah came of age and was not given to her Tamar realized she had been deceived by her father-in-law. She realized something else. Since her dead husband's next of kin had prior claim over anyone else to her as a wife, it was unlikely she would ever marry again, and she would remain a childless widow. She considered this neither desirable nor fair, and so took the law into her own hands. She seduced her father-in-law in order to bear his child.

The sacred writer does not tell us, and it is futile to speculate, what prompted Tamar to do what she did. Was her primary motive the desire to *humiliate Judah* for deceiving her? Was it simply the strong desire to *avoid the disgrace of childlessness?* Could it have been her determination to *be a mother in Judah,* to be part of the family that had received God's promises? Although we don't know what her motives were, her strategy was obvious. She would try to trap her father-in-law, to seduce him to sleep with her, so she could become pregnant by him. In our view her chances were slim, but her strategy worked.

Judah, now a widower, had gone to Timnah to shear his sheep. Knowing that sheep-shearing was a happy time, sometimes accompanied by boisterous celebration, Tamar laid aside the black garments she had worn as a widow and dressed in a way calculated to attract a lonely man's roving eye. Careful to veil herself so her father-in-law would not recognize her she sat down at the gate of Enaim, through which Judah had to pass.

It seems like a long shot to us, but her hunch proved correct. Judah did notice her, he was fooled by her disguise and her behavior, and he did proposition her, offering her as payment a goat from his flock. When she asked for some guarantee that he would send the goat, he gave her his *staff*, and his *seal* together with its cord. The seal was a small ceramic cylinder, custom-made, fastened to a cord and worn around one's neck. When this seal was rolled like a tiny rolling pin across a piece of clay it would produce a special design identifying the seal's owner. Herodotus, the Greek historian, reminds us that no Babylonian of any standing would ever be seen without his cylinder seal. Tamar requested these particular items as collateral not because they were so valuable, but because *they provided positive identification*. After spending the night with Judah, she returned to her father's home and put on her widow's clothes again.

²⁰Meanwhile Judah sent the young goat by his friend the Adullamite in order to get his pledge back from the woman, but he did not find her. ²¹He asked the men who lived there, "Where is the shrine prostitute who was beside the road at

Enaim? "There hasn't been any shrine prostitute here," they said. ²²Some went back to Judah and said, "I didn't find her. Besides, the men who lived there said, 'There hasn't been any shrine prostitute here.' " ²³Then Judah said, "Let her keep what she has, or we will become a laughingstock. After all, I did send her this young goat, but you didn't find her." ²⁴About three months later Judah was told, "Your daughter-in-law Tamar is guilty of prostitution, and as a result she is now pregnant." Judah said, "Bring her out and have her burned to death!" ²⁵As she was being brought out, she sent a message to her father-in-law. "I am pregnant by the man who owns these," she said. And she added, "See if you recognize whose seal and cord and staff these are." ²⁶Judah recognized them and said, "She is more righteous than I, since I wouldn't give her to my son Shelah." And he did not sleep with her again.

Naturally Judah wanted his pledge back from the woman — his staff, and especially his seal. He sent the agreed-upon payment through a friend, who asked the men of the town where the shrine prostitute was, the young lady who sold her sexual favors as an expression of her consecration to Astarte, the sister-spouse of the Canaanite fertility god Baal. The friend, of course, was unable to find her.

Three months later Judah learned that his widowed daughter-in-law was expecting a child. Now he added the sin of *hypocrisy* to his *lack of integrity*. He announced that as head of the family he felt himself responsible for seeing that an adulteress in his family was punished — properly and publicly. (Can't you just hear the self-righteous father-in-law: "...not only the widow of two of my sons, but the promised bride of my third son")?

Judah's self-righteousness had blinded him to the fact that he was equally guilty. And when the accused woman handed him his seal and his staff, thereby identifying him as the father of her unborn child, rather than including himself in

315

any punishment Judah could only stammer: "She is more righteous than I."

Jesus' strong condemnation of self-righteousness warns us that this sin still threatens God's children: "Why do you look at the speck of sawdust in your brother's eye and pay no attention to the plank in your own eye? ... You hypocrite!" (Matthew 7:3-5)

The closing words of verse 26 seem to imply that Judah took Tamar into his home, since she had married into his family and was going to bear his child.

It ought to be mentioned, in fairness to Judah, that his tragic lapse into sin, described so graphically in this chapter, seems to have *marked a turning point in his life.* He is mentioned three more times in the Genesis record, and in each of these instances his behavior contrasts sharply with his behavior here. Although he broke with his family when he married a Canaanite and moved away from his father and his brothers, yet in chapter 42 we see him traveling to Egypt with his brothers to buy grain for the family. In 43:1-5 and 46:28 Judah seems to have been especially close to his father, and a leader among his brothers. And when in Egypt Judah pleaded with Joseph not to imprison Benjamin (44:14-34) his words are not only eloquent and impassioned, but they give evidence of *true repentance* and of *spiritual maturity.* This is supported also by the fact that the LORD chose Judah to be the bearer of the Messianic promise (49:10).

²⁷When the time came for her to give birth, there were twin boys in her womb. ²⁸As she was giving birth, one of them put out his hand; so the midwife took a scarlet thread and tied it on his wrist and said, "This one came out first." ²⁹But when he drew back his hand, his brother came out, and she said, "So this is how you have broken out!" And he was named Perez.

³⁰Then his brother, who had the scarlet thread on his wrist, came out and he was given the name Zerah.

Six months later Tamar gave birth to twin sons. When one of the twins put out his hand the midwife immediately tied a scarlet thread on his wrist for identification, since so many privileges went with being the firstborn. But when that twin withdrew his hand, the twin who it had first seemed would be the younger moved ahead and became the firstborn. God made him prominent in another way.

When we compare verse 29 with Matthew 1:13, we see that God actually used an incestuous union to give us one of the Savior's ancestors. According to Genesis 49:12 Perez and his twin Zerah were included in the list of the members of Jacob's family that moved to Egypt, there to grow into a large nation. It was from Perez's line that great King David was born (Ruth 4:18-21; 1 Chronicles 2:5-15), as well as great David's greater son. As you read the lurid details recorded in this chapter of the Bible, perhaps the question occurred to you: "Weren't there more wholesome activities of Jacob's sons that Moses could have recorded? Why this?" Several reasons suggest themselves.

Genesis 38 certainly helps us to understand that *your family tree does not save you.* Jacob's sons were Abraham's great-grandsons, but they stood in constant danger of forgetting their high calling, of yielding to the sins of Canaan and of losing the Messianic blessing. It was only the grace of the Caller that saved them. This chapter helps us to understand better why God concluded that a stay in Egypt, away from constant contact (and intermarriage) with the Canaanites, was necessity for the family of Jacob.

This chapter gives a *beautiful picture of the condescending love of the Savior*, who did not hesitate to include sinners like Judah and Tamar in his family tree. Just as nobody should boast of his own righteousness, so no one need despair because of his sin.

And the chapter offers precious *assurance to those of us who are non-Jews*. The fact that God chose the descendants of Abraham does not mean that he has no use for Gentiles. We agree with Martin Luther: "Gentiles also may be the mother, brother, father, and sisters of our Lord Jesus."

Joseph Falsely Accused And Imprisoned

39 **Now Joseph had been taken down to Egypt. Potiphar, an Egyptian who was one of Pharaoh's officials, the captain of the guard, bought him from the Ishmaelites who had taken him there. ²The LORD was with Joseph and he prospered, and he lived in the house of his Egyptian master. ³When his master saw that the LORD was with him and that the LORD gave him success in everything he did, ⁴ Joseph found favor in his eyes and became his attendant. Potiphar put him in charge of his household, and he entrusted to his care everything he owned. ⁵From the time he put him in charge of his household and of all that he owned, the LORD blessed the household of the Egyptian because of Joseph. The blessing of the LORD was on everything Potiphar had, both in the house and in the field. ⁶So he left in Joseph's care everything he had; with Joseph in charge, he did not concern himself with anything except the food he ate. Now Joseph was well-built and handsome.**

After the interlude which related some of the shameful goings-on in the family of Judah, Moses once again picks up the thread of the story of Joseph. It is this thread that the remaining dozen chapters of Genesis will follow. What happened to Joseph in Egypt is of the greatest importance for the family of Jacob, the family of the promise.

There was a lively slave trade in the ancient Mediterranean world, and Joseph had involuntarily been swept into it. In that world a slave was considered little more than a piece of property. In the LORD's eyes, however, Joseph was vastly more. He was, first, a dearly loved child and, second, a valuable and chosen instrument through whom God was going to bless his people.

To bring that about, God arranged to have an official of the Egyptian royal guard purchase Joseph. Joseph's age (seventeen), his muscular build and his good looks were what probably attracted Potiphar's attention in the first place. But it didn't take him long to realize what a bargain he had gotten at the slave market that day. His new slave was not only strong, but intelligent. He had a good attitude; he was not bitter about his lot in life, giving his new master only sullen obedience. The Spirit of God had created in Joseph an attitude of resignation and a trust in the covenant God, although at the moment he was leading Joseph along a very perplexing and difficult path.

That same covenant God, the God of absolute constancy, prospered the work Joseph did in Potiphar's household. What an assurance that must have been for that lonely teenager in a foreign land! The LORD's hand of blessing became obvious as Potiphar gave Joseph one promotion after another.

He was *permitted to live in the master's house*, instead of in the slaves' quarters. He became *Potiphar's personal attendant*. Potiphar could only conclude that Joseph's God (whoever he was) must have been smiling on him. Joseph received still another promotion when his master put him *in charge of the entire household*, including supervision of the other slaves. Finally, Potiphar made him *manager of everything he owned*.

There was only one detail of household management which Potiphar reserved for himself, and we're not told exactly why. Potiphar seems to have been a religious man, who observed what the prescribed Egyptian ritual had to say about preparing and eating food. Potiphar preferred to supervise this himself, instead of leaving it up to his foreign slave.

With the benefit of hindsight we can see God's hand in Joseph's life even more clearly than Potiphar could. Not only was Joseph developing patience and growing in trust, but the years he spent as manager of a large household were God's way of building and honing his administrative skills. God was soon to find good use for them.

⁷After a while his master's wife took notice of Joseph and said, "Come to bed with me!" ⁸But he refused. "With me in charge," he told her, "my master does not concern himself with anything in the house; everything he owns he has entrusted to my care. ⁹No one is greater in this house than I am. My master has withheld nothing from me except you, because you are his wife. How then could I do such a wicked thing and sin against God?" ¹⁰And though she spoke to Joseph day after day, he refused to go to bed with her or even be with her.

It's estimated that Joseph may have spent ten years in Potiphar's household when he suffered another serious setback. Things had been going unusually well for him, and it seemed that a comfortable life in Potiphar's service lay ahead. But that is not what the covenant God had in mind. The LORD had bigger and better plans for Joseph, and slowly these began to take shape — again in a way that was painful for Joseph.

His master's wife began to express an unwholesome interest in the young slave, and the attraction she felt for him posed a much greater temptation for Joseph than the hatred of his brothers had. The more attractive and pleasing a temptation is, the harder it is to resist.

When the mistress of the household propositioned him, Joseph declined. In the first place, to accept her invitation would be to violate the trust his master had placed in him. But, even more important, to yield to her seduction would be to sin against God. The word translated "sin" means "to miss the mark." As our Creator, God is also our Master, who has determined the way he wants his creatures to live. *He* sets the goals for life: *we creatures* do not. And the goal God has set for life is not "Fun, fun, fun!" The only legitimate goals for life are (1) *God's greater glory* and (2) *our fellowman's welfare*. To substitute physical gratification for God's goals is to miss God's mark, and Joseph was afraid to do that.

"How could I do such a wicked thing?" Joseph asked. He spoke from a double motivation. First of all, *he stood in awe of God*. God's approval meant more to Joseph than a few moments of pleasure with another man's wife. Joseph was actually afraid to do something that would displease God. And, second, *he loved God*, the God who had chosen his family to be the cradle of the Savior. More than thirty centuries later Martin Luther put into words the double motivation which led Joseph to refuse to go to bed with Potiphar's wife: "We should *fear* and *love* God that we lead a pure and decent life in words and actions...."

Joseph's high moral standards made him all the more desirable to the lady of the household. Day after day she invited him to make love to her, and day after day he declined her invitations.

[11]One day he went into the house to attend to his duties, and none of the household servants was inside. [12]She caught him by his cloak and said, "Come to bed with me!" But he left his cloak in her hand and ran out of the house. [13]When she saw that he had left his cloak in her hand and had run out of the

house, ¹⁴ she called her household servants. "Look," she said to them, "this Hebrew has been brought to us to make sport of us! He came in here to sleep with me, but I screamed. ¹⁵When he heard me scream for help, he left his cloak beside me and ran out of the house." ¹⁶She kept his cloak beside her until his master came home. ¹⁷Then she told him this story: "That Hebrew slave you brought us came to me to make sport of me. ¹⁸But as soon as I screamed for help, he left his cloak beside me and ran out of the house."

The time came when Potiphar's wife refused to take no for an answer. When she grabbed Joseph by the cloak and commanded: "Come to bed with me!" he had no choice but to run out of the house, leaving in her hand his cloak, the outer robe that hung over the shoulders. Joseph may have lost his cloak, but he retained a good conscience. Later chapters of this narrative will document the fact that the Savior is very well able, should he so choose, to compensate us for what, in loyalty to him, we give up. A few years later the ruler of Egypt clothed Joseph in robes of fine linen (41:42).

With the same passion with which she had sought to seduce Joseph Potiphar's wife now sought revenge against him. With his cloak in her hands as circumstantial evidence she accused him before the members of her household and before her husband of having tried to attack her.

¹⁹When his master heard the story his wife told him, saying, "This is how your slave treated me," he burned with anger. ²⁰Joseph's master took him and put him in prison, the place where the king's prisoners were confined. But while Joseph was there in the prison, ²¹ the LORD was with him; he showed him kindness and granted him favor in the eyes of the prison warden. ²²So the warden put Joseph in charge of all those held in the prison, and he was made responsible for all that was done

there. **²³The warden paid no attention to anything under Joseph's care, because the LORD was with Joseph and gave him success in whatever he did.**

Potiphar was angry when he heard his wife's charges against Joseph, and we're not told specifically why he was angry. There is reason to think Potiphar may have suspected her of not telling the truth, and now it was going to cost him a competent and conscientious business manager. In the ancient world, for a slave to make sexual advances toward his master's wife would almost surely have earned him the death penalty. Joseph, however, got off with a prison sentence.

Potiphar could not publicly humiliate his wife by ignoring her charges; imprisoning the accused slave may have been his way of helping her to save face. At the time Joseph was led off to prison he was probably too upset to notice, but he was not assigned a cell on death row to await execution, and he was not left to rot in a dungeon. He was imprisoned where the king's prisoners were confined — apparently those accused of political crimes. This seemingly minor detail would later play a major role in getting Joseph out of prison and into a position of authority second only to the king.

God's loyal love followed Joseph into the prison, and this soon became apparent. God granted him favor in the eyes of the prison warden, who may very well have been tipped off by Potiphar to put Joseph's outstanding gifts to use in the prison. Joseph was actually put in charge of all the prisoners. Instead of being sentenced to solitary confinement, Joseph had access to all the prisoners — two of whom were, in God's plan, to be his ticket to freedom.

Since we know how this story comes out, we can see more clearly than Joseph could the strong and steady love of God that was guiding Joseph through these stormy years of his life. Perhaps that is a Bible truth Genesis 39 can teach us, especially when our lives, like Joseph's, take unexpected and unpleasant turns and detours. To remain faithful under temptation, to remain trusting under crushing personal tragedy, we must be convinced that the Savior has a good plan for us and that he's committed to carrying it out. The closing chapters of Genesis — as well as the story of Calvary — assure us that he has, and that he is.

Joseph, Interpreter of Dreams

40 Some time later, the cupbearer and the baker of the king of Egypt offended their master, the king of Egypt. ²Pharaoh was angry with his two officials, the chief cupbearer and the chief baker, ³ and put them in custody in the house of the captain of the guard, in the same prison where Joseph was confined. ⁴The captain of the guard assigned them to Joseph, and he attended them. After they had been in custody for some time, ⁵ each of the two men — the cupbearer and the baker of the king of Egypt, who were being held in prison — had a dream the same night, and each dream had a meaning of its own. ⁶When Joseph came to them the next morning, he saw that they were dejected. ⁷So he asked Pharaoh's officials who were in custody with him in his master's house, "Why are your faces so sad today?" ⁸"We both had dreams," they answered, "but there is no one to interpret them." Then Joseph said to them, "Do not interpretations belong to God? Tell me your dreams."**

In the course of time two new prisoners were placed in Joseph's charge — the cupbearer and the baker of the king of Egypt. Since ancient kings lived in constant danger of assassination, it became common practice for the king to select two of his most trusted servants to make sure that nobody in the palace kitchen poisoned his food or drink.

324

Now because of some sort of offense — real or imagined — these two court officials fell from favor and were imprisoned by the king. The captain of the guard (according to 39:1, that would be Potiphar, Joseph's former master) remembered the distinguished service Joseph had rendered him and assigned him to supervise the two prominent prisoners.

One morning when Joseph made his prison rounds, he noticed that the two special prisoners were disturbed about something. When he inquired he learned that both had had dreams the previous night. Both were convinced God was telling them something by means of the dreams, but they didn't know what. Ancient kings commonly had wise men whose job it was to interpret the royal dreams and to advise the king accordingly, but such help was not available to prisoners.

"Since God sent the dreams," Joseph told them, "only he can give the interpretation." When he then added: "Tell me your dreams," we see that Joseph was allowing for the possibility that God, who alone knew the meaning of the dreams he had sent, might enable him to give the interpretation.

9So the chief cupbearer told Joseph his dream. He said to him, "In my dream I saw a vine in front of me, 10 and on the vine were three branches. As soon as it budded, it blossomed, and its clusters ripened into grapes. 11Pharaoh's cup was in my hand, and I took the grapes, squeezed them into Pharaoh's cup and put the cup in his hand."

12"This is what it means," Joseph said to him. "The three branches are three days. 13Within three days Pharaoh will lift up your head and restore you to your position, and you will put Pharaoh's cup in his hand, just as you used to do when you were his cupbearer. 14But when all goes well with you, remember me and show me kindness; mention me to Pharaoh and get me out of this prison. ¹⁵For I was forcibly carried off from the land of the Hebrews, and even here I have done nothing to deserve being put in a dungeon."

The *cupbearer* told his dream first. In front of him was a vine with three branches, which budded and blossomed and produced grapes. He squeezed the grapes into Pharaoh's cup and offered it to the king. Joseph interpreted the dream to say: "In three days Pharaoh will *lift up your head*." The sacred writer uses the identical Hebrew expression three times (verses 13, 19 and 20) in a play on words, a pun. When Joseph told the cupbearer that Pharaoh would "lift up his head" he meant that the king would lift him up from disgrace and elevate him to his former position.

To this good news Joseph added the plea: "When you're released from prison, remember the one who brought you this good news. Please mention me to Pharaoh." To strengthen his plea, Joseph recalled that on two occasions he'd been the victim of injustice. Without mentioning either his brothers or Potiphar's wife by name, he emphasized that he had done nothing to deserve being forcibly torn from his homeland and later being thrown into prison.

¹⁶**When the chief baker saw that Joseph had given a favorable interpretation, he said to Joseph, "I too had a dream: On my head were three baskets of bread. ¹⁷In the top basket were all kinds of baked goods for Pharaoh, but the birds were eating them out of the basket on my head." ¹⁸"This is what it means," Joseph said. "The three baskets are three days. ¹⁹Within three days Pharaoh will lift off your head and hang you on a tree. And the birds will eat away your flesh."**

The favorable interpretation Joseph had given the chief cupbearer encouraged the chief baker to share the details of his dream. He sensed that the two dreams were so similar that he dared to hope for an identical happy outcome. He was going to be disappointed.

In his dream the royal baker saw himself carrying three baskets of baked goods for Pharaoh on his head, but birds were eating the contents of the topmost basket. The significant way the two dreams ended sealed the baker's doom.

Joseph interpreted: "Within three days Pharaoh will *lift off your head* and hang you. ..." Here the same expression is used as in verse 13, but in a drastically different sense. In three days the baker would be a dead man. He would be beheaded and his body hanged from a tree, where vultures would attack it. It took courage for Joseph to inform so prominent a prisoner of so terrible a doom awaiting him in so short a time, but Joseph was only announcing the truth God had revealed to him.

20Now the third day was Pharaoh's birthday, and he gave a feast for all his officials. He lifted up the heads of the chief cupbearer and the chief baker in the presence of his officials: 21He restored the chief cupbearer to his position, so that he once again put the cup into Pharaoh's hand, 22but he hanged the chief baker, just as Joseph had said to them in his interpretation. 23The chief cupbearer, however, did not remember Joseph; he forgot him.

Three days later there was a celebration in honor of Pharaoh's birthday. What happened at that celebration proved the correctness of Joseph's interpretation. It appears that the royal birthday was an occasion which the king might celebrate by declaring amnesty for certain political prisoners. Apparently the chief cupbearer's offense was considered pardonable, the chief baker's not. After he was released from prison, however, the cupbearer didn't bother to remember Joseph's plea. After all, what was a Hebrew slave in prison compared to an official of the royal court?

Joseph must have been down in the mouth when days and months passed and he heard nothing from the royal cup-bearer. The thought must have passed through his mind: "There went my last hope of gaining my freedom."

Joseph could not have understood that *God* was behind the cupbearer's forgetfulness. If that man had put in a good word for Joseph and the king had pardoned him, he would have left prison a free man and returned to everyday life in Egypt as an unknown. He might even have returned to his home in Canaan. But when Joseph left prison — and he was going to — God wanted him to take up a new and special career which would benefit God's people directly and would help to bring about the fulfillment of God's promises.

Meeting the chief cupbearer marked the turning point in Joseph's career. At that moment his humiliation had reached its lowest point. From here on everything would be looking up for him, although he was not aware of it.

"God is his own interpreter,
and he will make it plain."

Joseph's Dramatic Rise to power

41 When two full years had passed, Pharaoh had a dream: He was standing by the Nile, ² when out of the river there came up seven cows, sleek and fat, and they grazed among the reeds. ³After them, seven other cows, ugly and gaunt, came up out of the Nile and stood beside those on the riverbank. ⁴And the cows that were ugly and gaunt ate up the seven sleek, fat cows. Then Pharaoh woke up. ⁵He fell asleep again and had a second dream: Seven heads of grain, healthy and good, were growing on a single stalk. ⁶After them, seven other heads of grain sprouted — thin and scorched by the east wind. ⁷The thin heads of grain swallowed up the seven healthy, full heads. Then Pharaoh woke up; it had been a dream.

Another two years passed for Joseph in prison, perhaps the dreariest years of his life. He had now spent thirteen years in Egypt. That's a good share of one's lifetime, and now that Joseph realized he's been forgotten by the royal cupbearer he must have wondered if he would ever be a free man again. Now, however, *God's hour had arrived.* When Joseph's deliverance came, it came suddenly and unexpectedly.

Once again, God spoke by means of a dream, this time to Pharaoh. The *locale of the dream* was not unusual. Pharaoh himself was standing at the Nile, the river that brings life to a country that is ninety-five percent desert. But the *action of the dream* was most unusual. Seven sleek and fat cows came up out of the river and grazed along the shore. Then in his dream Pharaoh saw seven other cows, scrawny and ugly, also come up out of the river. But instead of grazing along the shore, they ate up the fat ones.

The king knew that cows are vegetarian animals, not carnivorous. Another thing. After the scrawny cows had eaten the fat ones they remained just as scrawny as they had been. The dream was so unusual, so disturbing, that it interrupted Pharaoh's sleep.

When he managed to fall asleep again he had a second dream, similar to the first but even stranger. Seven good-sized ears of grain grew on a single stalk. After them seven thin heads of grain sprouted and swallowed up the good-sized heads. Heads of grain eating other heads of grain — how odd! And, as with the first dream, the good ones came first, only to be destroyed by the bad ones. Again, the dream was so vivid and its message so foreboding that it disturbed the king's sleep.

⁸In the morning his mind was troubled, so he sent for all the magicians and wise men of Egypt. Pharaoh told them his

dreams, but no one could interpret them for him. ⁹Then the chief cupbearer said to Pharaoh, "Today I am reminded of my shortcomings. ¹⁰Pharaoh was once angry with his servants, and he imprisoned me and the chief baker in the house of the captain of the guard. ¹¹Each of us had a dream the same night, and each dream had a meaning of its own. ¹²Now a young Hebrew was there with us, a servant of the captain of the guard. We told him our dreams, and he interpreted them for us, giving each man the interpretation of his dream. ¹³And things turned out exactly as he interpreted them to us: I was restored to my position, and the other man was hanged."

The following morning the king was still bothered by what he had dreamed. He believed that the gods sometimes spoke to people in dreams; were his gods trying to tell him something here? Furthermore, both dreams ended on a note of tragedy.

Why should healthy cows have been swallowed up by scrawny ones, and healthy heads of grain by thin ones? Were these dreams bad news for the land of Egypt? Pharaoh had to find out. The dreams surely seemed to point to trouble ahead for the flocks and crops of Egypt, the very lifeblood of her existence as a nation.

The king assembled his wise men and his experts in magic, the most learned men in all Egypt, and asked them what his dreams meant. These men were a high rank of priests who specialized in determining the will of the gods and relaying this to men. But the experts stood speechless before their king. They could read their magic formulas for arriving at interpretations, and they could go through the rituals of their priestcraft, but they were completely out of touch with the sovereign Lord of nations, who had spoken to Pharaoh in the dream.

It was then that Pharaoh's chief cupbearer spoke up. He recalled that in prison he and the chief baker had met a young Hebrew who had interpreted their dreams. Although their dreams had been similar, each had a different ending. The Hebrew had interpreted both dreams, and events had unfolded exactly as he had predicted.

[14]So Pharaoh sent for Joseph, and he was quickly brought from the dungeon. When he had shaved and changed his clothes, he came before Pharaoh. [15]Pharaoh said to Joseph, "I had a dream, and no one can interpret it. But I have heard it said of you that when you hear a dream you can interpret it." [16]"I cannot do it," Joseph replied to Pharaoh, "but God will give Pharaoh the answer he desires." [17]Then Pharaoh said to Joseph, "In my dream I was standing on the bank of the Nile, [18] when out of the river there came up seven cows, fat and sleek, and they grazed among the reeds. [19]After them, seven other cows came up — scrawny and very ugly and lean. I had never seen such ugly cows in all the land of Egypt. [20]The lean, ugly cows ate up the seven fat cows that came up first. [21]But even after they ate them, no one could tell that they had done so; they looked just as ugly as before. Then I woke up.

[22]"In my dreams I also saw seven heads of grain, full and good, growing on a single stalk. [23]After them seven other heads sprouted — withered and thin and scorched by the east wind. [24]The thin heads of grain swallowed up the seven good heads. I told this to the magicians, but none could explain it to me."

Joseph was immediately summoned to appear before Pharaoh. From the moment the conversation between king and prisoner began, one senses that the balance of power had shifted. In his own nation the king may have been regarded as a god, but he was clearly not in charge of the situation here. He had been on the receiving end of a dream that bothered him.

Neither were his priestly advisers and magicians in control of the situation. For all of their pious mumbling and posturing they were unable to tell their king what he needed to know.

Who was in charge of the scene in the royal palace? Listen in on the conversation:

> "I have heard it said of you that when you hear a dream you can interpret it."
>
> "I cannot do it," Joseph replied to Pharaoh, "but God will give Pharaoh the answer he desires."

The sovereign Lord of nations was sending a message to a heathen king.

25Then Joseph said to Pharaoh, "The dreams of Pharaoh are one and the same. God has revealed to Pharaoh what he is about to do. 26The seven good cows are seven years, and the seven good heads of grain are seven years; it is one and the same dream. 27The seven lean, ugly cows that came up afterward are seven years, and so are the seven worthless heads of grain scorched by the east wind: They are seven years of famine. 28It is just as I said to Pharaoh: God has shown Pharaoh what he is about to do. 29Seven years of great abundance are coming throughout the land of Egypt, 30 but seven years of famine will follow them. Then all the abundance in Egypt will be forgotten, and the famine will ravage the land. 31The abundance in the land will not be remembered, because the famine that follows it will be so severe. 32The reason the dream was given to Pharaoh in two forms is that the matter has been firmly decided by God, and God will do it soon."

The king had reviewed the details of this double dream, and now it was Joseph's turn. God had given him a beautiful opportunity to witness the truth to a man who didn't know it. Because his own gods and his country's wisest men had been of no help to him, the king was receptive to what Joseph had to say, and Joseph made the most of his opportunity.

He had just come from prison to the palace, and the subject of the first two sentences he spoke was *God. "God has revealed to Pharaoh what he is about to do."* The Hebrew name for "God" here has the definite article attached to it; this usually emphasizes "the one true God."

"The dreams of Pharaoh are one and the same. The one true God, sovereign Lord of the nations, has sent you a message about what he's going to do in your country. *Seven years of great abundance* are coming, but *seven years of famine* will follow. Just as in your dreams the lean and ugly devoured the healthy and strong, so the seven years of famine will swallow up the supplies of grain stored up during the years of abundance.

"The matter has been firmly decided by God (the one true God) and he will do it soon." Here is further testimony that God was in control, regulating the flooding of the Nile, controlling Egypt's agriculture to serve his purposes. For God to have spoken to Pharaoh in dreams *twice* indicated that the full set of fourteen years would begin *soon.*

33"And now let Pharaoh look for a discerning and wise man and put him in charge of the land of Egypt. 34Let Pharaoh appoint commissioners over the land to take a fifth of the harvest of Egypt during the seven years of abundance. 35They should collect all the food of these good years that are coming and store up the grain under the authority of Pharaoh, to be kept in the cities for food. 36This food should be held in reserve for the country, to be used during the seven years of famine that will come upon Egypt, so that the country may not be ruined by the famine." 37The plan seemed good to Pharaoh and to all his officials. 38So Pharaoh asked them, "Can we find anyone like this man, one in whom is the spirit of God?" 39Then Pharaoh said to Joseph, "Since God has made all this known to

you, there is no one so discerning and wise as you. ⁴⁰You shall be in charge of my palace, and all my people are to submit to your order. Only with respect to the throne will I be greater than you."

Joseph did not stop with merely interpreting the king's dream; he added advice for the king. He listed some steps Pharaoh could take immediately to prepare for the famine, now only seven years away. The same Spirit of God who had given Joseph the key to unlock the mystery of Pharaoh's dreams suggested a method for meeting the emergency confronting Egypt.

"Since we're now in the first of the abundant crop years you'd be well advised to find the right man and put him in charge of Egypt's food supply. Take twenty percent of each farmer's harvest in each of the next seven years and put it in storage, so that there will be adequate supplies to supplement the poor harvests in the seven bad years that are coming." A twenty percent tax was surely not a heavy tax in prosperous years. Joseph had calculated that this would accumulate a food reserve adequate to see Egypt and her neighbors through the years of food shortage.

The king was mightily impressed by Joseph's words. His interpretation of the two dreams was *logical* and *clear*, and his suggestions for immediate action seemed *realistic*. Even more, the king realized that the words of Joseph were not just common sense; they were *supernatural wisdom*.

"I've already found the man you say I should look for. You shall be in charge." Is it unrealistic to think that an absolute monarch like Pharaoh would elevate a slave — and a foreign slave, at that — to the number two position in the kingdom? Pharaoh's own words answer the question: "Can we find anyone like this man, one in whom is the spirit of God?"

⁴¹So Pharaoh said to Joseph, "I hereby put you in charge of the whole land of Egypt." ⁴²Then Pharaoh took his signet ring from his finger and put in on Joseph's finger. He dressed him in robes of fine linen and put a gold chain around his neck. ⁴³He had him ride in a chariot as his second-in-command, and men shouted before him, "Make way!" Thus he put him in charge of the whole land of Egypt. ⁴⁴Then Pharaoh said to Joseph, "I am Pharaoh, but without your word no one will lift hand or foot in all Egypt." ⁴⁵Pharaoh gave Joseph the name Zaphenath-Paneah and gave him Asenath daughter of Potiphera, priest of On, to be his wife. And Joseph went throughout the land of Egypt.

Joseph was now permitted to enjoy not only the title but also the fringe benefits of high office: fine linen robes, a gold chain about his neck, and even the king's signet ring authorizing him to give orders in the king's name. Since this unknown foreigner was going to be instituting some sweeping changes in the Egyptian economy, the king thought it best to introduce him formally, by means of a parade through the streets of the capital.

Pharaoh took one more step to insure that the people of Egypt would cooperate with Joseph willingly. He gave Joseph *a new identity* as an Egyptian. No longer would he be referred to as "that Hebrew slave" (39:17). Joseph got a new Egyptian name and an Egyptian wife, daughter of the priest of On. Since the city of On, more familiar to us as Heliopolis, was the center of the worship of the sun-god Re, Joseph's father-in-law may very well have been the high priest. We're told that pharaohs also chose their wives from this family. Now, in addition to having a prominent position in Egypt, Joseph had *status* as well. He was regarded as the equal of the priests, the highest class of Egyptian society.

Joseph goes throughout Egypt

Some have wondered whether this might have posed a conflict of interest for Joseph. It is not stated, and we need not assume, that because Joseph was given rank equal to that of priests that he had to take part in the worship of the sun god. The duties Pharaoh assigned to him were political and economic, not religious.

⁴⁶Joseph was thirty years old when he entered the service of Pharaoh king of Egypt. And Joseph went out from Pharaoh's presence and traveled throughout Egypt. ⁴⁷During the seven years of abundance the land produced plentifully. ⁴⁸Joseph collected all the food produced in those seven years of abundance in Egypt and stored it in the cities. In each city he put the food grown in the fields surrounding it. ⁴⁹Joseph stored up huge quantities of grain, like the sand of the sea; it was so much that he stopped keeping records because it was beyond measure.

⁵⁰Before the years of famine came, two sons were born to Joseph by Asenath daughter of Potiphera, priest of On. ⁵¹Joseph name his firstborn Manasseh and said, "It is because God has made me forget all my trouble and all my father's household." ⁵²The second son he named Ephraim and said, "It is because God has made me fruitful in the land of my suffering."

⁵³The seven years of abundance in Egypt came to an end, ⁵⁴and the seven years of famine began, just as Joseph had said. There was famine in all the other lands, but in the whole land of Egypt there was food. ⁵⁵When all Egypt began to feel the famine, the people cried to Pharaoh for food. Then Pharaoh told all the Egyptians, "Go to Joseph and do what he tells you." ⁵⁶When the famine had spread over the whole country, Joseph opened the storehouses and sold grain to the Egyptians, for the famine was severe throughout Egypt. ⁵⁷And all the countries came to Egypt to buy grain from Joseph, because the famine was severe in all the world.

At this significant point in the narrative, Moses helps us to put Joseph's life in a time frame. "Joseph was thirty years old when he entered the service of Pharaoh." Since we learned earlier that he was seventeen when his brothers sold him (37:2), we realize he had already spent thirteen years of his life away from his home and family. And knowing the number of good and bad crop years, we can use this base number of thirty to calculate Joseph's age when he was reunited with his brothers (45:6).

But for now he had work to do. He made a tour throughout the land of Egypt to inspect existing grain storage facilities and to plan the new ones that would be needed. Under his supervision huge quantities of grain were stored up during the years of plenty. Storage sites were located in the cities, perhaps to simplify distribution of food to the populace during the drought years that lay ahead.

Before moving on to a description of those years, Moses gives us some information about *Joseph's family*. God blessed Joseph and his wife with two sons, and you've got to be impressed with the names Joseph chose for them. The firstborn was *Manasseh* ("he caused me to forget"). Instead of letting bitterness against his brothers or against Potiphar's wife simmer in his heart, Joseph let God erase the pain of those hurts. He concentrated on the fact that God had released him from slavery and from prison and equipped him to serve his Lord in a unique way.

The other son was name *Ephraim* ("double fruitfulness"). The name reflects Joseph's joy over this second gift of God. Joseph didn't know it at the time, but because his father Jacob was going to give him the right of the firstborn, both of his sons would be *heads of tribes* in the future nation of Israel.

Joseph occupied a position of power and privilege in an ancient nation which was a world power, but he did not

consider Egypt his home. We learn this from a remark
he made when naming Ephraim: "...God has made me fruitful in the *land of my suffering*." Egypt was very
obviously the place God wanted Joseph to be at that time,
and he was content to live there. But his heart was in
Canaan. That was the land of promise, and Joseph had
not forgotten.

Now the good years, the years of abundant crops, were
over, and the years of crop shortages and of famine began.
When the people of Egypt appealed to their king for help,
he directed them to Joseph. Joseph realized that the nation's
grain reserves from the years of plenty had to be guarded
carefully if the nation was to survive seven years of famine,
and so he did not simply *give* grain back to the people who
had originally grown it. Instead he *sold* it to them, as he did
to the people of other nations who came to Egypt to buy
food. This was the means God used to bring about the
migration of Jacob's family to Egypt.

Genesis 41 is a busy chapter, long and crowded with
detail. But we dare not let the mass of detail divert our
attention from a blessed truth. *Our Savior holds the destiny
of all people in his hands.* He so directs their course that
even the doings of the ungodly, though they may not realize
it, must contribute to God's glory and to the welfare of his
family of believers. God had overruled the evil designs of
Joseph's brothers, and now he controlled even the destiny of
the nation of Egypt in order to serve his good plans for his
chosen people.

Joseph's Reunion with His Brothers

42 **When Jacob learned that there was grain in Egypt, he
said to his sons, "Why do you just keep looking at each
other?" ²He continued, "I have heard that there is grain in**

Egypt. Go down there and buy some for us, so that we may live and not die." ³Then ten of Joseph's brothers went down to buy grain from Egypt. ⁴But Jacob did not send Benjamin, Joseph's brother, with the others, because he was afraid that harm might come to him. ⁵So Israel's sons were among those who went to buy grain, for the famine was in the land of Canaan also.

Sin is a great wrecker, a fact often lost sight of in an age when most people have an easy conscience about sin. For twenty years Joseph's brothers had lived with the knowledge that they had sinned — against God, against their father, against their brother. Over the years they had tried to dismiss the memory of their sin, perhaps by rationalizations ("What's done is done; we can't bring Joseph back"); perhaps by busying themselves with the nuts and bolts of making a living. To the casual observer it might have seemed that their crime against their brother was a thing of the past.

But you can't get rid of sin that easily. Sin is a wrecker. It had destroyed the relationship between the brothers and Joseph; it had destroyed a father's happiness over his children. Worst of all, the brothers' sin had destroyed the father-child relationship between them and God. Over the years *they* may have tried to forget, but *God* had not forgotten. The next four chapters of Genesis provide a detailed account of God's persistent — and successful — efforts to lead the brothers to repentance and reconciliation with Joseph and with God.

Father Jacob had learned, perhaps from friends, that foreigners were permitted to purchase food in Egypt. The family's supplies must have been running low, because Jacob asked his older sons to travel to Egypt for food, "...that we may live and not die" of starvation.

340

Jacob did not send Benjamin with his brothers. Benjamin, Rachel's second son, was now the special object of Jacob's love, and the aged father "was afraid that harm might come to him." Perhaps Jacob told himself: "Twenty years ago I sent Joseph on a trip to Shechem to visit his brothers, and I've regretted it ever since." That had been a trip of only fifty miles, a trip of only a few days, and it proved disastrous. A trip to Egypt was over three hundred miles; it would take weeks. The danger was too great for Jacob to let Benjamin go.

From Hebron the best route south would have been along the Via Maris, the Way of the Sea, which followed the Mediterranean shoreline all the way to Egypt. "Israel's sons," sons of the covenant bearer, joined others from Canaan who were making the same trip for the same reason, since God had permitted the famine to spread into other areas of the eastern Mediterranean. *The brothers'* chief concern on the trip was food for the family. *God* had other concerns. These sons of the covenant had grown indifferent to the blessings that went with being members of that special family. If they were not to lose these blessing completely, God had some work to do on their hearts, and Joseph would be his instrument.

⁶Now Joseph was the governor of the land, the one who sold grain to all its people. So when Joseph's brothers arrived, they bowed down to him with their faces to the ground. ⁷As soon as Joseph saw his brothers, he recognized them, but he pretended to be a stranger and spoke harshly to them. "Where do you come from?" he asked. "From the land of Canaan," they replied, "to buy food." ⁸Although Joseph recognized his brothers, they did not recognize him. ⁹Then he remembered his dreams about them and said to them, "You are spies! You have come to see where our land is unprotected."

Perhaps Joseph knew that eventually his brothers would have to come to Egypt to replenish their food supplies. Since Joseph was "the governor of the land," he could not be present at each grain transaction. Perhaps he had asked his sales people to notify him of any prospective buyers from Hebron, in Canaan. When the brothers finally did arrive, we might imagine the clerk asking them to wait while he notified Joseph. By whatever means, Joseph was present to deal personally with his ten brothers.

With the customary near-Eastern sign of respect they bowed with faces to the ground in front of this Egyptian official. Joseph's thoughts immediately ran back to his dreams (about his brothers' sheaves bowing down before his, and the sun, moon and eleven stars bowing before him, 37:5-9). He recognized that God had just fulfilled those dreams before his own eyes.

But he realized as well that God had some more work that needed to be done on those brothers. Their consciences needed to be awakened. Before he could identify himself to his brothers and assure them of his forgiveness and his good will, he had to learn whether they had repented. For Joseph the important consideration was not where his brothers stood *with him*, but where they stood *with God*.

Joseph therefore "...pretended to be a stranger and spoke harshly to them." It had to be that way. Before the surgeon can remove the cancer that threatens the patient's life, he has to cut deep; he has to wound the patient. For himself Joseph would have liked nothing better than to throw his arms around his brothers, but that would have interfered with God's higher and better plans for them.

The brothers did not recognize Joseph, and this is understandable. He was the last person they expected to meet. Remember, too, that more than twenty years had passed since they'd last seen him, a frightened seventeen-year-old stripped of his robe, pale with fear as he was led off into slavery. Now they saw a thirty-seven-year-old Egyptian official apparently suspicious of their motives. The fact that Joseph spoke to them through an interpreter in a language they could not understand heightened the illusion.

"You are spies!" They couldn't believe their ears. "Why would so many of you have to come down to buy food for one family?" Historically Egypt's greatest danger of invasion had been from the north, the direction from which the brothers had come. "You have come to see where our land is unprotected." The extended famine might have prompted Egypt's military leaders to pull back some of their defense forces from remote areas, perhaps on the fringe of the Sinai Desert, and station them closer to food storage areas.

There may have been irony in Joseph's charge. Two decades earlier his brothers had considered him a spy sent by their father to check up on them and report back; now the same accusation was directed at them. Joseph's charge was unjustified, and it stung the brothers. They were shortly going to have plenty of time — three days — to reflect on how unfairly they had once treated Joseph.

[10]"No, my lord," they answered. "Your servants have come to buy food. [11]We are all the sons of one man. Your servants are honest men, not spies." [12]"No!" he said to them. "You have come to see where our land is unprotected." [13]But they replied, "Your servants were twelve brothers, the sons of one man, who lives in the land of Canaan. The youngest is now with our father, and one is no more." [14]Joseph said to them, "It is just as I told you: You are spies! [15]And this is how you will be tested: As surely as Pharaoh lives, you will not leave this place unless your youngest brother comes here. [16]Send one of your number to get your brother; the rest of you will be kept in prison, so that your words may be tested to see if you are telling the truth.

If you are not, then as surely as Pharaoh lives, you are spies!"
¹⁷And he put them all in custody for three days.

The brothers continued to plead their innocence, but the only answer they got from the stern-faced Egyptian was: "I don't believe you!" They had once refused to listen to the tearful pleading of a younger brother; now somebody who held the upper hand over them would not listen to their pleas.

By repeating his accusation and offering them repeated opportunities to defend themselves Joseph was hoping to learn more about his father and his brother Benjamin. "Your servants were twelve brothers, the sons of one man, who lives in the land of Canaan. The youngest is now with our father...." *So Father is still alive! And Benjamin, too!"* "...and one is no more." *So their consciences hadn't let them forget.* But had they confessed their action as a sin against God and man? And did they still harbor resentment against the sons of Rachel, Jacob's favored wife?

Joseph devised a simple test. One of the brothers would be sent home to bring Benjamin to Egypt. And to make sure he would return, the remaining brothers would be confined to prison. If Benjamin did not come, Joseph would know they were spies. To add a note of realism to his proposal, and to underscore the seriousness of the situation, Joseph packed them all off into prison for three days. The bewildered brothers had time to think back to the awful treatment they had given their brother. They wondered, just as Joseph had, what was going to happen to them. This was harsh treatment, God's shock treatment, to bring them to acknowledge their guilt before God and to repent of it.

¹⁸On the third day, Joseph said to them, "Do this and you will live, for I fear God: ¹⁹If you are honest men, let one of your

brothers stay here in prison, while the rest of you go and take grain back for your starving households. ²⁰But you must bring your youngest brother to me, so that your words may be verified and that you may not die." This they proceeded to do. ²¹They said to one another, "Surely we are being punished because of our brother. We saw how distressed he was when he pleaded with us for his life, but we would not listen; that's why this distress has come upon us." ²²Reuben replied, "Didn't I tell you not to sin against the boy? But you wouldn't listen! Now we must give an accounting for his blood." ²³They did not realize that Joseph could understand them, since he was using an interpreter. ²⁴He turned away from them and began to weep, but then turned back and spoke to them again. He had Simeon taken from them and bound before their eyes.

Three days later the brothers were led out of prison and, expecting the worst, were again brought before the Egyptian governor. "I fear God," he announced. In other words, "you're not dealing with a tyrant. I will not condemn you merely on suspicion of guilt. And I have reduced the demand I made of you three days ago. Instead of imprisoning all of you except one, I'll have only one of you stay in prison, while the rest may go home to get your brother."

"But you must bring your youngest brother to me, so that your words may be verified and that you may not die." The implication was clear. "If you don't wish to do this, the case is closed. We will deal with you as we do in this country with spies." Even though Joseph knew what heartache his demand would cause his father Jacob, Joseph had to see how they reacted to Benjamin.

Just coming off of three days in prison, and then hearing talk about a possible death sentence, the brothers bared their hearts to one another, not knowing that the stern Egyptian was understanding every word they spoke. "Surely we are being punished because of our brother. We are bearing the consequences of our guilt." Their consciences, long silent, were speaking now.

Joseph must have been happy to recognize that his efforts to help his brothers confront their sin were beginning to bear fruit. Reuben's statement, "We must give an accounting for his blood," shows he knew their present misery came from God, who held them accountable for a crime that in his eyes was the same as murder.

When Joseph heard this, he had to leave the room. His emotions overwhelmed him, and tears flooded his eyes. After regaining his composure he returned and singled out Simeon. Simeon had been one of the ringleaders in the plot against the Shechemites (34:25). Had he also spearheaded the plot against his seventeen-year-old brother? Before their eyes Joseph had Simeon bound and led off to prison, to make sure the brothers would return with Benjamin.

²⁵Joseph gave orders to fill their bags with grain, to put each man's silver back in his sack, and to give them provisions for their journey. After this was done for them, ²⁶ they loaded their grain on their donkeys and left. ²⁷At the place where they stopped for the night one of them opened his sack to get feed for his donkey, and he saw his silver in the mouth of his sack. ²⁸"My silver has been returned," he said to his brothers. "Here it is in my sack." Their hearts sank and they turned to each other trembling and said, "What is this that God has done to us?"

Joseph then issued *two unusual orders* to his sales people. After the brothers' sacks had been filled with grain, each man's payment in silver was to be replaced in his sack. And secondly, the brothers were to be given provisions for their long journey home. Joseph didn't want them opening their sacks and finding their silver until a good portion of the return trip was behind them. Returning their silver seems to have been intended to keep the brothers bewildered, to strengthen their conviction: "There are things going on here that are not normal." Joseph's action may have been intended also to send a signal to the father that the Egyptian with whom the brothers were dealing did after all have a heart for the family.

It must have been with a feeling of relief that the brothers left Egypt, a subdued lot. At the end of the day they stopped off at one of the inns along the Via Maris. One man opened his sack to get feed for his donkey and found — his silver! The brothers could only look at each other and ask: "What is this that God has done to us?"

The name they used for "God" was an appropriate one. He is the *Almighty*, who as our *Creator* is also our *Master*, and who doesn't like it when his creatures, as it were, tweak his nose. With their question the brothers were not only admitting that God exists; they were admitting that God was the author of everything that had happened to them. We will learn later that they were so frightened that the other brothers didn't dare open their sacks, for fear of what they might find.

²⁹**When they came to their father Jacob in the land of Canaan, they told him all that had happened to them. They said, ³⁰"The man who is lord over the land spoke harshly to us and treated us as though we were spying on the land. ³¹But we said to him, 'We are honest men; we are not spies. ³²We were twelve brothers, sons of one father. One is no more, and the youngest is now with our father in Canaan.' ³³Then the man who is lord over the land said to us, 'This is how I will know whether you are honest men: Leave one of your brothers here with me, and take food for your starving households and go. ³⁴But bring your youngest brother to me so I will know that you are not spies but honest men. Then I will give your brother back to you, and you can trade in the land.' "**

It was a sober-faced group that perhaps ten days later reached Hebron and reported to Jacob the unbelievable experiences they had had in Egypt. And it was a grim-faced father who noticed that Simeon was missing and who learned the Egyptian governor had demanded that Benjamin accompany them the next time down.

We miss something in the brothers' report to their father. Although they had admitted their guilt to one another (verses 21, 22), and although they recognized the hand of God in their predicament (verse 28), they were not ready to confess their sin to their father (verse 32).

35As they were emptying their sacks, there in each man's sack was his pouch of silver! When they and their father saw the money pouches, they were frightened. 36Their father Jacob said to them, "You have deprived me of my children. Joseph is no more and Simeon is no more, and now you want to take Benjamin. Everything is against me!"

37Then Reuben said to his father, "You may put both of my sons to death if I do not bring him back to you. Entrust him to my care, and I will bring him back." 38But Jacob said, "My son will not go down there with you; his brother is dead and he is the only one left. If harm comes to him on the journey you are taking, you will bring my gray head down to the grave in sorrow."

As the men were emptying their sacks of grain, each man found in his sack the purchase price in silver. Now they had additional reason to dread the return trip to Egypt. If they brought Benjamin with them the Egyptian governor would know they were not *spies*. But now he could charge them with being *thieves*, and they would once again be at his mercy. The money-pouches they held in their hands brought them as little satisfaction as the twenty silver pieces they had once received for selling their brother. Sin is a great wrecker.

Father Jacob was thoroughly dismayed by the report his sons brought back. From his words we can see once again the intensity of the love Jacob had toward Rachel and her two sons. Although two decades had elapsed since Joseph had been taken from him, Jacob still felt that loss deeply. That wound had not healed. His life had not been the same ever since. And if, in addition, Benjamin were now taken from him, he would not be able to bear up under it. He would die of grief.

We're not impressed with the offer Reuben made to his father. He apparently felt that he, the oldest, ought to be the first to try to persuade Jacob to let Benjamin accompany them on the next trip to Egypt. Jacob simply ignored the offer. Could the senseless killing of two of his grandchildren compensate a grieving father for the loss of his favorite son?

The way God dealt with the ten brothers is the way he still deals with his erring children today. The curse announced by God's law still frightens people, producing sorrow over sin, which is the necessary first step of true repentance. The hard words the brothers heard from Joseph, the accusation of being spies, their three-day stay in prison, Simeon's months-long imprisonment — these were not evidences of God's anger raging against them, but of his determination to *convince them that the path they were following was leading them to certain destruction.* Joseph was not playing God with his brothers. He was the Lord's messenger here to transmit the harsh message of God's holy law. When it became clear that the brothers were listening to this preliminary message and that the law of God had done its preliminary work, then God would — again through Joseph — let them hear another message. Joseph's arms around

them would *assure them of his — and God's — forgiveness.*
True repentance, then, is first of all feeling the terrors of
God's anger over sin, and, secondly, trusting his offer of full
forgiveness, all for the sake of the Messiah, Jesus Christ.

Joseph's Brothers Visit Egypt a Second Time

This chapter records the second visit Jacob's sons made
to Egypt to buy food. The casual reader of Genesis may see
in this no more than the inevitable *consequence of pro-
longed famine.* The perceptive reader will, however, see the
hand of God again at work. There was some unfinished
business involving the eternal well-being of these brothers
God had to attend to.

43 Now the famine was still severe in the land. ²So when
they had eaten all the grain they had brought from
Egypt, their father said to them, "Go back and buy us a little
more food." ³But Judah said to him, "The man warned us
solemnly, 'You will not see my face again unless your brother is
with you.' ⁴If you will send our brother along with us, we will
go down and buy food for you. ⁵But if you will not send him, we
will not go down, because the man said to us, 'You will not see
my face again unless your brother is with you.' "

⁶Israel asked, "Why did you bring this trouble on me by
telling the man you had another brother?" ⁷They replied, "The
man questioned us closely about ourselves and our family. 'Is
your father still living?' he asked us. 'Do you have another
brother?' We simply answered his questions. How were we to
know he would say, 'Bring your brother down here'?"

The poor harvest of the previous year had brought famine
to the people living in Canaan. After doing all the belt-
tightening they could, they dipped into their cash reserves
and went outside of the country to buy food. It will be helpful to remember that in ancient Canaan there were no huge

silos and grain elevators holding tons of grain for future use. The average resident of ancient Canaan lived what we would consider a hand-to-mouth existence, using this year's crop to meet this year's needs. But when a second year of crop failure followed the first, the people of Canaan knew they faced a crisis.

Jacob had postponed asking his sons to make a second food run to Egypt because he knew the terms the Egyptian governor had set, terms spelled out twice here by Judah: "You will not see my face again unless your brother is with you." Jacob had been unwilling to meet those terms, but now he knew he had no choice.

"Why did you tell him you have a younger brother?" Jacob asked, his voice close to breaking. "You knew I wouldn't have wanted the Egyptian to know that! Why did you bring this trouble on me?"

"We didn't volunteer the information," the brothers replied. "The man asked us all sorts of pointed questions — about our father, and whether we had another brother. All we did was to answer his questions truthfully. How could we have known he would say: 'Bring that brother down here'?"

8Then Judah said to Israel his father, "Send the boy along with me and we will go at once, so that we and you and our children may live and not die. 9I myself will guarantee his safety; you can hold me personally responsible for him. If I do not bring him back to you and set him here before you, I will bear the blame before you all my life. 10As it is, if we had not delayed, we could have gone and returned twice."

To break the stalemate, Judah stepped forward. Perhaps he felt especially responsible for his father's grief, because twenty years earlier he'd been the one who suggested sell-

Genesis 43:11-14

ing Joseph into slavery (37:26f). In Judah's words we detect none of the bluster Reuben had previously expressed (42:37). Himself the father of two sons, Judah pleaded with his father: "Put the boy in my care; I'll be responsible for him. If I don't return him to you safe and sound, you can hold me accountable all my life." There's a *manliness* in Judah's words.

There's also a distinct note of *realism.* "We can't go on as we are. We'll die without food, and it's available only in Egypt. We've already waited too long. In the time that we've wasted we could've made two trips to Egypt."

¹¹Then their father Israel said to them, "If it must be, then do this: Put some of the best products of the land in our bags and take them down to the man as a gift — a little balm and a little honey, some spices and myrrh, some pistachio nuts and almonds. ¹²Take double the amount of silver with you, for you must return the silver that was put back into the mouths of your sacks. Perhaps it was a mistake. ¹³Take your brother also and go back to the man at once. ¹⁴And may God Almighty grant you mercy before the man so that he will let your other brother and Benjamin come back with you. As for me, if I am bereaved, I am bereaved."

When the father now responded, it is significant that Moses calls him by the new name God had given him: "*Israel* said to them... 'Take your brother. ...'" *Israel* responded — Israel, the man who had struggled with God in prayer and had won a blessing. In the present crisis he had once again struggled with God and had discovered what course of action the LORD wanted him to follow.

The aged patriarch — he was 130 at this time — did not give his permission from a feeling of *helplessness*, but in the *submission of faith*. This is not to say he knew Benjamin would soon be restored to his family circle; he

352

had no way of knowing that. But the patriarch *knew that God knew*, and he was content to let the outcome rest in the LORD's hands. In other words, his prayer was: "LORD, may your will be done!" And that settled the matter.

There were a few other details to be arranged. "Take a gift for the governor as evidence of our good will." Some of the gift items Israel listed were imported, brought by the camel caravans that regularly passed through Canaan. Some of the gifts — honey, pistachio nuts, almonds — were delicacies produced in Canaan and possibly less affected by the famine. "And to assure the Egyptian that you had no intention of cheating him," Israel added, "be sure you take double the amount of silver with you, enough also for the first purchase of grain."

¹⁵**So the men took the gifts and double the amount of silver, and Benjamin also. They hurried down to Egypt and presented themselves to Joseph. ¹⁶When Joseph saw Benjamin with them, he said to the steward of his house, "Take these men to my house, slaughter an animal and prepare dinner; they are to eat with me at noon." ¹⁷The man did as Joseph told him and took the men to Joseph's house. ¹⁸Now the men were frightened when they were taken to his house. They thought, "We were brought here because of the silver that was put back into our sacks the first time. He wants to attack us and overpower us and seize us as slaves and take our donkeys." ¹⁹So they went up to Joseph's steward and spoke to him at the entrance to the house. ²⁰"Please, sir," they said, "we came down here the first time to buy food. ²¹But at the place where we stopped for the night we opened our sacks and each of us found his silver — the exact weight — in the mouth of his sack. So we have brought it back with us. ²²We have also brought additional silver with us to buy food. We don't know who put our silver in our sacks." ²³"It's all right," he said. "Don't be afraid. Your God, the God of your father, has given you treasure in your**

**sacks; I received your silver." Then he brought Simeon out
to them.**

Nothing is said about the tedious, three hundred mile trip
to Egypt. The writer takes us at once to the scene at the end
of the journey. Joseph was happy to see his brothers had
returned with their younger brother. They had not taken
advantage of the opportunity, once they were out of their
father's sight, to vent their spite on Benjamin, as they had
done to Benjamin's older brother twenty years earlier.
Apparently without informing his brothers, Joseph gave
orders that they were to be taken to his home for dinner. He
wanted to put them at ease before testing them to find out
whether they were jealous of Benjamin.

Remembering the harsh treatment they had received on
their first visit to Egypt, the brothers were fearful. What
was behind this dinner invitation? Was this a trap? Did the
Egyptian merely want to get them away from the public
marketplace so that in private he could charge them with
stealing the silver and sentence them to slavery? Their consciences gave them no rest, and they anticipated the worst.

Before they entered Joseph's house, therefore, they
approached the steward of the household and offered him
the silver that had been returned in their sacks. To their surprise and perplexity, the steward (who must have been
briefed by Joseph) said: "You don't owe anything. My
books show that I received payment from you. The money
you say you found in your sacks must have been a special
gift from God." And before they could answer, he brought
Simeon out to them.

**²⁴The steward took the men into Joseph's house, gave them
water to wash their feet and provided fodder for their donkeys.
²⁵They prepared their gifts for Joseph's arrival at noon, because**

they had heard that they were to eat there. ²⁶When Joseph came home, they presented to him the gifts they had brought into the house, and they bowed down before him to the ground. ²⁷He asked them how they were, and then he said, "How is your aged father you told me about? Is he still living?" ²⁸They replied, "Your servant our father is still alive and well." And they bowed low to pay him honor. ²⁹As he looked about and saw his brother Benjamin, his own mother's son, he asked, "Is this your youngest brother, the one you told me about?" And he said, "God be gracious to you, my son." ³⁰Deeply moved at the sight of his brother, Joseph hurried out and looked for a place to weep. He went into his private room and wept there.

When Joseph arrived for the noon meal the brothers presented the gift they had brought along. They prostrated themselves at his feet, once again fulfilling Joseph's earlier dream (37:6-9).

Since they still anticipated the worst, the brothers didn't know what to make of the cordiality their host displayed — the friendly welcome, the questions about their father, the special warmth he extended to Benjamin and the special blessing he pronounced on him ("God be gracious to you, my son!").

Since at this point Joseph could not yet identify himself to them but had to restrain his emotions, he left the room so that in the privacy of his own chambers no one would witness the flood of tears. These were tears, first of all, *of joy* over seeing his own mother's son, but tears also *of gratitude* to God for producing what surely appeared to be a change of heart in his brothers.

³¹After he had washed his face, he came out and, controlling himself, said, "Serve the food." ³²They served him by himself, the brothers by themselves, and the Egyptians who ate with him by themselves, because Egyptians could not eat with

Hebrews, for that is detestable to Egyptians. ³³The men had been seated before him in the order of their ages, from the firstborn to the youngest, and they looked at each other in astonishment. ³⁴When portions were served to them from Joseph's table, Benjamin's portion was five times as much as anyone else's. So they feasted and drank freely with him.

After washing the tears away, Joseph returned to the dining room and the meal was served, with appropriate protocol. As Pharaoh's prime minister, Joseph was seated at a table by himself, his Egyptian guests by themselves, and the brothers by themselves. We know from history that Egyptians refused to eat the meat of certain animals commonly eaten by other people. For religious reasons, therefore, they would not be seated at the same table with foreigners. Joseph could not risk offending his Egyptian guests by flagrantly disregarding their customs.

The brothers were surprised to note that they were seated "in the order of their ages." ("How did he know who is the oldest? There's no way he could have known the order of our ages without supernatural help of some kind.") The entire setup made them feel uneasy.

It's mentioned specifically that Joseph arranged to have the brothers seated "before him," so he would be in a position to observe their behavior. Although they didn't realize it, Joseph was testing them for jealousy. When they noticed that Benjamin was receiving much larger portions than they, would they be envious of the preferential treatment he was receiving? Joseph couldn't detect any evidence of that.

Surely it must have dawned on the brothers that there was more going on in Joseph's home that day than appeared on the surface. First there was the *return of their silver*, then the *seating arrangement* at the table. In their father's household Benjamin consistently received *preferential treatment*, and now they observed that same thing in the Egyptian's dining hall. Luther points out that Joseph dealt with his brothers in a way that turned their attention away from that which was visible, and directed their attention to God's ruling. The brothers realized that *God had been intervening in their lives*.

As the eating and drinking continued, the brothers felt more and more at ease. Their host's gracious treatment had helped them to put aside the fear in which they had entered his home. If they had known what lay ahead for them the following morning, they might not have enjoyed the dinner as much.

Final Test of the Brothers' Repentance

One more testing was in store for Joseph's brothers, and it was by far the most difficult and the most painful. Twenty years earlier the brothers had *resented the preferential treatment* the favored son of the favored wife had received. At the dinner table the previous evening, however, the brothers had no longer seemed to be bothered by that. But twenty years earlier they had been *harsh and unfeeling toward the favored son* when danger threatened him. They had been just as cold and *unconcerned about their father's feelings* in this matter.

Had they changed in that respect, too? Joseph needed to know, and he devised a test to find out. He would put them in a situation where *they* would be free to return to their father but *Benjamin* would have to remain in Egypt. How would they react? Would they again think of themselves first, as they had the last time they faced a similar situation?

44 Now Joseph gave these instructions to the steward of his house: "Fill the men's sacks with as much food as they can carry, and put each man's silver in the mouth of his sack. ²Then put my cup, the silver one, in the mouth of the youngest one's sack, along with the silver for his grain." And he did as Joseph said.

The brothers were no doubt congratulating themselves on how well their second visit to Egypt had gone. Unknown to them, Joseph gave the order to insert his silver cup into Benjamin's sack, together with the silver he had brought as payment.

³As morning dawned, the men were sent on their way with their donkeys. ⁴They had not gone far from the city when Joseph said to his steward, "Go after those men at once, and when you catch up with them, say to them, 'Why have you repaid good with evil? ⁵Isn't this the cup my master drinks from and also uses for divination? This is a wicked thing you have done.' " ⁶When he caught up with them, he repeated these words to them.

The following morning the brothers were on their homeward way at the crack of dawn. They were barely out of the city when they heard hoofbeats behind them. They turned and saw the steward, the same man who the previous day had so cordially welcomed them to Joseph's dinner. Why was he coming after them?

"Yesterday my master showed you kindness by inviting you to be guests at his table, and today you repay his kindness with evil! Not only did you steal one of his personal possessions, his *drinking cup*, you stole the *sacred cup* he uses to find out secret information from the gods."

⁷But they said to him, "Why does my lord say such things? Far be it from your servants to do anything like that! ⁸We even brought back to you from the land of Canaan the silver we

found inside the mouths of our sacks. So why would we steal silver or gold from your master's house? ⁹If any of your servants is found to have it, he will die; and the rest of us will become my lord's slaves." ¹⁰"Very well, then," he said, "let it be as you say. Whoever is found to have it will become my slave; the rest of you will be free from blame."

The brothers couldn't believe their ears. These charges were preposterous, and they could do nothing but stutter: "Why do you accuse us of dishonesty? We demonstrated our honesty yesterday by returning the silver we had found in our sacks."

"Search our sacks." They spoke so confidently because they were absolutely sure none of them had stolen the cup. "If you find the cup with us, the man in whose sack you find it will die, and we will all be your master's slaves."

"Very well," he replied, "let it be as you say. Open your bags, and we'll see if the missing cup is there."

¹¹Each of them quickly lowered his sack to the ground and opened it. ¹²Then the steward proceeded to search, beginning with the oldest and ending with the youngest. And the cup was found in Benjamin's sack. ¹³At this, they tore their clothes. Then they all loaded their donkeys and returned to the city. ¹⁴Joseph was still in the house when Judah and his brothers came in, and they threw themselves to the ground before him. ¹⁵Joseph said to them, "What is this you have done? Don't you know that a man like me can find things out by divination?" ¹⁶"What can we say to my lord?" Judah replied. "What can we say? How can we prove our innocence? God has uncovered your servants' guilt. We are now my lord's slaves — we ourselves and the one who was found to have the cup." ¹⁷But Joseph said, "Far be it from me to do such a thing! Only the man who was found to have the cup will become my slave. The rest of you, go back to your father in peace."

The brothers untied the sacks from their donkeys and set them on the ground. Under the watchful eye of the steward, each man in turn opened his sack. To their surprise, in the mouth of each sack was their silver. The steward ran his fingers through the grain in each sack. To avoid any suspicion that he knew where the cup was, the steward intentionally began with the sack of Reuben, the oldest brother. The tension mounted as, one by one, the sacks of ten of the brothers were checked, and the cup was not found. Only one more sack to go! The brothers were confident that the search of the eleventh — Benjamin's — would prove that the charge of thievery was a mistake.

"The cup was found in Benjamin's sack." This couldn't be! But there was the evidence. In shock and grief the brothers tore their robes, as their father had done twenty years earlier when he saw Joseph's blood-stained robe. With hearts that were heavy and fingers that were numb they retied each sack of grain and loaded them all on their donkeys.

The steward had said: "Whoever is found to have (the cup) will be my slave; *the rest of you will be free from blame.*" That meant ten of the brothers could return home to their wives and families, if they wanted to. But not a one of them accepted the offer. At that moment they were not thinking about their own personal safety. They were thinking of their youngest brother and of their aged father. In stunned silence all of them returned to the city, dreading the confrontation that now awaited them.

"Joseph was still in the house when Judah and his brothers came in," since he knew the brothers would soon be returning. Of all the brothers, Judah is the only one named, because it was he who had guaranteed Benjamin's safe return and was determined to live up to his promise.

360

When the brothers saw Joseph they threw themselves to the ground in abject humiliation. While they were lying prostrate, hardly daring to look up to face their accuser, Joseph rebuked them: "Don't you know that a man like me can find out things by divination?" The reader will note that the text does not say Joseph, a child of God, practiced divination. God sternly forbids us to use the magic arts to try to find out information he has seen fit to withhold from us. But if Joseph's testing of his brothers' repentance was to be a valid test, it was important that they continue to think they were dealing with a foreigner, an Egyptian.

Judah's response to Joseph is noteworthy. "What can we say to my lord?...God has uncovered your servants' guilt." *Judah was not pleading guilty to the charge of thievery.* He was sure Benjamin had not stolen the cup. But behind Joseph's accusation Judah's ears heard another voice accusing the brothers of guilt for sins long past. *God had uncovered the guilt they had managed to conceal* for so many years. All the brothers had been involved; all therefore deserved to share in Benjamin's sentence; all were ready to submit to God's judgment and to be slaves for life. To make sure Judah had not spoken these words hastily and thoughtlessly, Joseph repeated his assurance that the older ten brothers were free to return to their father and their families.

Now the final and most difficult part of the test faced the brothers. Joseph's words were echoing in their ears: "The rest of you may go home." Their response to his offer would reveal the attitude of their hearts. Twenty years earlier they wouldn't have thought twice about saying: "Let Benjamin stay, let him rot in prison, as long as we get out of here safely!" And we can imagine them returning to their father say "Your favorite son, whom you always preferred to in jail in Egypt. He stooped to common

361

thievery, got caught, and now he's paying the price." Joseph waited eagerly to hear what Judah would say.

¹⁸Then Judah went up to him and said: "Please, my lord, let your servant speak a word to my lord. Do not be angry with your servant, though you are equal to Pharaoh himself. ¹⁹My lord asked his servants, 'Do you have a father or a brother?' ²⁰And we answered, 'We have an aged father, and there is a young son born to him in his old age. His brother is dead, and he is the only one of his mother's sons left, and his father loves him.' ²¹Then you said to your servants, 'Bring him down to me so I can see him for myself.' ²²And we said to my lord, 'The boy cannot leave his father; if he leaves him, his father will die.' ²³But you told your servants, 'Unless your youngest brother comes down with you, you will not see my face again.' ²⁴When we went back to your servant my father, we told him what my lord had said. ²⁵Then our father said, 'Go back and buy a little more food.' ²⁶But we said, 'We cannot go down. Only if our youngest brother is with us will we go. We cannot see the man's face unless our youngest brother is with us.' ²⁷Your servant my father said to us, 'You know that my wife bore me two sons. ²⁸One of them went away from me, and I said, "He has surely been torn to pieces." And I have not seen him since. ²⁹If you take this one from me too and harm comes to him, you will bring my gray head down to the grave in misery.'

³⁰"So now, if the boy is not with us when I go back to your servant my father and if my father, whose life is closely bound up with the boy's life, ³¹ sees that the boy isn't there, he will die. Your servants will bring the gray head of our father down to the grave in sorrow. ³²Your servant guaranteed the boy's safety to my father. I said, 'If I do not bring him back to you, I will bear the blame before you, my father, all my life!' ³³Now then, please let your servant remain here as my lord's slave in place of the boy, and let the boy return with his brothers. ³⁴How can I go back to my father if the boy is not with me? No! Do not let me see the misery that would come upon my father."

Judah now stepped before Joseph and spoke. Again we note the irony that he who once had suggested selling his brother into a lifetime of slavery now offered himself as a lifelong slave, in order to save his brother from a similar fate.

Judah spoke respectfully but passionately, in words charged with emotion. His plea returned repeatedly to his aged father and his special relationship to the son in whose sack the silver cup had been found. (The older brother fondly referred to his youngest brother as a "boy," although he was a man in his twenties, very likely already married and the father of children, 46:12). Without any bitterness Judah, son of Leah, spoke of the special love Jacob had for Rachel and of how, after Rachel's death, that special love had been transferred to her two sons, one of whom was now dead.

Judah proceeded to speak of the tug-of-war that had ensued between father and sons when they returned from their last trip to Egypt and announced that Benjamin had to accompany them the next time. Throughout Judah's plea one hears the heartbeat of love for his aged father, whose life was bound up with Benjamin's life and who would die if that son did not return.

Judah concluded with the simple but eloquent plea: "Since I have agreed to guarantee my brother's safety, you must let me take my brother's punishment. Make me your slave for life, but let him go home to his father! Please don't send me home without him and make me witness the misery and the death of my father!"

In commenting on this marvelous appeal, Martin Luther wrote: "I wish I knew how to pray to God as well as Judah prayed before Joseph." Earlier chapters of Genesis have recorded some details from the life of Judah that are anything but exemplary. Genesis 44 presents a totally different picture of Judah: *the picture of a man changed by the Spirit of God.* We can understand why Judah was the man God carefully trained for the position of carrying on the line of Jesus Christ, the Lion from the tribe of Judah (Revelation 5:5). Joseph's testing of his brothers was over. He had his answer.

Startling Revelation and Reconciliation

45 **Then Joseph could no longer control himself before all his attendants, and he cried out, "Have everyone leave my presence!" So there was no one with Joseph when he made himself known to his brothers. ²And he wept so loudly that the Egyptians heard him, and Pharaoh's household heard about it. ³Joseph said to his brothers, "I am Joseph! Is my father still living?" But his brothers were not able to answer him, because they were terrified at his presence.**

After hearing the moving appeal of Judah, there was only one thing Joseph could do. Judah's heart and lips had overflowed with loving concern for his father and with self-sacrificing love for his brother Benjamin. *Joseph knew now that his brothers had changed.*

The tender scene that was about to unfold in that room was much too private to be shared with outsiders. Joseph's gentle reminder to his brothers of what they had once done to him was *for their ears only*; nobody else in Egypt needed to know that. Joseph therefore dismissed from the room everybody but his brothers when he made himself known to them.

In the presence of his brothers Joseph broke down and wept. The brothers found it difficult to believe what they were seeing and hearing. The strangeness and sternness and sharpness were gone from his voice now, as Joseph spoke to his brothers in Hebrew, and no longer through an interpreter. "I am Joseph!" Now that he had seen a change of heart in his brothers he could tear off the mask he had been wearing, the mask of a harsh foreigner who seemed to do nothing but make trouble for them.

When they heard him say "I am Joseph!" they were terrified. Sin is the great destroyer, the great tension-maker. Until they had been assured by Joseph that the barrier between them and him was removed, there would be no peace of mind for them. Before they could bring themselves to speak Joseph had to assure them four times that God had used their evil deed for a good purpose. Joseph had previously asked about his father and had learned that Jacob was still alive. But he needed to hear that again.

⁴Then Joseph said to his brothers, "Come close to me." When they had done so, he said, "I am your brother Joseph, the one you sold into Egypt! ⁵And now, do not be distressed and do not be angry with yourselves for selling me here, because it was to save lives that God sent me ahead of you. ⁶For two years now there has been famine in the land, and for the next five years there will not be plowing and reaping. ⁷But God sent me ahead of you to preserve for you a remnant on earth and to save your lives by a great deliverance. ⁸So then, it was not you who sent me here, but God. He made me father to Pharaoh, lord of his entire household and ruler of all Egypt."

"Come close to me." We can easily imagine how the brothers had kept their distance. Joseph now showed them not only with words but with actions that he felt no bitterness toward them, that he had only feelings of love toward them. There was no sadness, no anger in his heart; there should be none in theirs, now that God had given them back to each other.

From the marvelous way things had developed in the past few months Joseph had been able to recognize what God, the Lord of nations, had been working to achieve. Using

such unlikely building materials as the hateful and misguided actions of the brothers two decades earlier, God had con-
structed a plan to save lives, the lives of the important family still living in famine-plagued Canaan. *"God* sent me
ahead of you...."

"...*to preserve a remnant* on earth." Joseph and his brothers and their families had escaped starvation in order to
grow into a great nation. Here is the key to the entire narrative. The brothers had once sold Joseph to Egypt in *hatred
and spite.* God had overruled their evil intent. His *steady
and sturdy love* had used their action to preserve a remnant,
a precious handful of his people, through a crisis that was
even now threatening them with starvation.

⁹"Now hurry back to my father and say to him, 'This is what
your son Joseph says: God has made me lord of all Egypt.
Come down to me; don't delay. ¹⁰You shall live in the region of
Goshen and be near me — you, your children and grandchildren, your flocks and herds, and all you have. ¹¹I will provide
for you there, because five years of famine are still to come.
Otherwise you and your household and all who belong to you
will become destitute.' ¹²You can see for yourselves, and so can
my brother Benjamin, that it is really I who am speaking to
you. ¹³Tell my father about all the honor accorded me in Egypt
and about everything you have seen. And bring my father
down here quickly." ¹⁴Then he threw his arms around his
brother Benjamin and wept, and Benjamin embraced him,
weeping. ¹⁵And he kissed all his brothers and wept over them.
Afterward his brothers talked with him.

There was no time to waste. For five more years the
famine in Canaan was only going to grow more severe and
cause more problems for their families. Joseph's main concern, however, was for his aged father. "Your father is anx-
iously waiting for you." The suffering Jacob had gone

through for twenty years had lasted long enough. To remedy that Joseph gave his brothers a tough assignment: "Tell my father: 'Your son Joseph is alive and well, and wants you to come down to Egypt!' Bring him down to me quickly! You can live in the region of Goshen." Although the exact location is uncertain, it's usually thought Goshen was east of the Nile delta, in the vicinity of what is today the Suez Canal.

The words kept pouring from Joseph's lips, because he could see his brothers were having difficulty believing that their long-lost brother was not only *still alive* but was *their friend.* He was not a powerful man who would now take revenge long overdue, but a loving brother who wanted only to restore the happiness and peace that had long been absent from Jacob's family. "You can see that it is really I who am speaking to you, and no longer through an interpreter."

Now Joseph let his arms do the talking. He embraced each of his brothers warmly, until finally the brothers found their voices and spoke to him. Tears flowed freely, and built-up tensions flowed out of them. At last they could speak freely, and they had much to tell him. Now they could confess how their vicious deed to him and to their father had for twenty years lain like a blight upon their personal and family lives, and how happy they were that this awful burden had now been lifted from them. No doubt they told him they appreciated the stern but salutary treatment he had given them.

¹⁶When the news reached Pharaoh's palace that Joseph's brothers had come, Pharaoh and all his officials were pleased. ¹⁷Pharaoh said to Joseph, "Tell your brothers, 'Do this: Load your animals and return to the land of Canaan, ¹⁸ and bring your father and your families back to me. I will give you the best of the land of Egypt and you can enjoy the fat of the land.'

¹⁹You are also directed to tell them, 'Do this: take some carts from Egypt for your children and your wives, and get your father and come. ²⁰Never mind about your belongings, because the best of all Egypt will be yours.' "

The news that Joseph's brothers had arrived spread through the capital and reached the palace. Nine years of the fourteen year emergency food conservation project were now over, and the king had been impressed with Joseph's wisdom and his faithfulness. In gratitude to Joseph for having saved his country from disaster, Pharaoh issued an invitation to Joseph's family to leave Canaan and come to live in Egypt.

Pharaoh gave the invitation in the form of an order: "You are directed to..." (literally: "commanded"; the verb root is the same as in the Old Testament word for the Ten Commandments). Pharaoh was issuing an order to Joseph: "Bring your family down here!" God had led Pharaoh to the same conclusion Joseph had reached with his brothers. Transplanting Jacob's family in Egypt had been in *God's plan* all along, and now things were falling into place. Pharaoh even told them not to worry about having to leave some of their household possessions behind; they could replace these when they arrived in Egypt.

²¹So the sons of Israel did this. Joseph gave them carts, as Pharaoh had commanded, and he also gave them provisions for their journey. ²²To each of them he gave new clothing, but to Benjamin he gave three hundred shekels of silver and five sets of clothes. ²³And this is what he sent to his father: ten donkeys loaded with the best things of Egypt, and ten female donkeys loaded with grain and bread and other provisions for his journey. ²⁴Then he sent his brothers away, and as they were leaving he said to them, "Don't quarrel on the way!"

As further evidence of his good will. Joseph gave each of his brothers a going-away present. They had once sent him into slavery without his richly ornamented robe; he gave each of them new clothing. Again, Benjamin got a particularly generous gift.

Joseph wanted nothing to spoil the brothers' homecoming, but he knew their job of breaking the news to their father was going to be tough. They were going to have to admit to Jacob that they had deceived him twenty-two years earlier, that Joseph had not been killed by a wild beast, that because of their cruelty Joseph was now in Egypt. During their long ride home, as they planned how they would break the news to their father, Joseph didn't want any of them arguing: "Selling our brother wasn't *my* idea." "*You* were more to blame than I." Tensions could rise and tempers could flare on that long trip home, and Joseph warned against that: "Don't quarrel on the way."

²⁵So they went up out of Egypt and came to their father Jacob in the land of Canaan. ²⁶They told him, "Joseph is still alive! In fact, he is ruler of all Egypt." Jacob was stunned; he did not believe them. ²⁷But when they told him everything Joseph had said to them, and when he saw the carts Joseph had sent to carry him back, the spirit of their father Jacob revived. ²⁸And Israel said, "I'm convinced! My son Joseph is still alive. I will go and see him before I die."

The aged father had been eagerly waiting for his sons to return. He was glad to see them, glad especially to see that Benjamin was with them. But he was not ready for the news his sons brought him about Benjamin's older brother: "Joseph is still alive!"

At first the news stunned Jacob. After he had believed a lie for almost a quarter century, hearing the truth about

Joseph was an emotional shock for the patriarch. He found it difficult to comprehend, let alone believe, what his sons were telling him.

The sons patiently repeated all the words Joseph had asked them to tell their father, and gradually the truth began to sink in. Jacob saw the costly gifts from his son, and the Egyptian carts Joseph had sent to transport his family to their temporary home so they could survive the famine. And finally Jacob was convinced: what my sons have told me is true. And then he had only one desire: "I will go and see Joseph before I die!"

A New Home for Jacob's Family

46 **So Israel set out with all that was his, and when he reached Beersheba, he offered sacrifices to the God of his father Isaac. ²And God spoke to Israel in a vision at night and said, "Jacob! Jacob!" "Here I am," he replied. ³"I am God, the God of your father," he said, "Do not be afraid to go down to Egypt, for I will make you into a great nation there. ⁴I will go down to Egypt with you, and I will surely bring you back again. And Joseph's own hand will close your eyes." ⁵Then Jacob left Beersheba, and Israel's sons took their father Jacob and their children and their wives in the carts that Pharaoh had sent to transport him. ⁶They also took with them their livestock and the possessions they had acquired in Canaan, and Jacob and all this offspring went to Egypt. ⁷He took with him to Egypt his sons and grandsons and his daughters and granddaughters — all his offspring.**

Israel, the patriarch, head of the covenant people, set out for Egypt with his entire household. It must have been an impressive procession — wagons carrying people and possessions, and the family's flocks and herds moving alongside the long line of wagons. After traveling about a day the caravan reached Beersheba, at the south border of Canaan, the place where Abraham had spent almost a century of his life. Here the caravan stopped. Jacob realized that once again he was at a significant juncture in his life. Once his household moved beyond Beersheba, they were outside the land God had promised them. Did he, the bearer of the promise, have any business leaving the land of promise?

Jacob had clearly seen God's hand in what had happened to Joseph, and Joseph's invitation to come to Egypt surely seemed like a God-given solution to the problem caused by the famine. But Jacob knew what trouble his grandfather Abraham had gotten into when he went down to Egypt to escape a famine (12:10-20). Perhaps Jacob remembered also how when his father Isaac contemplated traveling to Egypt to escape a famine, he was specifically forbidden by God to do so (26:1,2).

Jacob, therefore, stopped at the border. He offered sacrifices, perhaps on the same altar his father had built there (26:25), and took the matter to the Lord in prayer. He was unwilling to leave the land of promise without a specific directive from God.

God, the All-powerful, the one who controls nature and who guides the history of people and of nations, responded to the patriarch's prayer by speaking to him in a vision at night. God not only gave him permission to go to Egypt, he even promised blessing to Jacob's family in Egypt.

"I will make you into a great nation." In Egypt what was now a family would grow into a nation.

"I will accompany you," to protect you. Jacob's God was not a local deity whose power ended at his country's borders.

"I will surely bring you back" to the land of promise. Jacob would not live to see the fulfillment of this last promise. He would die in Egypt, and his beloved son would be with him at death to perform one last labor of love. He would be brought back to the promised land in a casket. But 400 years later his descendants would leave Egypt and occupy the land of Canaan as their homeland.

Reassured by God in the vision, Jacob could with a good conscience order the caravan to start moving again. After what must have been a journey of several weeks, they arrived in Egypt.

[8]These are the names of the sons of Israel (Jacob and his descendants) who went to Egypt: Reuben the firstborn of Jacob. [9]The sons of Reuben: Hanoch, Pallu, Hezron and Carmi. [10]The sons of Simeon: Jemuel, Jamin, Ohad, Jakin, Zohar and Shaul the son of a Canaanite woman. [11]The sons of Levi: Gershon, Kohath and Merari. [12]The sons of Judah: Er, Onan, Shelah, Perez and Zerah (but Er and Onan had died in the land of Canaan). The sons of Perez: Hezron and Hamul. [13]The sons of Issachar: Tola, Puah, Jashub and Shimron. [14]The sons of Zebulun: Sered, Elon and Jahleel. [15]These were the sons Leah bore to Jacob in Paddan Aram, besides his daughter Dinah. These sons and daughters of his were thirty-three in all.

[16]The sons of Gad: Zephon, Haggi, Shuni, Ezbon, Eri, Arodi and Areli. [17]The sons of Asher: Imnah, Ishvah, Ishvi and Beriah. Their sister was Serah. The sons of Beriah: Heber and Malkiel. [18]These were the children born to Jacob by Zilpah, whom Laban had given to his daughter Leah — sixteen in all.

[19]The sons of Jacob's wife Rachel: Joseph and Benjamin. [20]In Egypt, Manasseh and Ephraim were born to Joseph by Asenath daughter of Potiphera, priest of On. [21]The sons of Benjamin: Bela, Beker, Ashbel, Gera, Naaman, Ehi, Rosh, Muppim, Huppim and Ard. [22]These were the sons of Rachel who were born to Jacob — fourteen in all.

[23]The son of Dan: Hushim. [24]The sons of Naphtali: Jahziel, Guni, Jezer and Shillem. [25]These were the sons born to Jacob by Bilhah, whom Laban had given to his daughter Rachel — seven in all.

372

At this point, when the family of Jacob was about to become a nation, Moses gives us a listing of the families making up the larger household of Jacob. He lists first the six *sons of Leah* and their children (verses 9-15), then the two *sons of Zilpah*, Leah's maidservant, and her children (verses 16-18). Then follows the list of *Rachel's two sons* and their children (verses 19-22), and finally the two *sons of her maid Bilhah* and their children (verses 23-25).

What we have in these verses is clearly not a passenger list of all those who traveled to Egypt with Jacob's caravan. Some of the people named here were *already in Egypt* (verse 19); some had *not yet been born* (compare 42:32 with 46:9); some were *already dead* (compare 38:7-10 with 46:12).

The statement in verse 8: "These are the names of the Israelites...who went to Egypt" must therefore be understood as describing a genealogical table. Moses lists, first, *the ancestors of the twelve tribes* of Israel, and then those of their *descendants who founded the separate families* in each of the tribes. This may very well be the reason why, with only two exceptions, none of the daughters' names are included. Here, then, was the basic structure of the family from which the twelve tribes of Israel sprang, and which in Egypt grew into the nation of Israel.

²⁶**All those who went to Egypt with Jacob — those who were his direct descendants, not counting his sons' wives — numbered sixty-six persons.**

²⁷**With the two sons who had been born to Joseph in Egypt, the members of Jacob's family, which went to Egypt, were seventy in all.**

Two different totals are given here. The figure of sixty-six (verse 26) includes only Jacob's descendants; his sons' wives are not counted.

The figure of seventy (verse 27) apparently includes the patriarch himself, plus Joseph and his two sons, who were already in Egypt. In Acts 7:14 Stephen lists the total as seventy-five. He may have used a round number, or he may have included Joseph's five grandsons born in Egypt (Numbers 26:28-37).

Some have taken the number seventy (verse 27) to be symbolic. If seven is often the symbolic number for the covenant between the LORD and Jacob's family and ten symbolizes completeness (Genesis 31:7 and 41), then seven times ten might symbolize the fact that the family of Jacob, which stood in covenant relationship with God, was now complete.

28Now Jacob sent Judah ahead of him to Joseph to get directions to Goshen. When they arrived in the region of Goshen, 29Joseph had his chariot made ready and went to Goshen to meet his father Israel. As soon as Joseph appeared before him, he threw his arms around his father and wept for a long time. 30Israel said to Joseph, "Now I am ready to die, since I have seen for myself that you are still alive." 31Then Joseph said to his brothers and to his father's household, "I will go up and speak to Pharaoh and will say to him, 'My brothers and my father's household, who were living in the land of Canaan, have come to me. 32The men are shepherds; they tend livestock, and they have brought along their flocks and herds and everything they own.' 33When Pharaoh calls you in and asks, 'What is your occupation?' 34 you should answer, 'Your servants have tended livestock from our boyhood on, just as our fathers did.' Then you will be allowed to settle in the region of Goshen, for all shepherds are detestable to the Egyptians."

374

In just a few words Moses sketches a touching scene: the patriarch and his favorite son, meeting for the first time after twenty-two years of enforced separation. Joseph had been a lad of seventeen when Jacob had sent him to check up on his brothers. Now he was a mature man of thirty-nine, second in command in the government of Egypt.

As the aged father looked into the eyes of his beloved son he saw evidence of God's kindness to him, and he declared himself ready to die. Without the assurance of God's forgiveness, death was for sinners in the time of the Old Testament, as it is for sinners today, something to fear. But having the assurance of being at peace with God, the Old Testament saints could declare they were ready to die. And having that assurance, Jacob could also truly appreciate the other blessings God was showering upon him, such as his reunion with his long-lost son.

Now the matter of finding a place for his family to live had to be settled. Before introducing his brothers to Pharaoh, Joseph briefed them. When Pharaoh asked them their occupation they should answer: "We've never done anything but shepherding," inferring that in Egypt they would like to continue that occupation. This fact alone would be enough for Pharaoh to select a place for them to live which was away from the densely populated areas of the Nile valley. Since shepherds were "detestable to the Egyptians," Pharaoh would not have wanted the Israelites' presence to be a constant irritant to the feelings of his own people.

Ancient Egyptian inscriptions express contempt for cattle raisers. It seems this country, with its advanced culture, considered shepherds to be the lowest class. Joseph did not want Egypt to be a melting-pot for the children of Israel. They were to remain separate and not become egyptianized. Joseph therefore wanted them to live in Goshen, an area removed from the mainstream of Egyptian national life. Maintaining their occupation as shepherds would help to serve that purpose.

God may also have had his eye on the future when he selected Goshen as his people's temporary home. Four centuries later Goshen, in the region of what is today Suez, would be a more convenient point of departure when the Israelites escaped from Egyptian tyranny.

And so the family with whom God had established his covenant came to Egypt. The *immediate occasion* that brought them was the famine. But, as has been mentioned earlier, the God who controls history had *larger reasons*.

1. During the critical 400-year period while Israel was growing into nationhood, God wanted them removed from the influence of Canaanite religion and morals. God chose Egypt, not Canaan, to be the cradle for his chosen nation.

2. In this temporary home sharp religious and cultural differences would discourage intermarriage between Israelites and Egyptians and would make it easier for Israel to maintain its faith in the true God.

3. Egypt's advanced culture (law, arts, sciences) would give Israel much it could later use in setting up its own nation and government (see Acts 7:22).

With Israel's arrival in Egypt, a major phase in God's program to save a world of sinners was completed.

Spared from Famine

47 Joseph went and told Pharaoh, "My father and brothers with their flocks and herds and everything they own, have come from the land of Canaan and are now in Goshen."

²He chose five of his brothers and presented them before Pharaoh. ³Pharaoh asked the brothers, "What is your occupation?" "Your servants are shepherds," they replied to Pharaoh, "just as our fathers were." ⁴They also said to him, "We have come to live here awhile, because the famine is severe in Canaan and your servants' flocks have no pasture. So now, please let your servants settle in Goshen." ⁵Pharaoh said to Joseph, "Your father and your brothers have come to you, ⁶and the land of Egypt is before you; settle your father and your brothers in the best part of the land. Let them live in Goshen. And if you know of any among them with special ability, put them in charge of my own livestock."

After making sure that his family was temporarily settled, Joseph went to the palace, to have the arrangement ratified. "My father and brothers are in Goshen with their flocks (sheep/goats) and herds (cattle/oxen/donkeys). They're awaiting further instructions on where you want them to settle," he announced to Pharaoh, He had chosen five of his brothers and now presented them to Pharaoh.

Speaking through an interpreter, the king asked: "What is your occupation?" They replied just as Joseph had instructed them: "We're shepherds, from a long line of shepherds." This was the straightforward answer Joseph hoped would persuade Pharaoh that a location separate from the Egyptian populace would be preferable. The fact that the brothers even dared to suggest: "We would be perfectly happy to stay where we are in Goshen" leads one to conclude that Joseph may have previously suggested that to Pharaoh.

The brothers made it clear that they expected to be only temporary residents. "We have come to live here awhile." There was no way they could have known that the Lord of the calendar was going to stretch their temporary stay of half a dozen years — just until the famine was over — into a period of time that stretched over 400 years.

The brothers were delighted to hear Pharaoh say: "Very well; stay in Goshen." By giving his consent Pharaoh showed the high respect he had for Joseph. He granted Joseph's family land and food in his country, and even in a border area that was strategic to the defense of Egypt.

7Then Joseph brought his father Jacob in and presented him before Pharaoh. After Jacob blessed Pharaoh, 8 Pharaoh asked him, "How old are you?" 9And Jacob said to Pharaoh, "The years of my pilgrimage are a hundred and thirty. My years have been few and difficult, and they do not equal the years of the pilgrimage of my fathers." 10Then Jacob blessed Pharaoh and went out from his presence. 11So Joseph settled his father and his brothers in Egypt and gave them property in the best part of the land, the district of Rameses, as Pharaoh directed. 12Joseph also provided his father and his brothers and all his father's household with food, according to the number of their children.

At Pharaoh's invitation, Jacob himself had a separate audience with the king. The visit began and ended with Jacob pronouncing a blessing on Pharaoh. Since Jacob spoke as the patriarch who had received the Messianic blessing, his words were *more than just a pious wish*. He actually *conferred God's blessing on the king and his country*, since they had been God's chosen instruments for blessing his covenant people. We can see evidence of God's blessing, too, as king and country grew powerful and wealthy under Joseph's wise administration.

In response to Pharaoh's questions: "How old are you?" the patriarch responded: "The years of my pilgrimage are a hundred and thirty. My years have been few and difficult." Although 130 does not seem like "few" to us, Jacob felt sure he would not live to be as old as his grandfather

378

Abraham and his father Isaac, who had reached the ages of 175 and 180, respectively.

And his years had been "difficult." As a young man he'd had to leave home to escape the anger of his twin brother. For twenty years he'd been cheated by his father-in-law. He'd seen his own family torn apart by immorality, bloodthirst and lovelessness. And now, when he might have hoped to spend his declining years in the comfort of familiar surroundings, famine had forced him to pull up roots and move to a strange land. The years had taken their toll on Jacob. Life for him had indeed been difficult.

Does that sound familiar? Life for God's people is often difficult, where characters are shaped through trials of faith and where people are remodeled so that more and more they get to resemble what God originally had in mind when he designed the human race.

For a period of seventeen years Joseph had lived in his father's home before being sold into slavery. Now God gave him the opportunity to provide a home for his father for that same period of time (47:28). And by providing his brothers with food, each according to his family's need, Joseph repaid evil with good.

¹³There was no food, however, in the whole region because the famine was severe; both Egypt and Canaan wasted away because of the famine. ¹⁴Joseph collected all the money that was to be found in Egypt and Canaan in payment for the grain they were buying, and he brought it to Pharaoh's palace. ¹⁵When the money of the people of Egypt and Canaan was gone, all Egypt came to Joseph and said, "Give us food. Why should we die before your eyes? Our money is used up." ¹⁶"Then bring your livestock," said Joseph. "I will sell you food in exchange for your livestock, since your money is gone." ¹⁷So they brought their livestock to Joseph, and he gave them food in exchange for their horses, their sheep and goats, their cattle and donkeys.

And he brought them through that year with food in exchange for all their livestock.

It was a very special miracle of God that the family of Jacob had all its needs provided for at a time when all the other people living in Egypt were under severe economic stress. They had bought grain, as long as *their money* lasted. When that was gone, Joseph declared he would accept *their cattle* as payment for food.

By accepting their livestock as payment, Joseph enabled the people to make it through another year of famine. He could, of course, have *given* them food after he saw their money was gone. But with years of famine still ahead, the nation's food supply might not have lasted. Joseph also realized that complete subsidy by the government could easily have undermined the nation's morale.

¹⁸When that year was over, they came to him the following year and said, "We cannot hide from our lord the fact that since our money is gone and our livestock belongs to you, there is nothing left for our lord except our bodies and our land. ¹⁹Why should we perish before your eyes — we and our land as well? Buy us and our land in exchange for food, and we with our land will be in bondage to Pharaoh. Give us seed so that we may live and not die, and that the land may not become desolate." ²⁰So Joseph bought all the land in Egypt for Pharaoh. The Egyptians, one and all, sold their fields, because the famine was too severe for them. The land became Pharaoh's, ²¹ and Joseph reduced the people to servitude, from one end of Egypt to the other.

²²However, he did not buy the land of the priests, because they received a regular allotment from Pharaoh and had food enough from the allotment Pharaoh gave them. That is why they did not sell their land.

²³Joseph said to the people, "Now that I have bought you and your land today for Pharaoh, here is seed for you so you can plant the ground. ²⁴But when the crop comes in, give a fifth of it to Pharaoh, The other four-fifths you may keep as seed for the fields and as food for yourself and your households and your children."
²⁵"You have saved our lives," they said. "May we find favor in the eyes of our lord; we will be in bondage to Pharaoh."
²⁶So Joseph established it as a law concerning land in Egypt — still in force today — that a fifth of the produce belongs to Pharaoh. It was only the land of the priests that did not become Pharaoh's.

The following year all that the people had left to offer in exchange for food was *their land* and *their bodies*. "Buy us and our land in exchange for food, and we with our land will be in bondage to Pharaoh." Moses makes it clear that Joseph bought the land *for Pharaoh*; he himself did not benefit from these transactions. Joseph resisted the temptation to lay hands on some of the enormous wealth that was flowing into the national treasury.

More than one writer has called Joseph's action "enslavement of Egyptian peasants," and "shocking proof of Joseph's inhumanity." It is well to remember that it was *the people* who had suggested: "Buy us and our land" (verse 19). Joseph accepted that suggestion, although it was not his idea.

The people could continue to live on their farms as renters of state-owned land, with the right to keep eighty percent of what meager crops would grow during the famine. To ask a tenant farmer to pay twenty percent to the landlord does not seem an exorbitant demand. The people of Egypt did not consider Joseph ruthless. They understood his motive and praised him for bringing them through a crisis which could have been a national catastrophe.

²⁷Now the Israelites settled in Egypt in the region of Goshen. They acquired property there and were fruitful and increased greatly in number. ²⁸Jacob lived in Egypt seventeen years, and the years of his life were a hundred and forty-seven. ²⁹When the time drew near for Israel to die, he called for his son Joseph and said to him, "If I have found favor in your eyes, put your hand under my thigh and promise that you will show me kindness and faithfulness. Do not bury me in Egypt, ³⁰ but when I rest with my fathers, carry me out of Egypt and bury me where they are buried." "I will do as you say," he said. ³¹"Swear to me," he said. Then Joseph swore to him, and Israel worshiped as he leaned on the top of his staff.

Through Joseph's wise leadership God so guided affairs in Egypt that Jacob's family not only managed to survive but to flourish. "They were fruitful and increased greatly in number." The reader will remember that this was one of the purposes for which God had led the family of Jacob to Egypt.

Seventeen years had now passed since Jacob and his family had moved to Egypt. We're not told that God informed Jacob that his life was nearing its end. It's more likely that *the hard life* he had lived and *the grief* his sons had caused him had taken their toll on the patriarch, and his health began to fail. He felt his strength slipping and realized that the time had come for him to make some final arrangements.

The first of these dealt with choosing the site where he would be buried. Jacob specified the family plot Abraham had purchased in Hebron, in the land of Canaan. The significance of the patriarch's request "Put your hand under my thigh" has been treated in connection with Genesis 24:2. As he prepared for his death Jacob knew that God's promises regarding the possession of Canaan were certain. He clung to those promises and wanted to be buried in the land he knew his descendants would one day own. Even Jacob's burial was to give evidence of his faith in God's promises.

It should be emphasized that Jacob's faith held on to *all* of God's promises — not only the promise of a homeland for his descendants, but chiefly the promise of that famous Descendant through whom all nations of the earth would be blessed. *God's promise of the Savior was the heart of all the promises* he gave to the patriarchs. This is why God considered their faith in any part of that cluster of promises to be saving faith (15:6).

After securing his son's oath to bury him in the promised land, "Israel worshiped." The matter of coming to the end of his earthly life was something the patriarch wanted to share with God, as was the matter of preparing to enter a new life in the presence of God. The epistle to the Hebrews gives us this interesting commentary on this attitude of the patriarchs:

> These people were still living by faith when they died. They did not receive the things promised; they only saw them and welcomed them from a distance. And they admitted that they were aliens and strangers on earth. People who say such things show that they are looking for a country of their own. ... They were longing for a better country — a heavenly one. Therefore God is not ashamed to be called their God.
>
> (Hebrews 11:13,14,16)

Apparently too weak to prostrate himself on the ground, Jacob bowed his head on his staff in praise and thanksgiving to God. There were now several important matters involving his sons that needed his attention, and the next two chapters will deal with those.

Jacob Adopts Ephraim and Manasseh

The tenth and final "account" of Genesis, the Account of Jacob, is rapidly drawing to a close. In sharp contrast to the note of violence and treachery and immorality on which this "account" opened, it closes with two scenes which are full of tenderness and beauty. We have the first of those in chapter 48.

48 **Some time later Joseph was told, "Your father is ill." So he took his two sons Manasseh and Ephraim along with him. ²When Jacob was told, "Your son Joseph has come to you," Israel rallied his strength and sat up on the bed.**

Jacob himself may have suspected that this was his last illness and sent a messenger to notify Joseph. The fact that Joseph took his two sons along leads one to think the patriarch had probably informed Joseph previously that he intended to adopt two of his grandchildren as his own sons. It seems highly unlikely that the important transaction recorded here was an idea that occurred to Jacob on the spur of the moment.

The fact that Joseph brought his two sons to be adopted as co-heirs with Jacob's other sons says something about Joseph's sense of values. His sons could probably have expected positions of honor and influence in the Egyptian government. Joseph, however, renounced these, preferring that his sons think of their future in terms of the people of God.

With what little strength he had left, the aged patriarch sat up as his son and grandsons approached his bed. He wanted to perform the important ceremony that lay just ahead with appropriate dignity.

³Jacob said to Joseph, "God Almighty appeared to me at Luz in the land of Canaan, and there he blessed me ⁴ and said to me, 'I am going to make you fruitful and will increase your numbers. I will make you a community of peoples, and I will give this land as an everlasting possession to your descendants after you.' ⁵Now then, your two sons born to you in Egypt before I came to you here will be reckoned as mine; Ephraim and Manasseh will be mine, just as Reuben and Simeon are mine. ⁶Any children born to you after them will be yours; in the territory they inherit they will be reckoned under the names of their brothers. ⁷As I was returning from Paddan, to my sorrow Rachel died in the land of Canaan while we were still on the way, a little distance from Ephrath. So I buried her there beside the road to Ephrath" (that is, Bethlehem).

As he began to speak, Jacob reviewed some familiar history. Years earlier, when Jacob was fleeing from his brother, God Almighty had appeared to him at Luz (better known as Bethel). At that time God had promised to make the lonely fugitive into a great nation, which would one day own the land presently occupied by a number of Canaanite tribes. Jacob used an appropriate name for this God. He is *El Shaddai*, the God of awesome power, who can compel even nature to obey him.

Through a weak and dying man the Lord of nations announced some of his future plans for the nation of Israel. He who marches through history in judgment and in mercy would dispossess the present inhabitants of Canaan because of their persistent wickedness. And by an act of pure grace he would give their land to the descendants of Jacob as a homeland.

Joseph's two sons, perhaps in their twenties, now heard their grandfather call them by name. These two sons, born before Jacob had moved to Egypt, *would from now on be counted as Jacob's sons*, of equal rank with Reuben and

Simeon, Jacob's oldest sons. That meant that Joseph would now be represented among the twelve tribes of Israel not by a single tribe bearing his name, but that Ephraim and Manasseh would be separate tribes, each receiving a separate portion of the promised land. Joseph would thus receive the double share which usually went to the firstborn son.

The historical records in the opening chapters of 1 Chronicles substantiate this: "...(Reuben's) rights as the firstborn were given to the sons of Joseph" (1 Chronicles 5:1). Any other children born to Joseph after this would not be considered separate tribes, but would receive their inheritance through Ephraim and Manasseh.

We don't know why Jacob suddenly introduced Rachel into the conversation. Perhaps the fact that he was now facing death reminded him of her untimely death as Jacob's household was en route from Paddan-aram to Canaan. Or perhaps the provisions he was making for Rachel's two grandsons led him to think of her. She had never lived to see her son exalted to be ruler of Egypt and savior of his family. Rachel's memory was now to be honored as her two grandsons were placed on a par with Reuben and Simeon, Leah's firstborn. Now *three tribes* of Israel (Ephraim, Manasseh and Benjamin) would trace their ancestry to Rachel, although she had borne only *two sons*.

⁸When Israel saw the sons of Joseph, he asked, "Who are these?" ⁹"They are the sons God has given me here," Joseph said to his father. Then Israel said, "Bring them to me so I may bless them." ¹⁰Now Israel's eyes were failing because of old age, and he could hardly see. So Joseph brought his sons close to him, and his father kissed them and embraced them. ¹¹Israel said to Joseph, "I never expected to see your face again, and now God has allowed me to see your children too." ¹²Then Joseph removed them from Israel's knees and bowed down

with his face to the ground. ¹³**And Joseph took both of them, Ephraim on his right toward Israel's left hand and Manasseh on his left toward Israel's right hand, and brought them close to him.** ¹⁴**But Israel reached out his right hand and put it on Ephraim's head, though he was the younger, and crossing his arms, he put his left hand on Manasseh's head, even though Manasseh was the firstborn.**

Joseph now brought his sons to the bedside, so that they stood directly in front of their grandfather, facing him. Jacob embraced his grandsons and kissed them, marveling at the grace of God which he had experienced. He had never expected to see *Joseph* again, and now God had even let him see *Joseph's children.*

Joseph bowed to the ground before his father, as a token of respect and to express his appreciation for the privilege the patriarch was conferring on these two grandsons, who then knelt to receive his blessing. Joseph had so arranged it that *Manasseh*, his older son, was *at Jacob's right hand*, since the right hand was thought to typify a greater share of the patriarch's blessing. Ephraim, the younger son, was on the left. Joseph thought it was appropriate that the older son receive the greater blessing.

But as the patriarch pronounced the blessing he crossed his arms, placing his *right* hand on *Ephraim's* head. By crossing his arms Jacob intentionally and prophetically placed the younger son ahead of the older. Here, for the first time in the Bible, we meet the custom of laying on of hands, to symbolize that the Holy Spirit was conferring a special gift on these two young men, a gift they would otherwise not have had.

¹⁵**Then he blessed Joseph and said, "May the God before whom my fathers Abraham and Isaac walked, the God who has been my shepherd all my life to this day, ¹⁶the angel who has**

delivered me from all harm — may he bless these boys. May they be called by my name and the names of my fathers Abraham and Isaac, and may they increase greatly upon the earth." [17]When Joseph saw his father placing his right hand on Ephraim's head he was displeased; so he took hold of his father's hand to move it from Ephraim's head to Manasseh's head. [18]Joseph said to him, "No, my father, this one is the first-born; put your right hand on his head." [19]But his father refused and said, "I know, my son, I know. He too will become a people, and he too will become great. Nevertheless, his younger brother will be greater than he, and his descendants will become a group of nations." [20]He blessed them that day and said, "In your name will Israel pronounce this blessing: 'May God make you like Ephraim and Manasseh.' " So he put Ephraim ahead of Manasseh.

The phrase "(Jacob) blessed Joseph..." is to be under-stood in the sense that Joseph was receiving a blessing not directly, but indirectly, through his sons. In Jacob's words of blessing it is good to note that his memories of his earlier life were not bitter ones, but memories of the gentleness and goodness of God. The "Angel of God," the second person of the Holy Trinity, had appeared to Jacob in human form, guiding him, protecting him, assuring him, redeeming him from all evil.

When Joseph suspected that his father was mistakenly going to give the larger blessing to the wrong son, he took his father's hand to interrupt him. But Jacob's action was not an oversight. "I know, my son, I know." Jacob's cross-ing his arms to give a special blessing to the younger son was not the funny idea of an old man with failing eyesight. *Jacob was a patriarch*, and as he here transmitted the Lord's blessing he *acted with prophetic insight*. God had told him to bless the younger over the older. Centuries later, after the division of the kingdom, Ephraim assumed the leadership of the northern ten tribes. Next to the tribe of Judah Ephraim was the most powerful tribe in Israel. As a matter of fact, it became so dominant that the Old Testament prophets often refer to the northern ten tribes as "Ephraim."

"So (Jacob) put Ephraim ahead of Manasseh." In this patriarchal blessing God reversed the natural order, just as he had done in the case of Isaac's and Rebekah's twin sons before they were ever born (25:23). In years to come, when the Israelites would want to pronounce a blessing on someone, they would use the proverbial expression: "May God make you like Ephraim and Manasseh!"

²¹Then Israel said to Joseph, "I am about to die, but God will be with you and take you back to the land of your fathers. ²²And to you, as one who is over your brothers, I give the ridge of land I took from the Amorites with my sword and my bow."

Jacob concluded his blessing with the reminder that Canaan, not Egypt, would be the permanent home of the children of Israel. In this way God would make even the wickedness of the Canaanites serve his glory, although they would be completely unaware of it. When their cup of sin was full, God would step into their history with a condemning judgment, using their sin as the occasion to keep his promise to Abraham: "Your descendants will inherit this land."

Finally Jacob had a special gift for Joseph: "...the ridge of land I took from the Amorites." The words are not easy to explain. There are two possibilities.

The first understands the verb "I took" in a *historical* sense. In an event not recorded in the Scripture, Jacob had captured a special piece of land from the original inhabitants of Canaan.

Some scholars, however, have seen in the Hebrew verb translated "I took" an instance of the so-called "*prophetic perfect*," in which a future action is seen as already achieved. According to this view Jacob, through his posterity, would seize the land from the Amorites.

What a beautiful picture this chapter gives us of a believing child of God approaching the end of his life! Instead of being filled with bitterness as he looked back over a life that had its share of disappointments, Jacob preferred to focus his attention on the grace of God. He not only had gotten from God *more than he deserved*; Jacob knew he had gotten *the very opposite of what he deserved*:

> God's blessing instead of his condemnation;
>
> God's promise instead of his curse;
>
> God's constant guidance instead of his punishment.

It's a blessing to live as a child of God. It's an even greater blessing to die as a child of God.

Jacob Blesses His Sons

Jacob was now 147, and that was to be the full measure of years God allotted to him. He therefore gathered his twelve sons about his deathbed and spoke words which are at the same time *blessings* and *predictions*. What would happen to the twelve tribes of Israel in the future — for better or for worse — was not the result of chance. Jacob was aware that he was speaking prophetically, moved by the Spirit of God. Each son heard what the patriarch said to all the others. These last words of Jacob to his sons also became part of Israel's Old Testament scriptures, so that later generations of tribal members would also know what their ancestor Jacob had predicted for them.

49 Then Jacob called for his sons and said: "Gather around so I can tell you what will happen to you in days to come. ²Assemble and listen, sons of Jacob; listen to your father Israel."

Moses gives us Jacob's words *in the form of Hebrew poetry* (recognizable chiefly by its parallelism). This unusual literary form would make it easier, in years to come, for Jacob's descendants to remember his words. A problem facing the interpreter here is that the vocabulary used in poetry is often unusual, sometimes rare. In addition, many words Jacob used have more than one meaning. Sometimes the parallel structure of the verse offers a clue as to how the unfamiliar words are to be translated. In places, however, this interpretation will have to be tentative.

Jacob addressed the six sons of Leah first, in order of their ages. He then addressed the four sons of the maids, and finally Rachel's two sons.

³"Reuben, you are my firstborn, my might, the first sign of my strength, excelling in honor, excelling in power. ⁴Turbulent as the waters, you will no longer excel, for you went up onto your father's bed, onto my couch and defiled it."

The aged patriarch addressed *Reuben*, his oldest son, first. He described him as "turbulent as water" — unreliable, following the path of least resistance, just like water. Although Reuben was the firstborn, his moral instability made him unsuited to receive the birthright. He forfeited his position as leader (35:22), and never furnished a prominent leader for Israel — no judge, no king, no prophet. Reuben's tribe is hardly ever mentioned in Israel's history.

⁵"Simeon and Levi are brothers — their swords are weapons of violence. ⁶Let me not enter their council, let me not join their

Jacob and his sons

assembly, for they have killed men in their anger and hamstrung oxen as they pleased. ⁷Cursed be their anger, so fierce, and their fury, so cruel! I will scatter them in Jacob and disperse them in Israel."

Simeon and Levi were brothers in more than one sense. They were, first of all, *full brothers*, sons of Leah. But they were *two of a kind*, companions in evil. Simeon's and Levi's descendants were warned against hotheaded violence, such as these two brothers showed in the bloodbath at Shechem (Genesis 34). Jacob's words "they hamstrung oxen as they pleased" refer to a practice common in ancient warfare. When you defeated an enemy in battle and captured his livestock but couldn't take them with you as plunder, you might cut the sinews of the animals' hind feet, rendering them useless to the enemy. That horse would never again ride off to battle; that ox would never again pull a plow. Jacob pronounced his curse on that violence.

The father's final words to these two sons included a second curse: "I will scatter them...and disperse them in Israel." Neither of these two tribes would ever acquire territory in Canaan as their own, but would be scattered throughout the land. When the promised land was later divided among the tribes, *Simeon* received no block of territory but only about a dozen and a half towns within the tribal territory of Judah (Joshua 19:1-8). From the first census (taken shortly after the exodus from Egypt) to the second census (taken shortly before Israel occupied Canaan) the number of Simeon's fighting men declined from 59,000 to 22,000, making his the smallest tribe. The tribe of Simeon gradually lost its identity in the tribe of Judah.

The descendants of *Levi* later became the temple workers and teachers in Israel, and were distributed in forty-eight cities scattered throughout the twelve tribes.

So far Jacob's prophecies to his sons offered them little reason for hope. That would, however, change with the next prophecy, spoken to Judah.

⁸"Judah, your brothers will praise you; your hand will be on the neck of your enemies; your father's sons will bow down to you. ⁹You are a lion's cub, O Judah; you return from the prey, my son. Like a lion he crouches and lies down, like a lioness — who dares to rouse him? ¹⁰The scepter will not depart from Judah, nor the ruler's staff from between his feet, until he comes to whom it belongs and the obedience of the nations is his. ¹¹He will tether his donkey to a vine, his colt to the choicest branch; he will wash his garments in wine, his robes in the blood of grapes. ¹²His eyes will be darker than wine, his teeth whiter than milk."

"Judah, your brothers will praise you." Jacob's words involve a pun, a play on words, since the Hebrew name *Judah* means "praise." This son would be praised by his brothers, since God would accomplish wonderful things through him. The *covenant blessing*, which God had given to Abraham and Isaac and Jacob, would now be carried forward by Judah.

Judah would also assume the *position of leadership* which the older three brothers had forfeited. Judah's tribe is here pictured as a young lion, victorious over its enemies. From this tribe David would come, who would establish the dynasty that provided kings for God's people. The ruler's staff would be held by descendants of Judah, including great David's greater Son, Jesus Christ (Luke 1:32, 33).

There is some uncertainty about the Hebrew text of the phrase translated "...until he comes to whom it belongs." The King James Version translates these words "...until Shiloh comes," and "Shiloh" is usually understood as *"Rest"* or *"Rest-bringer,"* a name for the Messiah who brings rest for our souls. The NIV translation understands the Hebrew word to be a combination of two elements: "...*he to whom it* (the ruler's scepter) *belongs*." The Messiah alone deserves to rule as King; he is the only one who reconciled a world of sinners to a holy God. Many of Judah's descendants who sat on the throne in Jerusalem were not interested in Israel's Messianic hope, and did not deserve to be kings. Jesus Christ, Judah's great Descendant, is the one in whose hand the royal scepter belongs. His is a magnificent and universal reign, "and he will rule for ever and ever" (Revelation 11:15). When sinners are brought to see this and believe it, they bow before him in glad obedience.

Judah's tribe would enjoy prosperity; its rich tribal territory would offer its inhabitants plentiful supply. Normally you wouldn't tether a donkey to a grapevine for fear he might rip it right out of the ground. Judah's supply would be so plentiful, however, that he wouldn't have second thoughts about using a vine as a hitching post. His grape harvest would be so abundant that, if he chose to, he could have washed his clothes in wine. His eyes would sparkle from the juice of the grape.

¹³**"Zebulun will live by the seashore and become a haven for ships; his border will extend toward Sidon."**

Although the tribal territory of *Zebulun* was not situated right on the seacoast, it was close enough to acquire wealth from maritime trade, especially through the Phoenician port of Sidon, just to the north.

¹⁴**"Issachar is a rawboned donkey lying down between two saddlebags. ¹⁵When he sees how good is his resting place and**

how pleasant is his land, he will bend his shoulder to the burden and submit to forced labor."

Over the years Jacob apparently had noticed that his son
Issachar was lazy and unambitious. The patriarch foresaw
that Issachar's descendants would follow suit. In their home
in the beautiful and fertile Esdraelon Valley they would be
willing to offer hard labor in return for rest and creature
comforts. Jacob's words would serve as a warning for the
tribe of Issachar.

**[16]"Dan will provide justice for his people as one of the tribes
of Israel. [17]Dan will be a serpent by the roadside, a viper along
the path, that bites the horse's heels so that its rider tumbles
backward. [18]I look for your deliverance, O LORD."**

Two things are prophesied about *Dan.* In years to come
his tribe would provide leaders who would administer justice. And, like a serpent along the roadside, he would be a
dangerous opponent in battle. Samson, one of Israel's
national heroes, was a Danite (Judges 13-16).

Jacob had now moved more than halfway down the list of
his sons. As the Spirit opened the prophetic eye of the patriarch he could see far into the future. Suddenly he was filled
with a longing to see the fulfillment of the things he was
predicting. In humble faith he interrupted the flow of
prophecies about his sons and expressed his own heart's
desire: "I look for your deliverance, O LORD!" The patriarch
desired this fulfillment for himself, as well as for his children and children's children.

**[19]"Gad will be attacked by a band of raiders, but he will
attack them at their heels."**

The three Hebrew words which form the first half of this prophecy constitute a remarkable play on words which sound a note of warning. Gad's tribal territory would be situated east of the Jordan. Away from the nation's heartland, the Gadites would be exposed to the hit-and-run attacks of desert raiders. It would be reassuring for future generations of Gadites to hear that they would not be sitting ducks. The words "...but he will attack them at their heels" must have served to encourage them.

20"Asher's food will be rich; he will provide delicacies fit for a king."

The tribal territory of *Asher* was on Canaan's northern coastal plain. This rich farmland would produce food fit for the table of a king.

21"Naphtali is a doe set free that bears beautiful fawns."

A deer set free from confinement is a thing of grace and beauty as it bounds off into its native forest home. Jacob's words may point to *Naphtali's* ability to maneuver freely in battle. A footnote in the NIV, however, points out that the word translated "fawns" may also mean "words." If that's the intended meaning here, Jacob was prophesying that words of beauty would come from this tribe. Naphtali's most famous descendants were Barak and especially Deborah, who sang the beautiful song recorded in Judges 5.

22"Joseph is a fruitful vine, a fruitful vine near a spring, whose branches climb over a wall. 23With bitterness archers attacked him; they shot at him with hostility. 24But his bow remained steady, his strong arms stayed limber, because of the hand of the Mighty One of Jacob, because of the Shepherd, the Rock of Israel, 25 because of your father's God, who helps you,

because of the Almighty, who blesses you with blessings of the heavens above, blessings of the deep that lies below, blessings of the breast and womb. ²⁶Your father's blessings are greater than the blessings of the ancient mountains, than the bounty of the age-old hills. Let all these rest on the head of Joseph, on the brow of the prince among his brothers."

Jacob's final two blessings were spoken to the sons of his beloved Rachel. *Joseph* would be as fruitful as a vine planted near a spring of water. His offspring, the tribes of Ephraim and Manasseh, would be numerous. Others would feel antagonistic toward these successful tribes and would oppose them. Under the Almighty's protection, however, the two "Joseph tribes" would not be weakened by opposition, but would actually be strengthened by it. It is well to note that the specific blessings the patriarch promised to Joseph were *earthly* ones. The great *Messianic* blessing had already been promised to Judah.

As Jacob looked at his twelve sons and contemplated the numerous descendants who would be born to them, he was led to say: "I have enjoyed greater blessings than my ancestors."

²⁷"Benjamin is a ravenous wolf; in the morning he devours the prey, in the evening he divides the plunder." ²⁸All these are the twelve tribes of Israel, and this is what their father said to them when he blessed them, giving each the blessing appropriate to him.

The tribe of *Benjamin* became a very small tribe, situated between two more powerful tribes, Judah and Ephraim. But, like a vicious wolf, Benjamin would be a fierce opponent and would be successful in battle.

In bringing the long list of blessings and predictions to a close, the sacred writer emphasized that they apply not primarily to Jacob's sons, but to the tribes that would descend from them.

²⁹Then he gave them these instructions: "I am about to be gathered to my people. Bury me with my fathers in the cave in the field of Ephron the Hittite, ³⁰ the cave in the field of Machpelah, near Mamre in Canaan, which Abraham bought as a burial place from Ephron the Hittite, along with the field. ³¹There Abraham and his wife Sarah were buried, there Isaac and his wife Rebekah were buried, and there I buried Leah. ³²The field and the cave in it were bought from the Hittites." ³³When Jacob had finished giving instructions to his sons, he drew his feet up into the bed, breathed his last and was gathered to his people.

Jacob's last recorded words to his sons were instructions about his burial. He had previously made this request of Joseph (47:29-31); here he made it of all his sons. "Bury me with my fathers in the cave of Machpelah." That was the plot Abraham had originally bought when Sarah died. Later Abraham himself was also buried there, and Isaac, and Rebekah. There Jacob had also buried Leah. Although she was Jacob's less-loved wife, he chose to be buried with her instead of with his beloved Rachel because the connection with his fathers was dearer to him. Jacob wanted his burial in Canaan to tell his descendants that he believed God's promise to give them Canaan as their future homeland.

God's covenant promise, however, spoke not only about a future *homeland* God had in store for his people. God had promised also that Jacob's family would grow into a mighty *nation*, and that the world's *Savior* would be born from that nation of Israel.

Genesis 49 is a significant chapter in the history of God's Old Testament people. Jacob's prophetic words would *strengthen faith in God's promise* during the difficult days of slavery in Egypt. The patriarch's words would also *warn the Israelites*, during the days of independence, against character traits that would work against their welfare, against sins to which they were inclined. Most important, Jacob's words to his descendants *helped them to understand* how the blessings God had promised to Abraham were channeled to the twelve tribes.

Jacob's Burial; Joseph's Last Request

50 **Joseph threw himself upon his father and wept over him and kissed him. ²Then Joseph directed the physicians in his service to embalm his father Israel. So the physicians embalmed him, ³ taking a full forty days, for that was the time required for embalming. And the Egyptians mourned for him seventy days.**

Unlike the later Jewish custom of simply washing a dead body and anointing it with spices before burial, the ancient Egyptian process of mummification required forty days. The brain and internal organs were first of all removed. Body cavities were filled with spices, and the body was covered with salt for weeks, after which it was wrapped in linen and placed in a casket. Joseph now gave the order that this be done to preserve the body of his father, so that it could be transported to Canaan for burial.

⁴When the days of mourning had passed, Joseph said to Pharaoh's court, "If I have found favor in your eyes, speak to Pharaoh for me. Tell him, ⁵"My father made me swear an oath and said, "I am about to die; bury me in the tomb I dug for myself in the land of Canaan." Now let me go up and bury my father; then I will return.' " ⁶ Pharaoh said, "Go up and bury your father, as he made you swear to do." ⁷So Joseph went up

to bury his father. All Pharaoh's officials accompanied him — the dignitaries of his court and all the dignitaries of Egypt — [8] besides all the members of Joseph's household and his brothers and those belonging to his father's household. Only their children and their flocks and herds were left in Goshen. [9] Chariots and horsemen also went up with him. It was a very large company. [10] When they reached the threshing floor of Atad, near the Jordan, they lamented loudly and bitterly; and there Joseph observed a seven-day period of mourning for his father. [11] When the Canaanites who lived there saw the mourning at the threshing floor of Atad, they said, "The Egyptians are holding a solemn ceremony of mourning." That is why that place near the Jordan is called Abel Mizraim. [12] So Jacob's sons did as he had commanded them: [13] They carried him to the land of Canaan and buried him in the cave in the field of Machpelah, near Mamre, which Abraham had bought as a burial place from Ephron the Hittite, along with the field. [14] After burying his father, Joseph returned to Egypt, together with his brothers and all the others who had gone with him to bury his father.

Although the years of famine were long gone and Joseph's work of conserving Egypt's food reserves was finished, he was still an important government official. He therefore requested the pharaoh's permission to leave the country for an extended period of time.

The pharaoh did more than merely grant Joseph's request. He actually authorized an honor guard of prominent Egyptian officials to accompany the funeral procession to Canaan, in addition to a military escort to guarantee their safety during their trip through the desert.

The text does not make clear which route the funeral procession followed to Canaan. We are told "they reached the threshingfloor of Atad, *near the Jordan.*" Translated literally, those last three words mean "on the other side of the

Jordan," but the expression could indicate either side, depending on the writer's viewpoint. It's possible, as at the time of the exodus, that Jacob's family declined to take the most direct route along the Mediterranean coast, since that route led through the territory of the Philistines. They may have preferred to take the longer route — through the desert, around the Dead Sea — and approached Canaan from the east, as did their descendants several centuries later.

Here again the Egyptians who accompanied the funeral procession showed the high regard in which they held Joseph. Their observance of a period of mourning was so elaborate that even the natives of the area took notice. The memory of that incident was perpetuated in the new name given to the place: "Mourning of the Egyptians" (Abel Mizraim).

And so ended the earthly pilgrimage of Jacob, the "heel-grabber," the man who once thought his cleverness could help the LORD carry out his great plan. Through the LORD's patient training and tough love Jacob was transformed into Israel, "the man who struggled with God and overcame." Today in a mosque in the city of Hebron the traditional burial sites of Abraham and Sarah, of Isaac and Rebekah, and of Jacob and Leah can still be seen.

¹⁵When Joseph's brothers saw that their father was dead, they said, "What if Joseph holds a grudge against us and pays us back for all the wrongs we did to him?" ¹⁶So they sent word to Joseph, saying, "Your father left these instructions before he died: ¹⁷'This is what you are to say to Joseph: I ask you to forgive your brothers the sins and the wrongs they committed in treating you so badly.' Now please forgive the sins of the servants of the God of your father." When their message came to

him, Joseph wept. [18]His brothers then came and threw themselves down before him. "We are your slaves," they said.

[19]But Joseph said to them, "Don't be afraid. Am I in the place of God? [20]You intended to harm me, but God intended it for good to accomplish what is now being done, the saving of many lives. [21]So then, don't be afraid. I will provide for you and your children." And he reassured them and spoke kindly to them.

A guilty conscience is a terrible thing to live with. The brothers couldn't erase the haunting memories of what they had done thirty-nine years earlier. It also dawned on them that since their father was no longer around they were totally at the mercy of Joseph. Would he now finally settle accounts with the brothers who had treated him so shamefully?

They therefore sent a message to Joseph, perhaps through Benjamin. They had two things to say:

"Before our father Jacob died, he instructed us to relay his request to you: 'Please forgive your brothers for the evil they did to you.' We had the same father, and we serve the same God. For his sake please forgive us."

"Furthermore, we offer ourselves into lifelong slavery to you. You may do with us whatever you please."

Joseph wept when this message reached his ears. He wept tears of sadness — sadness over the torture his brothers must have been going through, sadness also over the fact that they had not believed him when he assured them of his forgiveness.

"Am I in the place of God?" Joseph asked his brothers. The person who takes vengeance tries to play God, and Joseph had no stomach for that. God had brought about a change of attitude in the brothers. God had furthermore overruled their evil deed and had actually used it to save people from starvation. We're told Joseph assured his brothers twice not to be afraid, since he had no intention of taking revenge. As he continued to speak kindly to them, his words calmed their fears.

²²Joseph stayed in Egypt, along with all his father's family. He lived a hundred and ten years ²³ and saw the third generation of Ephraim's children. Also the children of Makir son of Manasseh were placed at birth on Joseph's knees. ²⁴Then Joseph said to his brothers, "I am about to die. But God will surely come to your aid and take you up out of this land to the land he promised on oath to Abraham, Isaac and Jacob." ²⁵And Joseph made the sons of Israel swear an oath and said, "God will surely come to your aid, and then you must carry my bones up from this place." ²⁶So Joseph died at the age of a hundred and ten. And after they embalmed him, he was placed in a coffin in Egypt.

Joseph lived in Egypt another fifty-four years after his father died. He lived to be 110 — not as long as his father and grandfather. But he lived long enough to hold his children's children in his arms. He lived long enough to see with his own eyes that God was keeping his promise to multiply Jacob's family as the sand on the seashore.

Joseph's last recorded act was to renounce his ties with Egypt and to identify himself with the people of Israel. In faith he knew that Jacob's descendants would not live permanently in Egypt. Joseph trusted God's promises to lead his people *out of Egypt* and *into a new homeland in Canaan*. He therefore made his descendants swear they would take his remains with them when they left Egypt. He too wanted to share in the promised homeland, if only after his death. Several centuries later his request was honored. Moses took Joseph's mummified remains with him when the Israelites marched out of Egypt (Exodus 13:19). Joshua later buried those remains in Shechem, in the very heart of the promised land (Joshua 24:32).

Genesis 50 is more than just a fascinating page of Old Testament history. It says something crucially important to every human being about the way to solve the problem of sin. Sin is a disruptive factor in human life. Decades after Joseph's brothers had withheld their love from God and from their brother, the awareness of their sin festered in them like a hidden infection.

But the brothers' pain was unnecessary. *God has provided the solution* to the havoc sin raises in our lives. This solution consists of several parts.

1. *Confess sin honestly.* "He who conceals his sin does not prosper," God has told us (Proverbs 28:13). You don't solve the problem of sin by denying it or by excusing it or by trying to cover it up. You take it to the middle cross on Calvary and ask the Savior to wash it away with his blood. God has taught us to say: "Father, I have sinned."

2. *Believe the offer of forgiveness.* Although Joseph had assured his brothers he had forgiven them (45:4-15), they couldn't bring themselves to believe him. God has promised us that through Christ he has trodden our sins underfoot and hurled our iniquities into the depths of the sea (Micah 7:19). The remembrance of our past sins is painful, but it will be beneficial if it drives us back to the Savior's repeated offer of forgiveness. God wants us to believe his promise and then to live in the joy of his forgiveness.

The record of the death of Joseph concludes not only the "Account of Jacob," but also the early history of God's gracious dealing with mankind. The stage was now set for the next act in the drama of our redemption: God would lead his chosen nation to their promised inheritance in Canaan.

Conclusion

By tracing God's saving activity, first of all, *in the original world* (the first five "accounts"), and then *among the three great patriarchs* (the last five "accounts"), the book of Genesis has laid the foundation upon which the rest of the Scripture is built. Through all that has been recorded in the fifty chapters *we can detect God's great good plan* to gather a family for himself, a family of people who will love him, and trust him, and live for him until they one day live with him, at his side.

Jeremiah 29:11-13 - Memorize
Deut. 31:8   Philip. 3:7
Psalm   29:11   Psalm 68:11
I Chron. 29:12
   Psalm 27:8

189 Lakewood church
        Houston, TX. 4600 PO Box
              77210 Joel Osteen

1-800-435-8060